Cambridge Architecture

Sponsored by Cambridge Consultants

Cambridge Architecture

Tim Rawle

Trefoil Books, London

Sponsor's Foreword

Cambridge Consultants Ltd (CCL), since 1972 a part of the international consulting organisation Arthur D. Little, was founded in Cambridge in 1960, and has since grown into one of the UK's leading contract development and design companies.

The successful development of CCL owes much to Cambridge, especially those in the city, University and Colleges who have helped create the cultural, scientific and business environment enabling high technology companies to attract readily the talented people we need to flourish and grow. This is one reason why, when approached by Tim Rawle to sponsor this book, we were attracted to do so. We felt that in helping to bring into being this superb record of Cambridge's architectural history, we could in a small way, pay tribute to those who have created the environment to which I have referred and which we enjoy.

There is, however, another reason for supporting this book, and this concerns Tim Rawle's enthusiasm, quality of workmanship and dedication to complete this impressive project. Because this example of individual endeavour and committment so well reflects that which CCL has enjoyed from the many people who have worked in our company over the years, the publication of this book provides a welcome opportunity to record our gratitude.

Finally, we should like to thank Melissa Denny of Trefoil Books for publishing Tim's work in the form of this superb book. I am sure it will bring much pleasure to those who live and work here, as well as to those who are visiting, or are keen to learn more about this historic city.

Dr Robert Hook
On behalf of the Directors and Staff of
Cambridge Consultants Ltd.

Published by
Trefoil Books Ltd.,
7 Royal Parade,
Dawes Road,
London SW6

Copyright © Tim Rawle
Photographs © Tim Rawle
First published in 1985
Reprinted 1985

ISBN 0 86294 059 1 (cloth)
ISBN 0 86294 050 8 (paperback)

Set in Perpetua and Gill Sans by Typecraft (Home Counties) Ltd
and Words & Pictures
Printed in Great Britain

Title page: The east range of Downing College, designed by William Wilkins in 1806 and two-thirds built between 1807-13; finally completed by E.M. Barry between 1873-76 (see p. 140).

Half title: University officials in a procession leaving the Senate House via the east door (designed by James Gibbs and built in 1722-30, see p. 190)

Photographic data
Equipment – camera: Nikon FE body
lenses: Nikon 18, 28 (PC), 50, 85 & 135mm
The majority of the photographs were taken using a
28mm perspective control lens, with Ilford Pan F or
Kodak Tri X films.

All photographs and drawings by Tim Rawle unless otherwise credited

Contents

Acknowledgements

Among much reference material my four main sources of research were: Nikolaus Pevsner's invaluable *Cambridgeshire* of *The Buildings of England* series; Willis & Clark's *Architectural History of the University of Cambridge*; the *City of Cambridge* volumes of the *Royal Commission on Historical Monuments* (RCHM); and Philip Booth's and Nicholas Taylor's *Cambridge New Architecture*. (see select bibliography, p 223).

The original idea for this book was suggestd by John Cound and David Page of Cound Page Architects, the initial sponsors of the project, to whom I am most grateful.

I would particularly like to thank Richard Cutting, the ex Managing Director of Cambridge Consultants, for his enthusiasm in taking on the project at a crucial stage of threatened extinction. Upon his leaving the company I am indebted to the patience and encouragement of Bob Hook and Joanna Doxey in seeing the project to fruition. Equally, I am grateful for the considerable input of Melissa Denny of Trefoil.

For permission to photograph I would like to thank the university authorities, and the Masters, Fellows, and Scholars of the Cambridge colleges, and of Merton College and New College, Oxford — in particular the co-operation of the college Bursars and Porters. Also, to many individuals who tolerated a complete stranger clambering over balconies and rooftops in pursuit of good views, and to those who gave permission to photograph their private houses.

I owe much to the generosity of the directors and staff of Airship Industries for the flight above Cambridge on a freezing January afternoon to obtain aerial photographs (see photo opposite), particularly the senior pilot of Skyship 500, Nick Bennet. Thanks also to Brian Human for recording the experience.

Finally, I am extremely grateful to the following people: Phillippa Scoones and Alec Winton of Heffers; Nicholas Ray, Philip Lindley, and Sarah Baylis for most helpful comment and criticism; Paul Smith for photographic advice, and Charles Martinez for help with printing and for the portrait on the rear cover; Mr G.D. Bye and his staff, of the university library photographic department, for the excellent reproduction of old prints; Mark Lumley and the staff of the Cambridge Darkroom Gallery for their promotion of the photographs during the 1984 Cambridge Festival; Tony Maragna and Richard Kirk, of Cambridge Litho Plates, for their enthusiastic graphic experimentation on a number of my photographs; Jenny, Dundy, Richard and Margarida, for their hospitality on many return trips to Cambridge to complete the work; and my special thanks to Joanne and Bill for their help over the last year.

Tim Rawle October 1984

To my mother and father
&
Bob and Isobel
this book is dedicated

It was a dreary morning when the Chaise
Roll'd over the flat Plains of Huntingdon
And, through the open windows, first I saw
The long-back'd Chapel of King's College rear
His pinnacles above the dusky groves.

    Soon afterwards, we espied upon the road,
A student cloth'd in Gown and tassell'd Cap;
He pass'd; nor was I master of my eyes
Till he was left a hundred yards behind.
The Place, as we approach'd, seem'd more and more
To have an eddy's force, and suck'd us in
More eagerly at every step we took.
Onward we drove beneath the Castle, down
By Magdalene Bridge we went and cross'd the Cam,
And at the *Hoop* we landed, famous Inn.

    My spirit was up, my thoughts were full of hope;
Some Friends I had, acquaintances who there
Seem'd Friends, poor simple Schoolboys, now hung round
With honour and importance; in a world
Of welcome faces up and down I rov'd;
Questions, directions, counsel and advice
Flow'd in upon me from all sides, fresh day
Of pride and pleasure! To myself I seem'd
A man of business and expense, and went
From shop to shop about my own affairs,
To Tutors or to Tailors, as befel,
From street to street with loose and careless heart.

    I was the Dreamer, they the Dream; I roam'd
Delighted, through the motley spectacle;
Gowns grave or gaudy, Doctors, Students, Streets,
Lamps, Gateways, Flocks of Churches, Courts and Towers:

Strange transformation for a mountain Youth,
A northern Villager. As if by word
Of magic or some Fairy's power, at once
Behold me rich in monies, and attir'd
In splendid clothes, with hose of silk, and hair
Glittering like rimy trees when frost is keen.
My lordly Dressing-gown I pass it by,
With other signs of manhood which supplied
The lack of beard. - The weeks went roundly on,
With invitations, suppers, wine, and fruit,
Smooth housekeeping within, and all without
Liberal and suiting Gentleman's array!

    The Evangelist St. John my Patron was,
Three gloomy Courts are his; and in the first
Was my abiding-place, a nook obscure!
Right underneath, the College kitchens made
A humming sound, less tuneable than bees,
But hardly less industrious; with shrill notes
Of sharp command and scolding intermix'd.
Near me was Trinity's loquacious Clock,
Who never let the Quarters, night or day,
Slip by him unproclaim'd, and told the hours
Twice over with a male and female voice.
Her pealing organ was my neighbour too;
And, from my Bedroom, I in moonlight nights
Could see, right opposite, a few yards off,
The Antechapel, where the Statue stood
Of Newton, with his Prism and silent Face.

William Wordsworth (1770-1850)
The Prelude: Book III, Residence at Cambridge

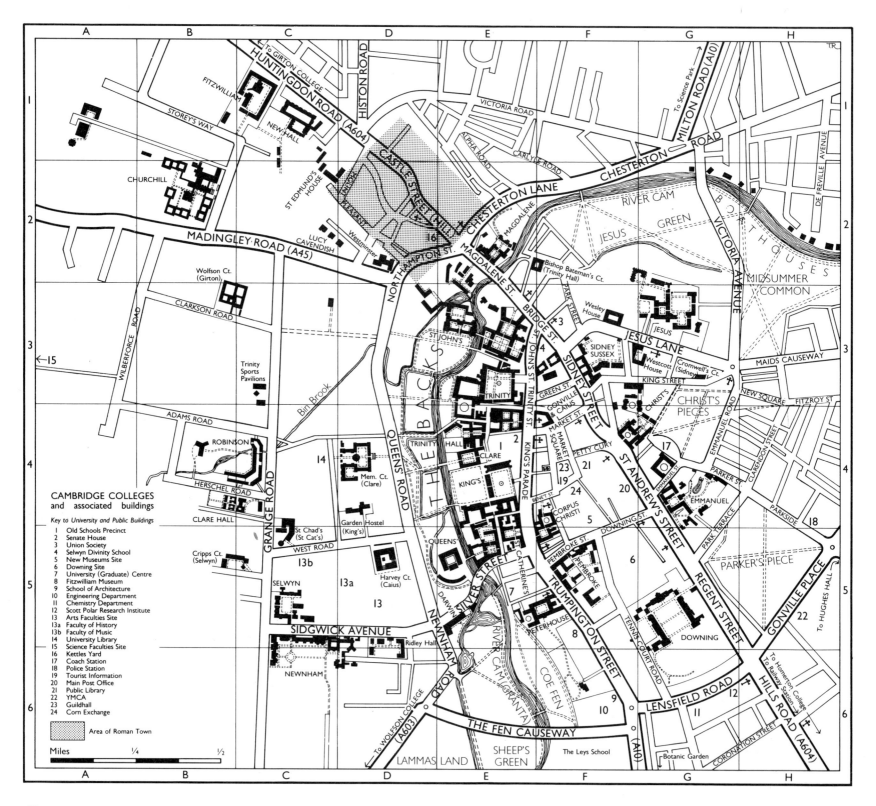

CAMBRIDGE COLLEGES
and associated buildings

Key to University and Public Buildings
1 Old Schools Precinct
2 Senate House
3 Union Society
4 Selwyn Divinity School
5 New Museums Site
6 Downing Site
7 University (Graduate) Centre
8 Fitzwilliam Museum
9 School of Architecture
10 Engineering Department
11 Chemistry Department
12 Scott Polar Research Institute
13 Arts Faculties Site
13a Faculty of History
13b Faculty of Music
14 University Library
15 Science Faculties Site
16 Kettles Yard
17 Coach Station
18 Police Station
19 Tourist Information
20 Main Post Office
21 Public Library
22 YMCA
23 Guildhall
24 Corn Exchange

Area of Roman Town

Miles   ¼   ½

viii

For most of the buildings in this book a grid reference relating to this map is supplied, either in the main text, on plans or in the captions. The grid reference consists of a letter followed by a number, for example E5 or B2, and will give the reader the approximate location of the building.

An aerial view of Cambridge looking south over the city from St John's College Chapel tower (see also back cover). In the foreground are the rooftops of the south range of Trinity's Great Court, beyond is Gonville & Caius' Tree Court, the back of the Senate House and King's Parade. On the left is the tower of Great St Mary's Church, the towers of the Emmanuel Congregational Church and Cambridge University Press's Pitt Building (both in Trumpington Street). To the right is the east end of King's College Chapel.

1 The source of the river Cam, Cambridge's *raison d'être*, at Ashwell, Hertfordshire, about 16 miles south-west of the city. The spring here and the surrounding ash trees gave rise to the name of the village, from the Old English *aesc*, 'ash tree', and *aewell*, 'source', and is first known to have been written down in about 990 AD as 'Aescewellan'. The water rises from nine holes in the chalk, at an average flow of one and a third million gallons a day, depending on the rainfall, or lack of it, of the previous summer, and feeds the river Rhee, the principal source of the Cam. The Cam meets the river Granta just south of Cambridge near the village of Trumpington, and they flow united through the city to join the Great Ouse 10 miles north near Ely. The Ouse enters the sea at the Wash in north-east Norfolk, approximately 65 miles from Ashwell.

I The Evolution of Cambridge

Cambridge has existed as a place of regular human settlement for about 2500 years, since the Early Iron Age. Although the Romans attached great strategic importance to Camboritum and established a considerable base there, no architecture pre-dating the late Anglo-Saxon period remains, the tower of St Bene't's church (c.1040, fig. 2) being the lone survivor from that time. With the Norman Conquest came a sturdy form of building, of which there are several good examples in Cambridge dating from the early twelfth century. However, buildings of brick or stone were a rarity as they were extremely expensive, and the more common wooden structures in the narrow streets of the mediaeval town were often destroyed by fire or simply rotted away.

Building Materials

The county of Cambridgeshire, some 550,000 acres, possesses abundant gault clay for brick-making, but there is no good local building stone. This is partly why the county has no strong individual architectural character of its own, and its vernacular buildings comprise an eclectic mixture of styles from the eight bordering counties. The great exception to this is the city of Cambridge itself, where, from the fourteenth century, the wealthy university and its associated colleges were able to import building materials from elsewhere. The only local building stone was a soft limestone known as 'clunch', which lends itself marvellously to carving, of which there are excellent examples throughout the town (eg in Great St Mary's Church). The nearest supply of good building stone is to the north-west, in Northamptonshire, where the limestone quarries, such as that at Ketton, have been the source of stone for many fine Cambridge buildings, such as King's College Chapel.

Because of the lack of local stone, Cambridge turned to brick-making at an early date, and this has resulted in one of the most noticeable differences between it and Oxford: a large number of Cambridge buildings are of brick, whereas at Oxford, which is situated in an area rich in limestone, they are predominantly of stone. Many important buildings in Cambridge were therefore built of brick as a matter of economic practicality; one of the first being Queens' College Old Court, built in 1448-49 of red brick with an inner core of clunch rubble. The local brick is of two colours; the yellow-grey which comes from the gault clay from the west bank of the river Cam, and the richer red brick made from the jurassic clays found mainly in the north of the county. These local clays are also responsible for the tiles of variegated colours often used together on many Cambridge roofs.

However, during the Classical Revival in the seventeenth and eighteenth centuries, the Gothic brick buildings of which Cambridge was almost entirely composed, became unfashionable, and several of the colleges embarked upon a vast 'cosmetic' operation to face many of their buildings with stone, especially those fronting the public streets. The buildings were thus fashionably classicised by the addition of a facade of stone by the process known as 'ashlaring'. As a result, the impression one receives today is that there are a considerable number of stone buildings, whereas, in fact many of them are built of brick. The fronts of Christ's College in St Andrew's Street and Pembroke College in Trumpington Street, both medieval brick buildings, now appear as stone structures because they were ashlar-faced, and there are numerous other similar examples throughout the town. To get an idea of the original appearance of the medieval Cambridge colleges, one should visit the Old Courts of Corpus Christi and Queens' (see figs 8 & 11).

It was not until the fifteenth century that brick and stone started to become more commonly used as building materials in Cambridge, and stone still only by those who could afford to import it. Consequently, it was the wealthy religious foundations, the colleges and the university who built in these lasting materials. Almost all the non-ecclesiastical and non-academic buildings, on the other hand, are of later date, and only a few medieval domestic structures survive intact.

It is not, of course, the buildings alone that have created Cambridge's particular 'ambience', but also the spaces around them - the streets, the courtyards and narrow passages, together with the river and the green areas - all are equally important. It is these things together which constitute Cambridge and which it is the purpose of this book to attempt to survey and illustrate.

Origins

To the immediate north of Cambridge lie the Fens, the extensive alluvial flood-plains of the rivers Great Ouse, Nene and Welland, which flow into the Wash. This vast area of reclaimed marshland, which accounts for about two-thirds of the entire county, is contained by the harder and higher belt of chalk to the east, south and west, on the northern edge of which is Cambridge.

The main river system in the Cambridge area is the Great Ouse which rises in the limestone Cotswolds about 55 miles south-west of the city, and enters the sea about 50 miles north-east in the south-east corner of the Wash at Kings Lynn. Two rivers, both tributaries of the Ouse, converge just south of Cambridge near the village of Trumpington; the Cam, which rises at Ashwell (Hertfordshire) about 16 miles south-west of Cambridge, and the Granta which rises near Safron Walden (Essex). They flow through the city united as the Cam to join the Ouse 10 miles to the north, near Ely. It is these two rivers, the Cam and the Granta, that have dictated the several different names by which the town has been known, depending on the river name chosen by successive occupiers of 'the place at the crossing of the river', and from which Cambridge takes its name (ie at the Cam bridge). There are basically five different names by which the town is referred to in this chapter: Camboritum (Roman); Grantacaestir (Anglo-Saxon); Grantabrycge (Anglo-Danish); Cantebrig (Norman); and Cambridge thereafter, a name which, according to Gray,[1] was not commonly used before 1600. It is interesting to note that when the name Grantabrycge appears in the Anglo-Saxon Chronicle of 875, that this was probably the earliest use of the word 'bridge' in written English. It could thus also be deduced that the original bridge at Grantabrycge, thought to have been built some-time between 696-875 probably by the great Anglo-Saxon King Offa (757-96), was the first of any importance to have been constructed in England after the departure of the Romans (prior to the construction of a bridge there would probably have been a ford to cross the river, though interestingly the name 'Camford' did not evolve).

Cambridge had both a river with fertile valleys and surrounding high ground to attract the original primeval settlers. In prehistoric times the area around Cambridge, particularly to its south and east, would have been regularly visited by packmen and tribesmen as it was in the vicinity of the ancient Icknield Way, a major route which followed the high chalk outcrop stretching from north Norfolk to south Devon, and providing unencumbered access to such centres of worship as Avebury and Stonehenge in Wiltshire. It must be remembered that most of the country at this time would have been covered in extremely dense forest and undergrowth, and these chalk downs provided fairly clear tracts of high ground.

The combination of land routes, a navigable waterway, the river-crossing and surrounding high ground, led to Cambridge acquiring strategic and military importance; first to the Romans, and then later to other occupying forces, the Saxons, Danes and Normans. The indigenous population was under constant threat of invasion. The ancient Belgic tribe of the Catuvellauni controlled the area in the last century BC; the Romans moved in from Camulodunum (Colchester) in the south-east in circa 43 AD; during the Dark Ages, the Saxons and then the Danes invaded from the north up the river from the Wash; and William the Conqueror and his men took it on their return from York in 1068.

There is one other geographical fact which had an important effect on the early development of Cambridge, its inaccessibility to and from London. This was due to the area of high ground known as the East Anglian Heights which stretch from Luton in the west round to Bury St Edmunds in the east. The dense forests and heavy clay soil to the north of the Heights, and the equally hazardous Essex Forest to the east, made direct access even more difficult. As a result the journey between London and Cambridge was a long and roundabout one, and this is why there is no 'London Road' in Cambridge today, as there is in so many other English towns.

In these early times in Cambridge, the local topography would have dictated settlement points on the few hilly outcrops rising above the floodplain of the river. On the left, or west bank of the Cam, a gravel-capped outcrop of the chalk ridge provided a suitable escarpment for habitation some 70 feet above sea-level, and this was soon to become the military vantage point controlling the river-crossing, subsequently named Castle Hill. On the right, or south-east, bank of the river, were three lower hills each about 30 feet above sea-level: Peas Hill, Market Hill, and St Andrew's Hill, all of which remain today but are hardly discernable as hillocks. Along the river banks, from what is now Magdalene Bridge to the Mill Pool above the Silver Street Bridge, stretched a wide area of marshy ground on both sides of the river, anciently known as 'The Thousand Willows', which was later gradually reclaimed and artificially raised to form building land which is now occupied by the central nucleus of Colleges and their beautiful gardens, or 'Backs', down to the river.

The present form of the city centre developed in response to the early problem of acquiring suitable land on which to build, and it is now difficult to imagine the area, from Castle Hill in the north to Trumpington Street in the south, as a collection of small settlements separated by marshy bogs and the river. However, from these primitive beginnings over a millenium ago, it is possible to visualise how, after the Romans departed, two Cambridges developed, one on the north and one on the south bank. Feuding tribes then fought for control of the river-crossing and in turn occupied either the dominating Castle Hill area, or the subservient settlement below on the east bank. However, it was the latter settlement that evolved as the main town when the military importance of the site was no longer paramount and it began to develop firstly as a centre of commerce, and then as a major university town.

The first settlers and the Romans

In the fourth millennium BC the first farmers settled in the district, as archaeological finds of neolithic artefacts have shown, and then in about 2000 BC the first makers of beaker pottery appeared. It was not until the Bronze Age (c.2000 – c.500 BC) that abundant finds show a great increase in the habitation of the Cambridge area. Concentration in the vicinity of Cambridge itself is supported by many Early Iron Age finds; including a flanged axe at Barnwell and a food vessel and pygmy cup from Midsummer Common.

A permanent settlement is thought to have been established in Cambridge in the Early Iron Age (c.500 – c.400 BC) when immigrants from the Low Countries came and settled along the Fen marshes and in the fertile valleys of the local rivers, evidence of such a settlement in Cambridge being found in the Hills Road area. Growing unrest and hostility among local tribes at this time is shown by the construction of fortifications, such as a hillfort at Vandlebury (Wandlebury, about three miles south east of the city), and war ditches at Cherry Hinton (a southeastern suburb of the present-day borough of Greater Cambridge). The grave of a tribal chief from this period was excavated at Newnham Croft in Cambridge and revealed the body of a middle-aged man accompanied by several interesting artefacts, one of which was possibly the remains of a wooden war chariot.

These archaeological and topographical remains are evidence that some form of organised social and political community had evolved around Cambridge at that time. A re-strengthening of the fortifications at the Wandlebury settlement by the ancient Britons was in response to the threatening presence of the strong Belgic tribe of the Catuvellauni, who were gradually expanding their territory northwards from the Thames during the late second century BC. That they eventually annexed Cambridge is proved by the existence of a settlement attributed to them excavated on Castle Hill covering an area of almost five acres.

Iron Age Cambridge thus lay in the territory of the Catuvellauni, ruled over by King Cassivelaunus and controlled from its capital Verulamium near St Albans in Hertfordshire, 40 miles away. It was during the reign of Cassivelaunus that Julius Ceasar made his two abortive expeditions across the Channel in 55 and 54 BC, from recently conquered Gaul. A hundred years later the Emperor Claudius returned to conquer Britain in AD 43. The Roman force, of about 40,000 men, sailed from Boulogne that summer, landed at Richborough in Kent, forded the Thames, and then proceeded to take the new capital at Colchester. From there they spread out, the 14th and the 9th Legions marching in the direction of Cambridge, and it was probably the 9th which first set foot in the settlement where they subsequently established an important camp.

The centres of government of Roman Britain were at Verulamium, Colchester, Lincoln, Gloucester and York, with London already a great mercantile town though not yet a political one. Apart from these, there were other towns of lesser importance which were laid out on the characteristic rectangular plan. This was the case at Camboritum where a camp was established on the hill overlooking the river-crossing. There were numerous strongholds of this kind, all being connected by a network of roads. Although there is a good deal of conjecture as to the importance of Camboritum in Roman Britain, there is evidence to support its being equal in military terms to the main centres such as Colchester and York. Bede (673-735) tells us that this 'city' had walls of masonry, whereas an ordinary camp would have had earthen ramparts. Bede's documentary evidence is supported by the discovery of portions of Roman brick walls on the Castle Hill site excavated in the early nineteenth century, and the number of archaeological finds in this area since then indicates a considerable settlement. Undoubtedly, Camboritum was important because of its location as the northernmost point before the marshy Fens, and its river-crossing provided, effectively, a gateway to the north or south-east.

Of the many important roads built by the Romans during their occupation, two passed through Camboritum: Akeman Street and the Via Devana, bringing even greater importance to the settlement, though it is unclear as to exactly where these roads entered Camboritum. Akeman Street ran from south-west to north-east, from Cirencester (Gloucestershire) to Brancaster (north Norfolk), in the Camboritum district roughly parallel to, but north of, the ancient Icknield Way. It entered the area via Barton in the south-west and left by Ely in the north-east. The Via Devana ran from south-east to north-west, from Colchester (Essex) to Chester (Cheshire) entering the area near Wandlebury in the south-east, and leaving by what is now the Huntingdon Road out past Girton Village in the north-west. Both these roads were important and branched off the great Ermine Street, the main north-south artery which connected Verulamium (and London) with York, via Lincoln.

By the second century AD, a town had been established, and by 300 AD it is thought to have been fortified by a wall of Northamptonshire limestone surmounting extensive earthen ramparts. The boundaries of the settlement (see p.8) enclosed an area of about 25 to 28 acres, and the buildings within it were probably of timber, clay and thatch construction. To the south-east of the camp, below the hill, was marshland and the river, with the crossing located slightly downstream of the present Magdalene Bridge. The Via Devana crossed the river here and proceeded towards the hill through what is now the Old Court of Magdalene College, through the present St Giles's churchyard, entering the camp at the centre of its south wall at a point which is now roughly in the middle of the south side of St Giles's church. It probably left the camp at what is now the junction of Mount Pleasant and Castle Street, and was crossed by Akeman Street which is thought to have run along the northern boundary of the camp. The river-crossing itself was probably a ford rather than a bridge and, indeed, the architect James Essex supports this supposition, as when he was building a stone bridge on this site in the mid-eighteenth century (the predecessor of the present iron structure) he remarked that the ford 'very plainly shewed itself in the year 1754 as a firm pavement of pebbles.'[3]

Today, there is no visible trace of the Roman occupation of Cambridge, except that the main axis of the present city follows roughly the route of the Via Devana (the present A604).

It was the construction of Roman roads at such places as London, Cambridge and Oxford, where navigable rivers also existed, that helped to ensure the later emergence of those towns as major centres. These roads also greatly assisted later conquests by Saxons, Danes and Normans, and aided them in their attempts to unite the country. No hard roads were made after the departure of the Romans until the eighteenth century, by which time many of the thousands of miles of Roman road had disappeared, much of it having been used as building stone by medieval Englishmen.

Northern Invaders: Saxons and Danes

The Romans left England in 410 AD, leaving the peoples of East Anglia, now accustomed to the protection of the Roman army, vulnerable to attack by barbarian raiders. During the Dark Ages invasions by Saxons and Jutes, and later Danes and Norsemen, in vast numbers over a period of about six centuries, had a pronounced and lasting effect.

The Roman settlements were generally left empty, and we know from a story told by Bede that the Roman camp at Camboritum was left abandoned for several centuries.[4] The tale concerns Etheldreda, a daughter of one of the Kings of the East Angles, and who established the minster at Ely in 673, where she died in 680. According to Bede 'Etheldreda was succeeded in the office of abbess by her sister Sexburga, who had been married to Earconberct, King of Kent. When Etheldreda had been buried sixteen years the same abbess resolved to raise her bones, place them in a new coffin and remove them to the church. She ordered some of the brethren to look for a stone wherewith to make a coffin with this object. They took ship – as the district of Ely is entirely surrounded with waters and fens, and has no large stones – and came to a certain desolate little city, situated not far away, which in the English language is called Grantacaestir. And presently they found near the walls of the city a coffin beautifully fashioned of white marble, closely fitted with a lid of the same material. So, perceiving that the Lord had prospered their journey, they gave thanks and brought it with them to the monastery.' Grantacaestir was Cambridge, and the name should not be confused with the present day village of Grantchester which lies about two miles to the south of Cambridge.

Grantacaestir suffered much during the Dark Ages because it was situated between the two rival Kingdoms of Mercia and East Anglia, and was, in effect, a battleground over which the two tribes fought for control of the river-crossing. It appears that the Mercians were generally the stronger tribe as shown, for instance, in King Penda's destruction of the settlement on Castle Hill after his victory over the East Angles in 634, and King Offa controlled the area in the second half of the eighth century when he is thought to have been responsible for the first bridge. It was during this period that two settlements began to evolve at Grantacaestir, with the Mercians being firmly established on the west bank, or Castle Hill; and the Anglians below on the east bank, in what is now the main city centre.

Archaeological finds at Girton, St John's College playing fields off Madingley Road, and at Newnham Croft (all west bank sites), all dating to the fifth century, show that the first Nordic settlers had close connections with the region of lower Saxony between the rivers Elbe and Wesser in Germany, and with the Schleswig area of Denmark. These early Saxon invaders, from about 450 AD, were mainly farmers and they did much to transform forest and fen into agricultural land; whereas the later Danish invaders, of the ninth and tenth centuries, were great seafarers and traders who brought commerce and prosperity to the places in which they settled, almost always situated on a river navigable from the sea, of which Grantacaestir was one.

The Grantacaestir district was the subject of almost continuous warfare between Mercia and East Anglia for about 250 years, from circa 600-850, but then the threat of invasion by the Vikings united most of the English kingdoms to defend the coastline. East Anglia, in particular, was vulnerable to attack and the Norsemen and Danes soon penetrated the region by sailing up its many rivers into the interior whence they spread out into middle England. The Cam was just such an artery for Viking infiltration as it was a tidal waterway as far inland as Waterbeach, which is only about eight miles north of Cambridge, and from there the river in those days formed a deep channel enabling sea-going vessels to reach Grantacaestir. A great Viking army had ravaged the area continuously from 865-869, and the *Anglo Saxon Chronicle* records that in 875 Danes wintered at Grantacaestir, whilst three years later, by the Treaty of Wedmore, the area passed into the Danelaw, as did the whole eastern side of England from Teeside to the Thames estuary, reaching as far inland as Chester.

The effect of Danish occupation on Grantabrycge was extremely important, for they formed a major inland port at this convergence of land-routes and waterway. By establishing their settlement next to the river – in what is now the area around Bridge Street and St Clement's Church (St Clement is the patron saint of Danish sailors) – they fused the two communities as one. Moreover they brought unprecedented importance to the right, or east bank of the river where they built the port itself, constructing numerous wharves and hythes. The port soon became the regional centre for trade, and, as a result, the town prospered greatly for several centuries. Danelaw continued into the early tenth century until the Saxons, under Edward the Elder, King of Wessex, recovered the region by 921. Edward passed a law soon after, which stated that all trading must take place in a market town under the supervision of the justices, thus aiding the concentration of commerce in the new centres, such as Grantabrycge.

The Danes laid the foundations of the English Borough and its Town, and it was they who introduced the division of the country (their Danelaw) into 'shires' or 'counties', which were later named after their central towns; as with Cambridge and Cambridgeshire. From this time onwards Cambridge was firmly established as the main county town, whilst Ely was the religious centre.

Edward did not put an end to the Viking invasions and further attacks took place throughout the tenth and eleventh centuries, with possibly the most fierce at Grantabrycge resulting in the burning of the town in 1010 just prior to the last Danish Conquest by King Cnut (or Canute). The Danes restored peace and organisation to the county and an important town such as Grantabrycge would have been quickly rebuilt, though once again of such perishable materials as wood, cob, wattle, daub and thatch.

Danish ingenuity in trading combined with the Saxon market law of King Edward (who also established a royal mint at Grantabrycge) brought great prosperity to the town during the tenth and eleventh centuries. The market was one of the most important trading centres for products such as good quality hay from the Fens and also sedge which was one of the main heating and building materials. The architecture of the town at this time, around the new centre of the port, would have consisted of a collection of wooden buildings with mud walls and thatched roofs. There is evidence of two major structures in the area of Castle Hill; possibly the original church of Cambridge (Christianity having come to Britain in the seventh century), and a fortress guarding the river-crossing. The existence of the church (since named 'All Saints by the Castle') is supported by a find of seven gravestones of Anglo-Saxon detail, which were excavated on Castle Hill in 1810. This led to conjecture that before the Norman Conquest the main church of Grantabrycge was located in the area of the old Roman town, and was almost certainly a wooden structure, probably destroyed in the great fire of 1010. The existence of some form of wooden fortress (a 'burh' in Anglo-Saxon) overlooking the river-crossing is extremely likely, and is supported by the fact that a tax (known as 'burhbote') was levied in the county for the maintenance of such a building.

The Danish invasion of Grantabrycge marked the beginning of the town as a prosperous community, a prosperity which resulted in the first stone buildings, parts of which have survived to the present day: the Anglo-Saxon tower of St Bene't's church (fig. 2), and smaller details in other early churches, since rebuilt, such as St Mary the Less.

Norman Cantebrig

The Norman Conquest instigated a swing away from the influence of northern Europe towards the mainstream of Western European culture. In terms of architecture the Conquest was most important, as the Normans brought with them an advanced Romanesque style of building from which was to develop English Gothic.

The symbol and instrument of Norman domination was the castle. William subdued Middle England between 1067-69 and established castles at Lincoln, Huntingdon and Grantabrycge in 1068. Like his predecessors, William recognised the military importance of the settlement on the edge of the Fens. The castle at Grantabrycge, which has not survived, was built on the high ground overlooking the river-crossing, on 'Castle Hill', and thus focused attention once again on the west bank of the river. These early castles were of the earthenwork 'motte-and-bailey' type, consisting of one or more fortified enclosures (baileys) dominated by a steep-sided earthen mound with a flat top (the motte) on which stood the tower (the keep) normally built of stone; the whole structure being surrounded by ditches, banks or palisades. This was the type of construction employed here and the surviving castle mound shows (fig. 3) that the motte was about 40 feet high by about 200 feet across, and required the demolition of 27 houses at the time of its construction.

The castle at Cantebrig was built by William's Sheriff, Picot, who was not very popular with the citizens, one of whom described him as 'a hungry lion, a ravening wolf, a filthy hog'. The Conquest was responsible for a revival of church building in England and Picot's wife, Hugolina, having been taken seriously ill, vowed that if she were to recover she would build a church at Cantebrig in honour of her patron Saint, Giles,

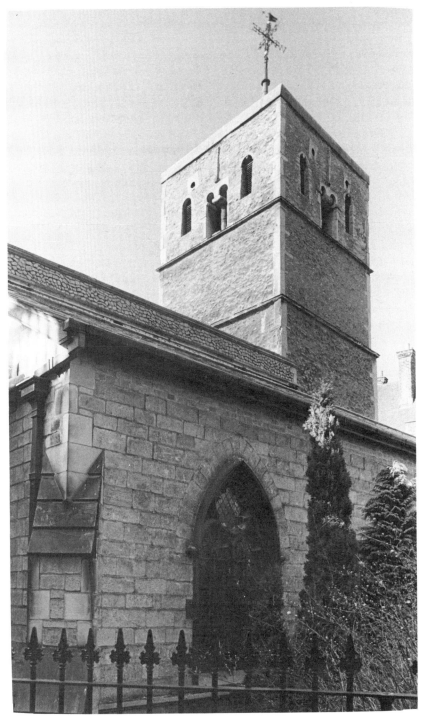

2 The oldest building in Cambridge — St Bene't's Church, with its pre-Conquest tower built sometime during the second quarter of the eleventh century (see also fig. 71).

and establish a religious household with it. She recovered and founded the original Church of St Giles, on Castle Hill (since rebuilt) and a house of Regular Canons in 1092. Two decades later, Picot's successor, the crusading knight Pain Peverell, enlarged the foundation from six to thirty clergy and moved it to a more spacious and pleasant setting in the fields on the eastern side of the town. A local chronicler of the period informs us that: 'Moreover in the middle of the place some springs, fresh and pure, welled forth, in English called Barnewelle, that is, the Children's Wells, at the time so called because once a year, on the Vigil of the Nativity of St John the Baptist, boys and youths used to meet there, and, as is the English habit, engaged in wrestling and other youthful games, and with songs and instruments of music applauded each other'.[5] Hugolina's foundation subsequently became the Augustinian Barnwell Priory of which little has survived (see chapter 7).

Pain Peverell established the Priory at Barnwell in 1112, and in the 1130s several other monastic foundations arose at the newly-named Cantebrig: the Benedictine Nunnery of St Radegund was founded, (also in the fields east of the town) and the nuns' church and conventual buildings survive today as the most substantial religious 'house' in Cambridge, forming the nucleus of Jesus College (the Nunnery itself was taken over in 1496). Two hospitals, both administered by monks, were also established around this time: the Leper Hospital beyond Barnwell on the Newmarket Road, none of the domestic buildings of which have survived, though the superb little chapel of St Mary Magdalene (see chapter 7) still exists; and the Hospital of St John in the town centre of which nothing remains, although this foundation was perpetuated as St John's College. The most spectacular Norman building to survive in Cambridge is the round Church of the Holy Sepulchre (fig. 4), in the town centre. Apart from these, Romanesque details exist in some of the churches since rebuilt; for example St Giles and St Peter on Castle Hill, and St Mary The Less in the southern part of the town (see chapter 7).

The building of these religious foundations during the twelfth century, reflects the existence of a prosperous community at Cantebrig. Sometimes townsmen united to finance such ventures, or, as in the case of St John's Hospital, one man (a burgess named Henry Frost) was able to support a foundation of Augustinian monks to tend the poor and sick. Around 1200, the first stone house was built at Cantebrig (the earliest surviving in the county), the so-called 'School of Pythagoras' (fig. 5) which was located only a short distance away from the Hospital of St John and is now in the grounds of St John's College.

Further religious foundations were established in Cantebrig in the thirteenth century,[6] some of which formed the basis of later college foundations at the time of the Reformation and Dissolution of the Monasteries under Henry VIII some three centuries later.

3

The Medieval Town

Domesday Book, the great survey of England made under William The Conqueror in 1086, records that much of the dense woodland in the Cantebrig area had been cleared, the open field system of communal cultivation was well organised, many villages started, parish boundaries created, and law and order firmly enforced by the new Norman Overlords. Cantebrig flourished as an important commercial centre, and was one of the most prosperous towns in the country; its port, markets and fairs attracting traders on an international level. In particular, the medieval town was famous for its many fairs, of which the most renowned was that held on Stourbridge Common, later described by Queen Elizabeth in 1589 as 'by far the largest and most famous fair in all England'. The origins of this great trading event may go back to the early twelfth century, or beyond. The Barnwell Chronicler, referring to Pain Peverell's Augustinian foundation of 1112, continues '...so it happened that owing to the multitude of boys and girls resorting thither for their sports it became a custom for a crowd of merchants to meet there on the same day to traffic and buy and sell.' The day referred to for this original festival was on the Vigil of the Nativity of St John the Baptist (ie Midsummer Day). In about 1211, King John granted a licence to the Leper Hospital of St Mary Magdalene, near Stourbridge Common, to hold the fair each year during late August and early September, this probably being its inauguration as a national event. As the fair grew in size and popularity it may even have stretched as far west as the present Midsummer Common, the name of which possibly comes from the day on which the original festival was held, as much as a thousand years ago.

Stourbridge Fair was undoubtedly one of the great annual trading events in Europe, where exotic goods such as Italian silks and French wines were exchanged for East Anglian wool or Cornish tin. Many other goods were also sold; such as leather, ironmongery, coal, tallow, books, horses and fish. However, the fair was not just a trading event: its associated entertainments - theatre, puppet shows, bear-baiting, beer drinking - endowed the town with considerable national importance every year for many centuries. The Fair continued well into the eighteenth century, along with other smaller events, such as the Garlick Fair held by the Benedictine Nuns of St Radegund. Of these Cambridge events none has survived on any scale, though the annual Strawberry Fair, held for one day every June on Midsummer Common, may have something of the atmosphere of the medieval fairs which so engrossed the town for a large part of each summer.

4

5

3 William the Conqueror built the castle at Cambridge in 1068, but only the motte remains on Castle Hill. **4** The Norman Round Church of the Holy Sepulchre, built soon after 1130 but with extensive Victorian restoration. **5** The oldest surviving house in the county, known as 'The School of Pythagoras', of c.1200.

The boundaries of the medieval town were precisely defined. For defensive purposes the King's Ditch had been dug around two sides of the settlement, probably in the first half of the eleventh century. It was re-cut and cleaned out in 1267-68. The King's Ditch contained the town within its protective boundary to the east and south, whilst the loop of the river did the same to the north and west (the course of the ditch ran from the Mill Pool in the south, at the western end of the present Mill Lane, and pursued a north-east to north-west curve to rejoin the river east of the Great Bridge).

Within these boundaries, the area of the town was divided into four distinct parts: the centre of the settlement was around the Market Place between what is now King's Parade/Trinity Street in the west, and Sidney Street in the east; then there was another smaller concentration of houses in the Bridge Street area, the old Danish centre near the port; between these two built-up settlements, in what is now the St John's Street area, there was a 'green belt' which was to be built on during the thirteenth century; and, finally, there was the extensive strip of land to the west of the old High Street (now King's Parade, Trinity and St John's Streets) which was then marshy and unsafe for building, but which is now occupied by several colleges. The military settlement on the opposite bank was quickly becoming a suburb of the new commercial east-bank town.

Settlement outside the town boundaries had begun with the establishment of Barnwell Priory and St Radegund's Nunnery in the eastern fields. Other monastic Orders, such as the Carmelite Friars at Newnham, and the Friars of the Sack and the Gilbertine Canons of Sempringham in Trumpington Street, later established themselves to the south of the town perimeter; thus encouraging settlement in the area beyond the Trumpington Gate. The Hospital of St John, built to the west of the old High Street in the town centre, was the first instance of building on land reclaimed from the river.

The floodplain of the river constituted a large area in the town which could not be built upon, and thus in order to obtain more building land, the medieval townsmen diverted the Cam on a new course along the eastern edge of its floodplain (its original course was probably further to the west nearer the present Queens' Road, in fact marked by the line of the smaller ditches that exist there today) so that buildings such as mills, warehouses and wharves could be erected on the now hard east bank near the town centre. As a result a new commercial area arose between the river and the High Street, dissected by a network of lanes and hythes which connected the busy wharves with the town centre and the market place: the names reflecting the goods unloaded at the quayside; such as Cornhythe, Salthythe, and Flaxhythe. By this time, the busy port with its heavy barge traffic, had spread far upstream from the original Danish wharves, east of the Great Bridge, and now covered a distance of almost half a mile to the Mill Pool in the south. The floodplain of the river had, thus, been almost entirely confined to the west bank and its rich, fertile soils were later to form the gardens, or

'backs', of the Colleges which were to take over this area during the next few centuries.

Medieval Cantebrig was able to expand only to a limited extent to east and west owing to the existence of the great fields; the Barnwell Field to the east, and the Cambridge Field to the west. The Open Field system of cultivation existed in every English town and the fields were an essential part of the livelihood of the medieval community, but normally there was only one great field, and at Cantebrig it is thought that two fields evolved because of the dual origins of the town itself. This hypothesis is supported by the fact that tithes for the land were distributed for the Barnwell Field mainly to churches in the southern part of the town; and for the Cambridge Field to churches in the old northern part.

At Cambridge it is still possible in places to trace the medieval farming system in the great West Field, but the great East Field has been heavily built on since the nineteenth century and only a few areas of common land survive, such as Jesus Green, Stourbridge and Midsummer Commons, to attest to its existence. Illustrations of the two Cambridge Fields, although at a rather later date, are given in David Loggan's superb *Cantabrigia Illustrata* of 1690 (fig. 6).

Academic Invaders

By the year 1200, Cantebrig had emerged as a prosperous centre of commerce efficiently organised by the Normans, and still at that time under the control of the local Sheriff. Its trading inhabitants enjoyed unprecedented wealth, and the town had one of the largest Jewry's in England at that time – a sign of a successful and prosperous business community – and the peasant classes probably also lived comfortably above subsistence level, with ample work in the markets and fairs and the two great fields on either side of the town. The burgesses of the town had been campaigning for the 'freedom' of the borough from the crown, and this was successfully achieved in 1207, only two years before the conjectured date of the founding of the University, an event which was to be comparable in its effect on the town to any of the previous invasions. Ironically, therefore, as soon as the community thought they had gained their autonomy, they found they had a new master in the powerful University authorities to whom they would play the subservient host for many centuries to come.

At some time in the last years of the reign of Henry II (1154-89), the first Plantagenet King, the townsmen purchased the 'farm' (leasehold) of Cantebrig from the crown, although there was nothing in the undated writ to ensure that this act was in perpetuity. It was not until the two charters of King John, in 1201 and 1207, that the townsmen could rest assured that their purchase was secure: the 1207 charter stated conclusively that the burgesses of the town were 'to hold for ever of us and our heirs to them and their heirs'.

The origins of Cambridge University are, like those of Oxford, somewhat obscure. It is generally accepted that Oxford was started earlier than Cambridge as it is known that a group of scholars left Oxford in 1209, after riots between the townspeople and the academics had resulted in the hanging of three of their colleagues, and came to Cantebrig to resume their studies. In 1229, another group of scholars left Paris, under similar circumstances, and also migrated to Cantebrig. It is 1209 which is generally recognised as marking the beginning of Cambridge University. It must be remembered, however, that Cantebrig already possessed a learned community by 1209 in the form of the religious houses established there and which provided the basis for the university system (see chapter 3 & 6). Thus, it would not be unreasonable to assume that the small group of academic refugees who headed for

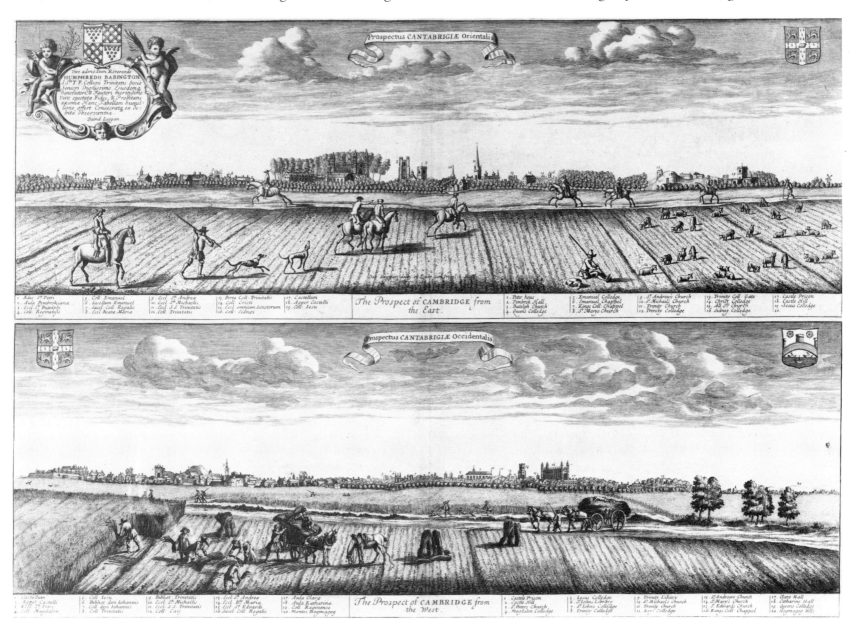

6 David Loggan's illustrations of the two great fields at Cambridge *c.*1690: the Barnwell Field and the Cambridge Field. These extensive tracts of open farmland flanked the town, preventing urban expansion until the Acts of Enclosure (see p. 32) in the early nineteenth century.

Cantebrig from Oxford and Paris did so in the knowledge that an intellectual society of teachers already existed there.

The University has not always lived in close harmony with its host the town, as it does today, and for many centuries there was much friction between the academic community and the townspeople or, as it came to be known, between 'Town & Gown'. The grievances between the two parties seem too have been equally the fault of both sides in that neither was really willing to tolerate the other.

At first, owing to the definition of a scholar and to what was then termed the 'benefit of Clergy', which could be claimed by anyone who could read and write, many undesirable characters came to the town in the guise of scholars and gave the genuine academics a bad reputation among the townspeople for causing trouble. On the other hand, the well-intentioned scholar suffered from the extortionate rents charged by the local landlords. The present day situation of students living in their colleges or college-owned property in and around the town, did not become commonplace until the fifteenth century: before then students were left to fend for themselves in the town and, later, in their own organised hostels. The Colleges were initially intended to house teachers only (see chapter 3). The University and Corporation elected Taxors to administer the rents charged in the town, and the powers of the university were soon extended to such matters as the control of weights and measures and ale house licencing.

Apart from such minor problems, there were other more serious grievances which led to rioting, resulting in the hanging of townsmen, while the equally guilty academics involved often escaped lightly. The university gained the power of Conusance, which meant that the Chancellor and Masters were granted the privilege of trying all civil and criminal cases in which a clerk (teacher) was either plaintiff or defendant. This was the Chancellor's Court and it soon became known as 'The Townsmens Scourge', as, undoubtedly, many university members took advantage of the protection it afforded. The situation between 'Town & Gown' continued to worsen and a major riot broke out in 1261, the outcome of which illustrates the strength of the hold the university now had over the town. During the riot many houses were damaged and university records were burnt, and when the case was tried by three judges appointed by Henry III, 16 townsmen and 28 scholars were found guilty; the scholars received the King's pardon, but the townsmen were hanged for inciting the riot. Similar cases, though not as serious, were tried in the following centuries, such as that linked to the Peasants Revolt of 1381.

Without the University it is reasonable to assume that Cambridge would not have the stature, or the architecture, that it has today, as it is the Colleges and University that have made it more than just an ordinary East Anglian market town and created a city of architectural renown. It was not, however, the university itself but the evolution of the individual colleges which had such an impact on the town (today there are over 30). In fact until the mid-nineteenth century, when it was forced to expand its teaching and administrative facilities on an unprecedented scale owing to the introduction of many new subjects into the curriculum at that time, the university did not make its architectural presence felt in the town to any great extent. Although the function of the University and the Colleges are inter-related the two have developed architecturally along quite separate lines.

7   8

The first College at Cambridge was founded in 1280 by Hugh de Balsham, Bishop of Ely, when he arranged to house his endowed scholars with the monks at the Hospital of St John. This proved unsuccessful, and in 1284 the academics were moved to their own building outside the city boundaries, south of the Trumpington Gate, next to the church of St Peter (now St Mary the Less), and the establishment consequently became known as 'Peterhouse'. The Bishop had based his foundation on the statutes of the first official College at Oxford, Merton, founded by Walter de Merton in 1264. It is interesting to note that Merton also owned property in Cambridge; the area now in the north-west corner of St John's College containing Merton Hall and the 'School of Pythagoras' (The 'Merton Arms' Public House, in Northampton Street, still bears his name), and it may only have been chance that he chose to found his college on his land in Oxford rather than in Cambridge.

The first building at Peterhouse - the Hall (fig. 7) - was built in 1286 and is the oldest surviving collegiate structure in the town. No further colleges were founded until the fourteenth century when seven were established in less than three decades: Michaelhouse (1324, to become part of Trinity College in 1546); University Hall (1326, to become Clare Hall in 1338, and then Clare College in 1856); King's Hall (1337, also part of Trinity from 1546); Pembroke (1347); Gonville Hall (1348, Gonville & Caius College from 1557); Trinity Hall (1350); and Corpus Christi (1352, fig. 8). These colleges were quite different to those of the present day, as they were endowed foundations to house teachers and there were no students resident in them. It was only following the innovatory ideas of William of Wykeham at Oxford in the late fourteenth century, who founded his 'New College' there, that students joined the teachers in the colleges at Cambridge.

By the fourteenth century, most of the suitable building land within the confines of the medieval town had already been built on and, consequently, the colleges had to settle for what was left. If they wanted to stay within the town boundaries, then the only site remaining was the land on the east bank of the river, alternatively they would have to leave the town proper and build on one of the numerous open sites around the perimeter, as was the case with Peterhouse and Pembroke. Corpus Christi was the only exception; its site, in the centre of the town on the east side of the ancient High Street, was possibly obtained because the college was founded and endowed by two town guilds, both composed of local merchants, a rare case of the propagation of the College system by the townsfolk themselves.

Coinciding with the birth of these early colleges, there was a decline in the river trade at Cantebrig and, subsequently, in the prosperity of the town. This was reflected in the country as a whole and was partly due to the continual drain on national funds in heavy taxation to finance the Hundred Years War (1337-1453). The Black Death, which swept the country on several occasions during this period, was particularly bad in the Eastern Counties in the mid fourteenth century.

Cambridge was not a particularly healthy place to live; its location on the edge of the marshy Fens, combined with the hot summer of 1349, made it extremely vulnerable to disease. It received a regular flow of traders and scholars, who probably acted as carriers for the plague, and its sanitary arrangements were greatly neglected. This was one of the grievances of the university authorities who had tried on several occasions to force the corporation to improve the situation, and, in particular, to clean out the King's Ditch which had become virtually an open sewer encompassing the whole east and south sides of the community. For several years the mortality rate at Cantebrig was such that it was deserted by traders, and the scholars now regularly vacated the town during the summer months to live in the country away from the dangers of the Black Death, which had taken its toll of so many of their colleagues; 16 of the 40 scholars of Kings Hall, for instance, died between April and August 1349.

This was a harsh time for both academics and townsmen, but it gave the colleges the chance to establish themselves in the area between the wharves and the High Street, in the wake of the decline of the heart of commercial Cantebrig — the river industry. The later expansion of these early foundations, and others joining them in that area, resulted in the central nucleus of Colleges and their extensive gardens flanking the river. Today that whole area is simply known as the 'Backs' and comprises the typical picture of the famous University town (fig. 9).

In the second half of the fourteenth century the first university buildings were also started, on the site known today as the Old Schools. This land was given to the university by a Nigel de Thornton in 1278 but its first building, the Divinity School, was not built until c.1350-1400 after which much else followed in the vicinity (see chapter 6).

9

7 The first college building — the Hall at Peterhouse of 1286.   **8** The Old Court of Corpus Christi College, built 1352-77 but with late fifteenth century buttressing.   **9** The College 'Backs' towards Clare from King's water meadows (*see also fig. 63*).

Late Medieval Cantebrig

The Peasants' Revolt of 1381, which started in Kent and Essex, quickly spread east and north reaching Cantebrig by the middle of June, where its leaders were the brothers James and Thomas of Grantchester, and it gave the townspeople the opportunity to express their grievances against the increasingly dominant University. During the two days of rioting at Cantebrig the angry mob, led by many of the town's officials, forced the university authorities and the Masters of the colleges to renounce their privileges and to abide by the laws common to all. The rioters broke into Great St Mary's Church, which had been taken over by the university as its administrative headquarters, and statutes, charters, and other effects of the university and the colleges were publicly burnt in the market place. The revolt in the Cantebrig area was suppressed by Henry le Spencer, Bishop of Norwich, with a small troop of soldiers. The following November the Mayor and Bailiffs of the town were summoned to Westminster where their forcibly obtained concessions were declared void and they were severely reprimanded for their actions against the scholars.

'Town & Gown' feuds continued as the University increased its presence in the new academic quarter between the High Street and the river. A severe fire in the town centre in 1385 destroyed over 100 properties and left many homeless, adding to the exodus resulting from the plague. In 1402 an order was passed to try and combat the pestilence now associated with Cantebrig stating that no dung or filth was allowed to be left in the streets or market place for more than seven days! Some of the ancient street names attest to the state of the medieval town, such as 'Foul Lane' (now Trinity Lane) the condition of which was thought to be the cause of much illness in the bordering colleges of Trinity Hall and Gonville Hall.

The fifteenth century saw the foundation of six new colleges at Cantebrig. In 1428 Henry VI gave a site on the north west bank of the river for the accommodation of Benedictine monks from the Abbey of Crowland who were studying at the University; this was the origin of Magdalene College (1542). At some time around 1437 William Byngham, a London parish priest, founded God's House as a training college for grammar school teachers, on a site just east of Clare, later to be relocated and then refounded as Christ's College in 1505. In the early 1440s, Henry VI founded his initially modest college, King's, in the same area as Byngham's, which he soon decided to expand on an unprecedented scale, resulting not only in the relocation of God's House, but in the demolition and eventual transformation of a large part of the medieval town. In 1446, Henry gave a small piece of land to the Rector of St Botolph's Church, Andrew Dockett, who established his College of St Bernard to the south-east of King's; this was re-founded by Henry's Queen, Margaret of Anjou, to become 'the Queen's College of St Margaret and St Bernard'; and, later, was further augmented by Edward IV's Queen, Elisabeth Woodville, thus gaining its present name –

Queens' College. The third Provost of King's College, Doctor Robert Woodlark, founded St Catherine's Hall in 1473 to the south-east of King's. The Benedictine Nunnery of St Radegund was taken over by Bishop Alcock of Ely in 1496 with the permission of Henry Tudor, and was converted into the 'College of the Blessed Virgin Mary, St John the Evangelist, and the Glorious Virgin St Radegund', commonly known as Jesus College.

Of this new group of colleges, the monks' hostel (Magdalene) was the first to be established on the west side of the river. God's House, (though only temporarily), King's, Queens' and St Catherine's added to the growing academic sector along the east bank; while Jesus was located outside the town's perimeter. By far the most controversial of these foundations, and undoubtedly the most important single event in the topographical history of medieval Cantebrig, was King's College. King's was to stretch from the High Street in the east (now King's Parade) to the river in the west, and from Clare College in the north to the site of the Carmelite Friars in the south (now Queens' College). This was an enormous area and one of the busiest in the town centre, being crowded with tenements and commercial properties, and dissected by streets connecting the market place with the wharves of the industrial riverside.

Henry VI's acquisition of this site for his college effectively divorced the commercial town centre from the river in that area, dealing yet another severe blow to the ailing river trade. At this time a major street, Milne Street, ran through this area parallel with the High Street and the river, on a line which today would be the continuation of Queens' Lane

10

in the south to Trinity Lane in the north (see p. 8). The central portion of Milne Street was demolished and so, eventually, was all the property around it, including the parish church of St John Zachary, the Blue Boar Inn, the river wharf known as Salthythe, and many other commercial buildings fronting onto the High Street. To compensate for depriving it of access to the river in this area, Henry gave the town some land to the north of his site, upon which the corporation created what is now Garret Hostel Lane.

The foundation of King's marks the beginning of the transition of the town centre from civic to academic control. In 1447 Henry obtained a large area of land on the west side of the river, today comprising the Water Meadows of King's – known as 'Scholars Piece' – and what later became the Fellows Garden of the neighbouring Clare College; this acquisition inaugurated the famous 'Backs'.

Henry VI had obtained his enlarged site by the middle of the fifteenth century, but owing to the outbreak of the Wars of the Roses in 1455 did not live to see its completion. In fact, building proceeded very spasmodically, with only the famous chapel being completed by the early years of the following century, and it was not until the eighteenth and early nineteenth centuries that the college arrived at its present form.

The foundation of King's on such a large site in the centre of Cantebrig, coupled with the plague epidemics and the severe fire of 1385, resulted in a marked decline in population. In 1446, the burgesses complained that houses previously occupied by artisans were now taken over by scholars, and, as a consequence of the vast influx of academics, craftsmen were now leaving the district.

The transition from market town to academic centre had a marked effect on the town's topography and, in particular, on its architecture. The fifteenth century saw the construction of some of the finest Cambridge buildings: King's College Chapel (fig. 10) was begun in 1446, though it was not completed until 1515. Queens' first court (fig. 11) was built between 1448-49 and much of its second, or Cloister Court, was also constructed. Magdalene's first court was begun; Pembroke's first court, and much at Gonville and Trinity Halls also. The Schools precinct of the university continued with the completion of the south, west and east ranges.

The architectural activity in the town itself was almost nil at this time, and although many of the parish churches were enlarged, the additions were almost all for college purposes. Many of the early colleges did not have chapels and were sited next to parish churches in which they could worship, as was the case, for instance, at Peterhouse and Corpus Christi. Others only had to walk a short distance to their parish churches. As a result, some churches added extra side chapels at this time to accommodate the enlarged congregations; as, for example, at St Edward, St Botolph and St Clement. The most extensive rebuilding scheme of this period was that undertaken by the university of Great St Mary's Church (fig. 12) which was begun in the late fifteenth century but not fully completed for over a hundred years.

11

10 King's College Chapel (1446-1515) from the south-east — for many the finest building in Cambridge (see pp. 120-123). **11** The west and north ranges of Queens' College medieval Old Court (1448-49). **12** Great St Mary's Church from the market square, rebuilt 1478-1608.

12

Reformation Cantebrig

Henry VIII acceded to the throne in 1509 and by 1534 the divorce of the Church of England from Rome was complete. After the Dissolution of the Monasteries an act was passed in 1545 authorising the similar suppression of the colleges, which were in effect religious foundations, of both Oxford and Cambridge. In 1546 a university commission inquired into the state of the colleges and its report was submitted to the King. The university authorities approached Katherine Parr, Henry's sixth wife, for help. This campaign evidently succeeded for in that same year Henry not only dismissed the act of 1545 but also established a foundation of his own at Cantebrig, Trinity College (fig. 14).

Cantebrig was no exception to the great religious and social changes that followed on from the Reformation. Quite apart from this, the architecture of Cantebrig began to reflect a new classical influence based on the Italian Renaissance, although a truly classical style of architecture did not develop in England until the seventeenth and eighteenth centuries.

In the sixteenth century, before the Reformation, the town was dominated not by the Colleges (although there were fourteen of them), but by the wealthy religious houses now well established in Cantebrig. Barnwell Priory, the oldest and richest of the local monastic institutions, was the first to submit in 1538, after which the others followed suit. Many of the dissolved monasteries were to be swallowed up into existing or new college foundations. The sixteenth century saw the birth of six colleges, some re-foundations and some completely new: Lady Margaret Beaufort, the mother of Henry VII, re-founded God's House as Christ's College in 1505, and posthumously founded St John's College in 1511 on the site of the former Hospital of St John. In 1542 the Lord Chancellor, Lord Audley of Walden, refounded the almost extinct monks hostel as Magdalene College; and in 1546 Henry VIII founded Trinity, to be the largest college at Cantebrig. To achieve this large-scale foundation, the King combined the existing colleges of Michaelhouse and King's Hall, with other hostels and properties in the vicinity, and there is perhaps some truth in the idea that he embarked on this scheme partly to out-do Thomas Wolsey's large foundation of Cardinal's College at Oxford, of a few years earlier (now Christ Church).

There were two Elizabethan foundations; Emmanuel, founded on the site of the dissolved Dominican Priory, by Sir Walter Mildmay in 1584; and Sidney Sussex, on the site of the dissolved Franciscan Priory, by Lady Frances Sidney, Dowager Countess of Sussex, in 1594. Although this new group of colleges was to have a great effect on the architecture of the town they did not alter its topography, as they simply took over the sites of existing foundations.

During the sixteenth century there was a general awakening to the plight of the students, who were still expected to provide their own lodgings and food in rented accommodation, or in the numerous student hostels flourishing at that time (see chapter 3). The Masters and Fellows of the Colleges saw the need to include the student body as a resident

13

part of the college community, as Wykeham had done at Oxford over a century earlier. Thus, students began to be housed within the colleges themselves and, consequently, extra buildings were required to accommodate them. This resulted in the first major expansion of the colleges and for that purpose many new buildings were erected during the sixteenth and seventeenth centuries.

By the early sixteenth century Cantebrig had sunk to the 29th wealthiest town in England, as calculated by its tax contributions. However, there was a recovery in the English river trade during the century which was to culminate in the golden age of river transport in the eighteenth century, before its final collapse following the introduction of the railways in the nineteenth. At Cantebrig the revival of the river industry, though severely diminished, brought back the town's lost prosperity, rising to rank ninth wealthiest in the country by the mid-seventeenth century. Corn had become the most important commodity and Cantebrig was one of London's major corn markets during the reign of Elizabeth I (1558-1603). The Reformation had had the effect of bringing attention to one of the few industries introduced into Cantebrig by the university - book production and selling. Books and their associated crafts, such as paper making and illuminating, had been present in the town since the early days of the University, and bookselling was a major trade at the famous Stourbridge Fair where the 'Booksellers Row'

consisted of several stalls. Gray tells us that there were bookbinders working in Cambridge in the early years of the sixteenth century, such as Garret who was a friend of Erasmus, the Dutch Humanist, who was teaching here at the time; and also that the first Cambridge printer, John Lair de Siberch, was practising in the early 1520s after settling in the town from his native Cologne. Gray also informs us that at the end of the fifteenth century, hops had been introduced into Eastern England from the Netherlands, and by the early 1500s Cantebrig had its first major brewery between the river and Magdalene, run by a Dutchman called Francis van Hoorn.

There are two excellent illustrations depicting Cambridge in the late sixteenth century, both aerial views from the south: the first, by Richard Lyne of 1574, is interesting but its accuracy questionable; whereas the second, by John Hammond of 1592 (fig. 16) is thought to be an extremely precise and detailed picture of what the town was like at that time. From Hammond's drawing it is easy to see that Cantebrig was still very much a rural town, and that there were still open green areas at its centre, such as that between what is now Trinity and Sidney Streets, in the vicinity of the appropriately named Green Street. On the west bank of the river there were as yet no college 'Backs', and the only college-owned property that interrupted the extensive town green all along that bank were the water meadows of King's.

14

13 The picturesque, timber-framed, President's Gallery in Queens' College Cloister Court, *c.*1540 (*see also fig. 308*). **14** Henry VIII's Trinity College; founded in 1546 by combining the older colleges of King's Hall and Michaelhouse, later re-organised to form the present Great Court (see p. 90). **15** The Gate of Virtue (west elevation) at Gonville & Caius College, designed by Dr Caius and built in 1565-67, is one of the earliest predominantly classical structures in Cambridge (*see also fig. 84*).

15

25

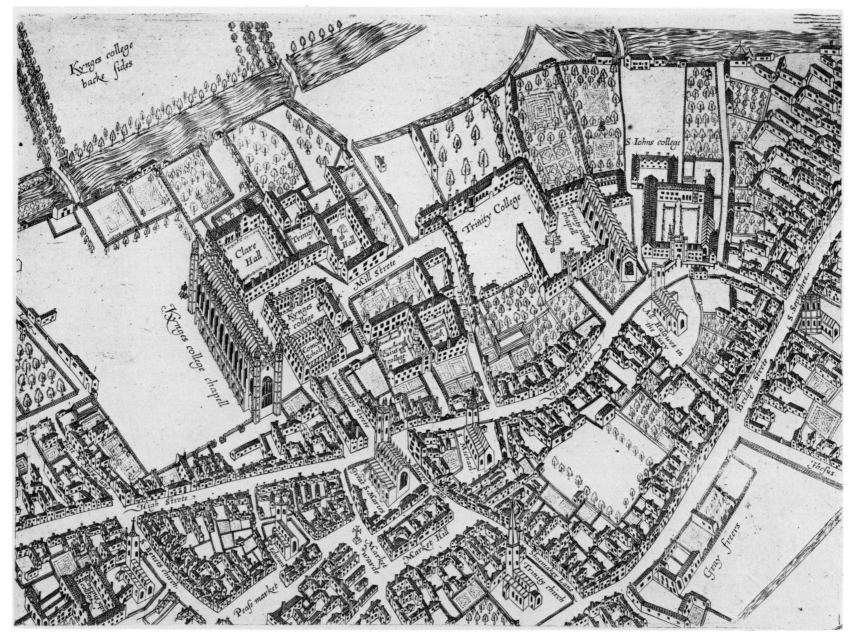

16 John Hammond's aerial perspective of Cambridge, drawn in 1592, gives an excellent idea of the town at that time. The college 'Backs' had not yet been created, nor were there any stone bridges over the river. King's consisted solely of the vast chapel and the original small Old Court, now part of the university's Old Schools precinct. The old High Street — now King's Parade, Trinity and St John's Streets — differed greatly from its present form, with such buildings as Kings' gatehouse and screen, and the Senate House, being absent. Trinity is shown in its original state, just prior to the re-organisation by Dr Nevile, and, next door, St John's consists only of two courts. The former church of All Saints in the Jewry (All Hallowes) faced Trinity (*see fig. 563*) but this was demolished in 1865 when St John's Street was widened. To the south-east of the church was an open green area, through which today runs Green Street. To the east is the site of the Gray Friars Priory, which was dissolved under Henry VIII, and which only two years later was to be taken over by Sidney Sussex College. In the same vicinity can be seen part of the King's Ditch, forming the by then redundant eastern protective boundary of the town, soon to be filled-in.

26

Seventeenth and Eighteenth Century Cambridge

Cambridge was actively involved in the Civil War (1642-51), which emphasised the split between 'Town & Gown' and brought added venom to the now traditional feud: the townspeople were Parliamentarian in their sympathies, while the University was predominantly Royalist. During this period 'Town & Gown' were virtually at war with each other and it was widely known that the colleges were often used to store munitions for the Royalist cause. Scholars walked the streets in fear of attack by the townsmen, and none of them was allowed to leave the town unless they could produce a voucher signed by a leading townsman stating that they were a 'confider' and sympathetic to the Parliamentarian cause.

Oliver Cromwell, himself a native of the eastern counties, had been elected Member of Parliament for Cambridge in 1640, and was no stranger to the place as he had been a student at Sidney Sussex College some years earlier. Cambridge became, once again, an important strategic and military stronghold, controlling as it did the roads between East Anglia and the Midlands. In the early stages of the Civil War the town was the base for the armed forces of the Eastern Counties Association, and Gray tells us that in defence of the town a large cannon called a 'drake' was placed on the Great Bridge, and the castle was strengthened employing materials that had been set aside for use in the rebuilding of Clare College. The other bridges of the town, from Silver Street to St John's, were all destroyed by Cromwell's men to hinder a possible attack by Royalist forces. Such an attack was thought to be imminent in February, 1643, when Cromwell raised an army of 30,000 men to defend the town, but it was a false alarm and they were not required.

The most important topographical event of this period took place when the large and rather muddled site of Trinity College was re-organised and virtually transformed between 1597-1605 by its Master, Dr Thomas Nevile. This was a huge task which Nevile executed with great planning ingenuity, resulting in one of the town's most famous compositions - Great Court (see Trinity College). In 1610 and 1613 St John's and Trinity purchased from the town the land on either side of the river to the west of their main sites (Trinity in exchange for what is now Parker's Piece), and at about the same time Clare bought from King's the northern section of the Water Meadows. These acquisitions extended the College Backs. In 1615, Dr Stephen Perse, a fellow of Gonville & Caius, died after founding a 'Free School' in what is now Free School Lane; this was then to become the Perse Grammar School. The last outbreaks of the plague took place in 1630, 1665 and 1666, after which the town was not troubled again by serious pestilence. In 1655 there is a reference, for the first time, to a regular stagecoach service between London and Cambridge carrying passengers and mail. There were two routes; either via Bishops Stortford or Ware, depending, presumably, on whether one was going to north or south London.

Samuel Pepys (1633-1703), the seventeenth century diarist, records making many journeys between London and Cambridge both by coach and on horseback; it was either an easy journey taking two days, visiting his favourite inns en route, or one very long day from 4am to 8pm.

In 1719 another famous Cambridge man, Dr John Addenbrooke, died and left in his will provision to build a hospital, of which there are now two in Cambridge bearing his name. Between 1760-63 the first Botanic Garden was established in Cambridge by the university on a five-acre site to the east of Free School Lane in what were originally the gardens of the Austen Friars; this was moved in the nineteenth century to its present 40 acre site south of the town centre (see chapter 6). In 1788 an Act was finally passed to ensure the regular cleansing of the towns sanitary system, as well as for better paving of the streets, and lamps were first installed along the Cambridge streets. There are three excellent volumes of illustrations depicting seventeenth and eighteenth century Cambridge: Loggan's *Cantabrigia Illustrata* (1690); Harraden's *Cantabrigia Depicta* (1811); and Ackerman's *History of Cambridge University* (1815).

During the seventeenth and eighteenth centuries, there was very little enlargement of the area of the medieval town, even though the population almost doubled. This confinement was due to the great fields on either side of the town and to the marshy land unsuitable for building along the west bank of the river. Thus, the increase in population must have been accommodated by increasing the density of the built-up area. Some contemporary eye-witness reports of the town are revealing: 'The buildings in many parts of the town were so little and so low that they looked more like huts for pigmies than houses for men...The place is not at all large and about as mean as a village, and were it not for the many fine colleges it would be one of the sorriest places in the world.'[7]

No new colleges were founded in the seventeenth or eighteenth centuries, though it was a time of expansion and much building activity. Up until then the colleges had kept a fairly discreet profile with their enclosed courts on a domestic scale, the exception being King's College Chapel which dominated the town as it still does today. The only emphasis given to the street facades of the colleges were the towered gatehouses which appeared from the fifteenth century onwards, and by 1600 there were half a dozen of these sturdy structures scattered throughout the town (see chapter 4).

From the Tudor period onwards classical details and complete classical structures (such as the screen in Kings College Chapel), though not yet entire buildings, started to appear in Cambridge and College buildings were gradually to become more elegant and ornate over the next two centuries. Those who commissioned the new buildings, the Masters and Fellows of the Colleges, began to change their requirement from simple buildings to house academics to those creating a fashionable public display, particularly in their street facades.

The early years of the seventeenth century in Cambridge saw both medieval Gothic and classical details combined in the same building, but it was not until 1640-1643 that the first predominantly classical building was erected, the Fellows Building at Christ's College (fig. 17). The architect of this building is unknown and although it was unique at Cambridge, and innovatory in the country as a whole, it still referred in certain details to medieval forms. In the 1660s Cambridge received its first wholly classical building with Christopher Wren's Pembroke College Chapel (fig. 18). This was Wren's first completed work (1663-65), and the Chapel at Emmanuel followed a few years later. Between 1676-1695 Wren completed his Cambridge masterpiece, Trinity College Library. The influence of Wren on the local Cambridge architects was immense and can be seen in many other contemporary buildings.

The early eighteenth century was a time of great proposals for magnificent building schemes in Cambridge such as had not been contemplated since Henry VI's dream of King's in the mid fifteenth century. However, none of these projects was to be realised in their entirety and at best one or two buildings were executed as parts of larger schemes.

In 1714 Dr John Adams, the Provost of King's, had invited ideas for the completion of the college along the lines of the founder's original intentions (see King's College). Among the architects asked to submit drawings, Sir Christopher Wren had strongly recommended his former assistant and collaborator Nicholas Hawksmoor. However, the only building to be completed from the King's competition was the Fellows, or Gibbs Building, by James Gibbs some twenty years later. Gibbs was another architect who was also to be frustrated in that his ambitious scheme was only partially completed, as was also the case with his other building of the same period, the Senate House (fig. 19). Apart from the famous London-based architects who were building in Cambridge at this time there were other local architects, two in particular, who could design competently in the classical manner: Sir James Burrough and

James Essex, who added several fine classical buildings to the colleges in the eighteenth century. However, Burrough and Essex were also responsible for much of the 'ashlaring' that took place at this time; the process by which medieval brick buildings were dressed in an Italianate facade of stone.

Undoubtedly the most fascinating of the eighteenth century building schemes was that put forward by Hawksmoor (whilst also working on the King's competition) for the reorganisation of the entire town centre based on a Classical Baroque forum. Hawksmoor attempted to transform a still rather unimpressive and congested little market town into something more fitting to one of the leading universities in Europe.

17 18

Looking at Hawksmoor's sketch plan (fig. 20) the most noticeable aspect was his intention to open-up the old narrow streets of the medieval town, concentrating on the main south-east to north-west axis (A604) from Regent Street to Magdalene Bridge, and on the ancient High Street from the south end of King's through to the Round Church. At the south-east approach to the town from London there was to be an enormous gateway, approximately opposite what is now Downing College in Regent Street. This would have emphasized the point of entry into the town and have acted, in the true Baroque manner, as a prelude to the main theme; the town centre. At the other end of this axis, there were to be two piazzas, one on either side of Magdalene Bridge, marking the point of exit from the town. As one progressed along the route between the triumphal gateway and the piazzas, powerful vistas would have opened up: firstly, by the new emphasis given to Petty Cury, which was widened and set in a direct east-west line from Christ's College Gatehouse through to the east end of King's College Chapel in the distance; secondly, by a new street cut through from the gateway of Sidney Sussex to the gatehouse of Trinity; and, finally, by the much widened St John's Street which now visually connected the Round Church with the gatehouse of St John's College. Thus, as one travelled through Cambridge one's attention was arrested by hints of the magnificent buildings that existed further into the architectural heart of the town, around which the main theme of the composition was set.

Sadly, both Hawksmoor's scheme for King's and his plan for rebuilding the town remained on paper and there are no Hawksmoor buildings at Cambridge. *The Town of Cambridge As it Ought to be Reformed,* by the late David Roberts and Gordon Cullen, explains Hawksmoor's scheme in detail and, more importantly, translates it into visual form (figs 21-26):

By an act of the imagination, as realised in the following drawings, it is possible to see in Hawksmoor's plan for Cambridge his conception of a university town as a stately and grand spectacle...He preserves carefully the existing form of the town with its two converging main streets...The main theme of Hawksmoor's plan lies, however, between Trumpington Street and St John's Street. The colleges and churches are like fountains and statuary in a baroque garden, merely diversions and invitations on the approach to the climax....The University Forum itself is a masonry enclosure peopled by obelisks and surrounded by buildings of great size, each complementary to the other and with apertures which reveal the Backs, the 'reformed' market place, Trinity Street and Christ's...Old and new are merged into an ideal scene, the abstract qualities of mass, space, line and silhouette are employed to create a breath-taking architectural picture. The spectator is assaulted by giant porticoes, belittled by obelisks, and invited towards other dominating spaces and impelling avenues....The vista into the new court of King's leads into one of Hawksmoor's finest conceptions....As at Greenwich and Blenheim there is a strong sense of movement, in this case towards the Backs and a bridge over the river.....The Cambridge streets have become a baroque progression...By his plan medieval Cambridge would have been given unity and visual meaning. It would have been transformed into lucid, broad spaces set in front of a series of masonry back-drops....Against it the dignity of university life and ceremony would have been performed....

17, 18 & 19 Three of the most important classical buildings at Cambridge of the seventeenth and eighteenth centuries: **17** The south-west elevation of the Fellows' Building at Christ's College, designer unknown, and built in 1640-43. **18** Pembroke College Chapel of 1663-65, in the main west front of the college towards Trumpington Street; Christopher Wren's first completed work. **19** The Senate House, by James Gibbs of 1722-30, only part of a larger scheme which was never fully executed (see chapter 6). *See also figs 83-99, pp 54-57.*

19

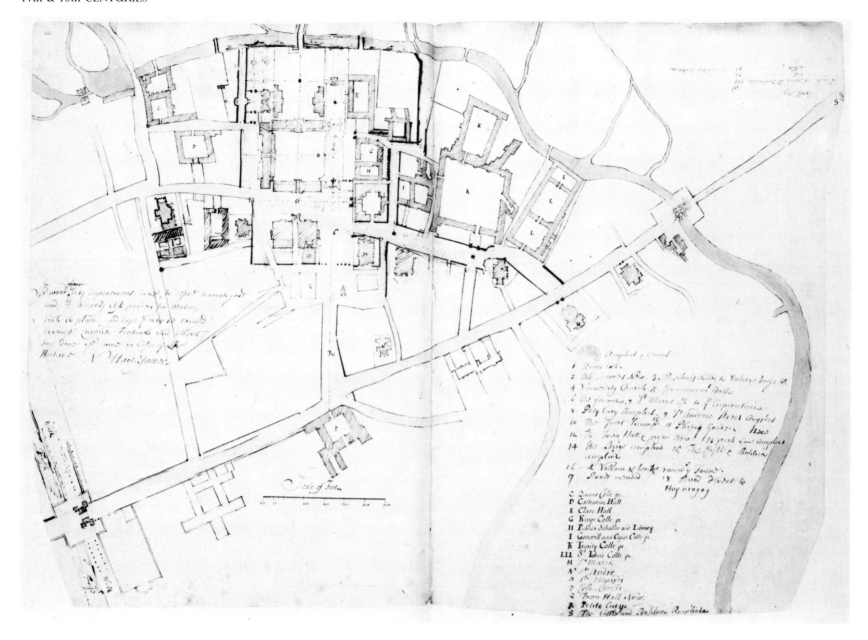

20 Nicholas Hawksmoor's scheme for the re-planning of the centre of Cambridge, *c.*1714 (Trustees of the British Museum). Hawksmoor intended to open up the narrow streets of the medieval town, concentrating on the Regent Street to Magdalene Street axis in the east, and the Trumpington Street to St John's Street route in the west, linking them with augmented or new streets, and creating dramatic vistas employing existing buildings. The giant gateway, marking the point of entry into the composition, can be seen in the south-east area of the plan, and the piazzas marking the point of exit in the north-west around Magdalene Bridge. **21-26** Modern drawings illustrating Hawksmoor's ideas for the centre of the town and what actually exists today. (The drawings shown in figs. 21, 23 & 25 are reproduced with the permission of the artist, Gordon Cullen; the extract of David Roberts's text, on page 29, is reproduced with the permission of Mrs M.M. Roberts and Brooke Crutchley). **21** The intended University Forum, now King's Parade, where the street is transformed into a piazza surrounded by grand Baroque buildings, and **22** the same area as it is today. **23** Hawksmoor's idea for the view towards Trinity College from the forum — another piazza surrounded by college fronts and shops, and **24** Trinity Street as it is now — tightly enclosed and congested. **25** The University Forum as it might have appeared from the market place, and **26** the view today.

21

22

23

24

25

26

Enclosure, Expansion and Reform

The nineteenth century at Cambridge was a time of great change both in the social and political structure of the town and the university, as well as in the vast expansion that was to take place with an acceleration of growth unprecedented in the town's history. This was to be the beginning of an improved relationship between 'Town & Gown', when the age of university privileges and its ancient suzerainty over the town, were to be superseded by Act of Parliament. The university itself underwent much internal reform, and the whole academic scene was drastically changed with the introduction into the curriculum of many new subjects, particularly the natural and social sciences, in the middle years of the century. John Steegman describes Cambridge at the beginning of the period; 'Byron was up at Trinity, boxing, pistol shooting, swimming in the pool above Grantchester which still bears his name, doing little work in the academic sense, but forming close intellectual friendships as well as friendships rather less intellectual but a good deal more passionate'. – such was the life of a Georgian undergraduate. Steegman continues 'However, this Cambridge of the "Bucks" of great drinking, of riotous driving of tandems through the narrow streets, of fashionable prize-fighters, of privileged noblemen undergraduates, of mail-coaches and flying-coaches and stage-coaches – was soon abolished by progress and reform'.[8]

Topographically the event which was to vastly increase the built-up area of Cambridge was the passing of the Acts of Enclosure which, in effect, removed the 'corsets' in the form of the great East and West Fields, which contained the over-full town, and resulted in a long overdue explosion of urban development on all sides.

The Acts of Enclosure were those by which the open field system was broken down into much smaller units, each being 'enclosed' by a landlord with hedges, walls or fences, thus creating the patchwork of fields so characteristic of the English countryside today. Enclosure at Cambridge came fairly late and it was not until 1802 and 1807 respectively, that the great East and West Fields were broken up by Act of Parliament.

By the division of these large areas (see fig. 6; the East Field was 1150 acres, the West 1284) into smaller units, it was possible to put aside sections for urban development – of which congested Cambridge was in desperate need, and the town started to expand, to begin with along the east side. Large areas of housing were built between the Newmarket Road and Hills Road, through which a new route, Mill Road, was created. Starting in the 1820s and continuing until after 1850, the most intensive area of building was between Hills Road and Trumpington Road, soon to be known as 'New Town'. This area of south and east Cambridge began to take on a new character, quite different to the old town, as most of the new housing was in the form of continuous terraces, all constructed over a relatively short period. The subsequent result was an outer residential district with strong homogeneity of character, in contrast to the older and much more varied town centre. This was not to be the only area of intensive expansion, and, owing to the rapid growth of population in nineteenth century Cambridge, similar areas of terraced housing developed to the north and south-west.

The population explosion in Cambridge in the nineteenth century was not as great as elsewhere, perhaps owing to the lack of local industry. That it was not inconsiderable is shown, for example, in the parish of St Andrew the Less, in the eastern area of the town on the Newmarket Road, where the population rose from 252 in 1801 to a staggering 9486 by 1841. The prosperity now enjoyed by the Eastern Counties was a result of the improved agricultural production in this extremely fertile quarter of England, much of which passed through the Cambridge markets. The Eastern Counties Railway station at Cambridge was opened in 1845 after much debate as to its location; the university authorities eventually won the argument, having it situated outside the town to the south-east in what was formerly the Middle Field of the great East Field. This was a deliberate move by the university in order to discourage the use of the railway by undergraduates who could now reach the joys of London in a fraction of the time that it had taken previously. Locating the station here also encouraged more suburban development in the surrounding area, even further to the south and east.

The university and colleges became the largest single employer in the town. By the end of the century, there were over twenty colleges housing several thousand fellows and students, all of whom had to be looked after and fed. Even today the tradition of service has survived, and every Cambridge undergraduate living in college property has his or her daily 'bedder' to attend to their needs. Many amenities were supplied to the town at this time for the benefit of all; such as gas lighting in the 1820s, a public water supply in 1853, and the first drainage system in 1895 at a cost of £150,000, before which the river had carried the towns sewage and had always been a health hazard.

The Reform Act of 1832 and the Municipal Corporations Act of 1835 gave the Cambridge townspeople a larger say in the running of the town. The re-structuring of the town's corporation eventually led to the all-important Cambridge Award Act of 1856. Sir John Patterson, formerly a judge in the Court of the King's Bench, acted as arbitrator in 1855 to resolve the age-old grievances between 'Town & Gown'. By this time the university was more concerned with its own internal problems, trying to bring itself into line with modern subjects and contemporary teaching, and its old quarrels with the town must now have seeemed rather insignificant. The oaths and declarations binding the Town Council to conserve the privileges and liberties of the university were abolished; the right of the university to claim conusance via the Chancellors Court in actions of law involving a university member was to cease; the power of the Vice-Chancellor to grant ale house licences, to supervise weights and measures and the running of markets and fairs, etc, was transferred to the justices of the peace of the borough; and all property of the university and colleges, with a few exceptions, was to be assessed for rates as every other property in the borough. A few privileges did remain, but most of these ceased before long, such as the power of the university authorities to arrest 'common women' whom it considered to be meddling with its undergraduates: a case of wrongful conviction caused considerable uproar and, as a result, this right was also surrendered to the civil authorities in 1894.

Within the university itself, the fight for equally important reform was also taking place amongst its members, who were trying to shake-off many of the now outdated, and medieval, customs which controlled their lives. Most college statutes required that a certain proportion of their fellows had to be in religious orders and that all fellows were subject to the university's Religious Test Act, which excluded dissenters. It is easy to see how such a restriction was to become a serious problem in the Cambridge of Charles Darwin, whose *Origin of Species* was published in 1859, and encouraged a very controversial form of atheism, particularly among the recent influx of natural scientists at that time. Although the anti-subscription movement had been fighting for the repeal of the Test Act since the middle of the eighteenth century, it was not repealed until 1871. Similarly, there was a requirement of celibacy for most of the fellows, unless that is, they were Master of a College, a Professor, or a Fellow also holding a university post. A Fellow belonging in none of these categories and wishing to marry, did so at the forfeiture of his fellowship as the view of the colleges was that marriage would only detract from the Fellow's loyalty to his foundation. This issue also became a serious problem in the mid 1800s, resulting in both frequent abuse of the regulations and the resignation of numbers of college fellows, until the statutes were finally changed in 1882 allowing them to marry. The fellow and his family could not, however, be housed within the college, and a new type of housing need therefore arose. At the time of Enclosure the university and many of the colleges acquired most of the land immediately west of the river realising the potential and convenience of the area for later expansion. Colleges such as Trinity, Clare and King's established Fellows' gardens, and St John's, Trinity, Caius and Trinity Hall, created sports grounds in the area, as there was no room for such facilities in the colleges themselves.

Unlike the other areas of new development around the town, to north, east and south, which were being crammed-full of rows of terraced houses, the character of West Cambridge was to be one of comparative wealth. Large detached houses with extensive gardens were built for dons with private means, or rich professionals, who could afford to build there to the high standards imposed by the colleges by the restrictive covenants which they placed on the building leases. The development of the area was initiated by Gonville & Caius who were the first college to grant building leases for their land around Queens' and West Roads. Throughout the Victorian period and into the early years of the twentieth century, many large houses of architectural note were built in the area from Barton Road in the south to the Huntingdon Road in the north (see chapter 8)

After more than 200 years without any new colleges being established at Cambridge, the year 1800 saw the foundation of Downing College (fig. 27). This college should have been founded in the latter half of the eighteenth century after the third Sir George Downing had died heirless,

27

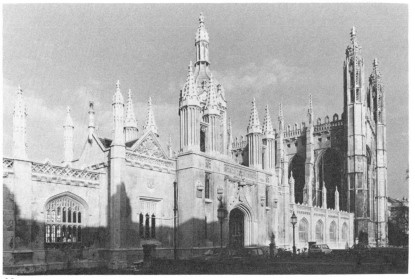

28

27 & 28 Two buildings of the early nineteenth century: the Greek Revival Hall at Downing College, of 1818-20, and the Gothic Revival screen and gatehouse at King's College, of 1824-28 — both designed by William Wilkins and illustrating the versatility of this architect who built much in Cambridge.

leaving his fortune for the building of the college. However, owing to lengthy and expensive litigation by his widow, its building was delayed and its scale much diminished. The site was finally chosen for Downing, and an Act of Enclosure of 1801, preceding the main Acts of 1802 and 1807, provided for the enclosing of a large area of land, previously known as St Thomas Ley's and Swinecroft and then as Pembroke Leys, on the southern edge of the town. This was mainly marshland, popular for snipe and duck shooting in the eighteenth century, and it is a curious fact that even today duck still fly in to waddle around Downing's extensive lawns, though it is almost half a mile from the river, the nearest water.

The colleges of the second half of the nineteenth century all arose out of a definite need, rather than from beneficence. The fight for women's emancipation was, at Cambridge, associated with the cause for higher education for women. Three women's colleges arose at this time: Newnham and Girton, both located away from the town centre for reasons of Victorian prudery, and the Cambridge Women's Training College, which was later to become a 'recognised foundation' of the university in 1949 when it changed its name to Hughes Hall.[9] Just before the foundation of these ladies' colleges in 1869, another new type of foundation was established in the form of the 'non-collegiates' society, an institution set up specifically to cater for students who wanted to study at Cambridge but could not obtain membership of one of the wealthy, endowed colleges. This later developed in the twentieth century to become Fitzwilliam, a now fully recognised university college.

During the last quarter of the century, several theological colleges were founded at Cambridge. Only one of these, Selwyn College, was a university foundation, and between 1877-1921 five independent theological colleges emerged around the town (see chapter 3). Finally, in the 1890s, two colleges, already established elsewhere, migrated to Cambridge: Homerton, which is the local teachers training college, affiliated to the university as an 'Approved Society' in 1976; and St Edmund's House, originally a Roman Catholic lodging house, which became an 'Approved Foundation' in 1975.

The nineteenth century was a period of unprecedented architectural development in the whole town, but particularly in the colleges and the university. The busy Victorians built a phenomenal number of new buildings, expanding many college sites, but also sometimes restored too severely or completely demolished older buildings, replacing them with not always very appropriate additions. With the introduction of certain new subjects, in particular the practical natural sciences, the university took on an added responsibility in both teaching and administration, and, as a result, had to expand its premises considerably (see chapter 6). New university sites began to spring up all over the town, with a particular concentration in the area today known as the New Museums Site and the Downing Site, in the southern quarter of the town centre. The design of many of these buildings reflects the nineteenth century's diverse tastes, and Cambridge is a showcase for the work of numerous famous architects of the period. The town of today really started to take shape in the latter half of the nineteenth century.

29 The Gothic Revival south screen and gate of St John's College New Court, by Rickman & Hutchinson of 1826-31, the largest single college building to that date in Cambridge (*see also fig. 346*). **30** The Victorian Baroque Fitzwilliam Museum, Trumpington Street, designed by George Basevi, and built between 1837-75. **31** The pretty 'Queen Anne' of Newnham College, founded in 1871 and here represented by Sidgwick Hall of 1880 by Basil Champneys. **32** 'Elterholm', 12 Madingley Road, an 'Olde English', half-timbered 'magpie' manor house of 1900, designed by the Liverpool firm of Grayson & Ould.

30

31

32

The Twentieth Century

At the beginning of the nineteenth century the population of Cambridge was about 10,000, by 1921 it had increased to almost 60,000. In 1911 under the Local Government Boards Act the area of the borough was also greatly increased by the addition of land on its east and south sides: 1300 acres was added from the Chesterton district in the north-east; 300 from the parish of Cherry Hinton in the south-east; 495 from Trumpington in the south; and 167 from Grantchester in the south-west, bringing the total area of 'Greater Cambridge' to 5497 acres. With the steady peripheral growth that had started after enclosure in the nineteenth century the gradual coalescence of the surrounding local villages was inevitable, as the suburban sprawl slowly stretched out to the many village 'satellites' that were within a radius of only a mile or two of the city centre: Girton in the north; Chesterton, Fen Ditton, and Cherry Hinton on the east side; Trumpington and Shelford to the south; and Grantchester and Newnham in the south-west. The housing 'sprawl' took on a varied character in the different areas (see chapter 8). The historic centre of Cambridge had evolved over a period of more than 800 years, and yet within about one eighth of that time a built-up area many times its size encompassed it to the north, east and south. In 1800 the town had been surrounded by green fields, by 1900 it was surrounded by a multiplicity of houses which were steadily increasing in number. However, from the west the countryside was still able to come almost into the city centre – as it still does today (see fig. 63).

The expansion and development of Cambridge in recent years has taken on a very precise pattern: the university and colleges are building westwards while the city council is basically building eastwards. A lot has happened in planning terms during the twentieth century, much of which, particularly in the city centre, has been dictated by the introduction of the motor vehicle.

Before the Second World War some of the colleges were responsible for a large amount of unfortunate demolition, mainly in the area of the bridgeland around Magdalene and St John's Colleges, but the effect of the war and the subsequent preservation of historic buildings, whether monumental or domestic, fortunately checked the pre-war habit of arbitrary destruction for purposes of expansion.

This northern area had evolved with the main section of the port in the days of the river industry. It was an intimate and lively district with rows of terraces dissected by narrow lanes and courtyards from Northampton Street in the north to the Round Church in the south. However, Magdalene and St John's needed to expand, and in order to do so began to demolish the 'slums' that surrounded them, mainly down the western side of Magdalene and Bridge Streets. Magdalene wished to build a large new court opposite the main college, and St John's new courts and a car park and bicycle shed along the strip of land to the east between its older courts and Bridge Street. Between them they demolished about a third of all the property in that area, to build what at St John's turned out to be a disaster as far as the townscape is concerned, but at Magdalene the results were eventually rather more sympathetic to the local environment, though only because of a temporary lack of funds and the intervention of the Second World War. The ambitious scheme by Sir Edwin Lutyens, of which only the west range was completed, would have resulted in the demolition of even more property. By the 1950s, when building was resumed, attitudes had changed, and the existing, older buildings were restored with a few new additions to the same scale. Magdalene's own fellow in architecture, David Roberts, was engaged to adapt the plan to provide new college courts, similar in atmosphere to the existing surroundings. One of the most important inter-war events was the crossing of the Backs by Clare College to build their Memorial Court on the west side of Queens' Road, initiating a new area of college and university development.

In the 1960s property on the east side of Bridge Street was demolished by the council in order to widen the roads and to accom-

34

33 One of the earliest modern buildings in Cambridge, Caius' Market Hill Hostel of 1934 by M. Easton. **34** Churchill College, 1959-68, by Richard Sheppard, Robson & Partners.

33

modate Cambridge's first multi-storey car park in Park Street. It is a great pity that this whole area was so savagely mutilated by the colleges and the council, as it would have been an area of great charm[10] (see figs 54-56).

After Clare College had built on the west side of the river, that whole area started to become a secondary 'campus', together with other smaller sites in the north and south of the town. Several new colleges were founded: New Hall (1954), Churchill (1958), Darwin (1965), Clare Hall (1965), Lucy Cavendish (1965), University College, later Wolfson (1965), and Robinson (1974), so that by the mid-seventies Cambridge had 31 university colleges, 5 independent theological colleges (one no longer exists), and the large Cambridgeshire College of Arts & Technology on the east side of the town. Undoubtedly it is the college authorities which have, with a few exceptions, handled their modern development and expansion most successfully in Cambridge.

The standard of university expansion and development in twentieth century Cambridge has been generally poor, as can be seen on a walk around the New Museums site, the Downing site, the Engineering Laboratories, the Chemistry Laboratory, or the Mill Lane site, all near to the town centre. The Arts Faculties site, off Sidgwick Avenue and West Road, is an improvement on these though it still lacks the quality of the Old Schools and the Senate House precinct in the town centre. Like the shopping developments that the authorities have forced on the town, the equally large university departments, such as the Chemistry block, would have been better located outside the city centre. The Deer Report, of 1965, recommended a move to the open west fields site, where such famous Cambridge departments as the Cavendish Laboratory now operate and have room to breathe and expand in the future if necessary, but this proposal came too late, and land that should have been used for more appropriate purposes, such as housing, or shops, now contains monolithic buildings. Out of the dozens of university structures built since 1900 a few exceptional buildings have evolved. Hopefully, in the future the university will leave the few sites that remain within or just around the city centre for other purposes, and locate whatever buildings are yet to come in the designated area to the west.

As for the 'Town', it was decided that Cambridge needed bigger and better shopping facilities, as was the trend throughout the country in the fifties, sixties and early seventies. Cambridge has recently received its second, and indeed equally controversial shopping precinct in two decades. After much discussion in the fifties as to the extent and design of these new precincts, it is a curious and ironic fact that there was an initial argument to leave the historic centre untouched, and to place the new commercial development on the east side of town around Fitzroy and Burleigh streets in the area known locally as the 'Kite'. The final result has been that Cambridge today posesses both the Lion Yard and the Kite developments! A link between the two shopping centres has been long intended, via Christ's Pieces, and such buildings as Bradwells Court were prematurely built along this axis to lure the consumer from one to the other.

As in every other English town or city, serious problems started in the 1920s in Cambridge when the motor car became a common feature. The initial effects can be seen on the formerly narrow streets of the town, many of which were widened to accommodate the increasing number of vehicles: Jesus Lane in 1922, Bridge Street in 1938, Park Street in 1956, and Round Church Street in 1961, to name but a few. This, coupled with the demolition of some street facades, as in Bridge Street, completely changed the character of many parts of the town. Bridge Street is probably the best example, where, at the junction with St John's Street and Round Church Street, it can be seen that all three were widened to cope with the excess traffic that was using the multi-storey car park, just around the corner in Park Street, in the early 1960s. The former character of the street can be imagined if one looks at the collection of half-timbered houses that were recently restored on its southeast corner (see fig. 56).

35

36

35 The Cripps Building at St John's College, 1963-67, by Powell & Moya. **36** The History Faculty of 1965-68 by James Stirling (photograph Richard Einzig).

37

38

37 The Senior Combination Room (west elevation) Downing College, of 1966-70, by Howell, Killick, Partridge & Amis — one of the most satisfying and successfully integrated modern buildings in the city (see p. 140). **38** The most recent college foundation, Robinson; founded in 1974, designed by the Glaswegian firm of Gillespie, Kidd & Coia, and built (first stage) between 1977-80. **39** The first 'High-Tech' building at Cambridge: the headquarters of Sinclair Electronics, off Mill Road, of 1981-82 by the local practice of Lyster, Grillet & Harding. **40** An unusual structure on the city outskirts — the large NAPP Laboratories in the Science Park, of 1981-83, by the Canadian firm of Arthur Erickson & Associates.

An exciting area of industrial development is now growing in Cambridge with the recent Science Park on the nothern outskirts; while to the south is the abominable form that is New Addenbrookes Hospital, thankfully well away from the historic city centre. As to the quality of twentieth century architecture at Cambridge, there is a considerable variation; from excellent and internationally renowned buildings, mainly in the colleges and university, to numerous uninspiring schemes executed by the university and the council. The styles are also varied, ranging from late 'Arts & Crafts' to the adventurous early 'Modern Movement'; 'Traditionalist'; 'New Brutalist'; 'Modern Vernacular'; and, even most recently, to 'High-Tech', all being designed by an equally varied array of local and internationally famous architects. Once again, as in the nineteenth century, a phenomenal amount of building was accomplished, mainly in the boom of new college and university expansion from the fifties through to the seventies.

39

40

When one thinks of Cambridge, whether having lived there for years or just having visited for a day, certain images – mainly topographical and architectural – and no doubt different for each person, dominate the picture. The famous buildings, such as King's College Chapel or the Senate House, the medieval cottages in Magdalene Street, or the numerous churches or college fronts with their battlemented gatehouses, together with the narrow streets, the market place, and the 'Backs' along the river, create a unique environment which has taken over 800 years to evolve. And, of course, there are the swarms of bicycles, the punts, ducks, rowing 'eights' and so on to complete the picture. The following photographs (figs 41-69) are a selection of just some of these Cambridge scenes.

41 The annual Rag Week 'Bed Race', King's Parade. The Senate House and Caius College are in the background.   **42** King's Parade (east), a mixture of sixteenth, seventeenth and eighteenth century houses and shops with Great St Mary's Church beyond.

41

42

43

45

46

47

44

43 Trinity Lane. **44** Sidney Street, with Sidney Sussex College. **45** A typical 'full-term' college scene — lunchtime at Trinity Hall. **46** St Andrew's Street. **47** A winter's day looking east through the central arch of the Gibbs Building, King's College. **48** A summer's night at Magdalene May Ball (1981), with a steel-band entertaining guests.

48

49

51

50

52

53

55

54

56

49 The city from the west, from the university library tower; Clare College's Memorial Court is in the foreground. **50** The market square from Great St Mary's. **51** Trinity's massive Wolfson Building in amongst the older city fabric like an ocean liner in dock. **52** King's College chapel from the Guildhall. **53** Lanterns at St John's and Trinity. **54** Portugal Place, behind St Clement's Church. **55** The sixteenth-eighteenth century cottages of Magdalene and Northampton Streets. **56** The sixteenth century and later cottages in Bridge Street, restored in 1982.

57

58

60

59

61

57 The sixteenth-eighteenth century cottages of Little St Mary's Lane, facing the church of St Mary The Less. **58** Trumpington Street looking north, with the sixteenth century Little Rose Inn, and Pembroke and Peterhouse Colleges beyond. **59** A conflicting juxtaposition of architectural styles: the neo-classical Master's Lodge of Downing College, and the late Gothic Revival church of Our Lady and the English Martyrs. **60** A teak-framed greenhouse in the University's Botanical Gardens on the southern edge of the city. **61** The continuous row of cottages in Orchard Street, with their mansard roofs and large chimney stacks, built sometime between 1820-1830. **62** The Methodist Wesley Church and some delicate trees on Christ's Pieces. **63** Sheep grazing on Scholars Piece on the west side of Kings College 'Backs'.

62

63

64

65

66   67

64 Punting on the 'Backs' between King's and Clare bridges.   **65** Two rowing eights returning home up the Long Reach through Fen Ditton Meadows.   **66** Rowing on the lower river past Fen Ditton Tea Rooms.   **67** The Bridge of Sighs connecting the east and west bank sites of St John's College.   **68** The early eighteenth century iron gates to Clare College bridge, with King's College Chapel in the distance.   **69** A misty morning along the college 'Backs', from Trinity bridge; the clear, uninterrupted span of Garret Hostel bridge pierces the willows, and Clare bridge can be seen faintly in the distance.

68

69

2 The Changing Styles of Buildings at Cambridge: a pictorial survey.

Introduction

Cambridge is well equipped to illustrate the general changes of style that have taken place in English architecture, and possesses fine examples from several periods. These changes were not, of course, unique to Cambridge, but were common to England as a whole.

There is a wealth of medieval architecture in Cambridge. The Romanesque style is represented by a late Anglo-Saxon church and two Norman churches, one of which is a rare example of the circular church plan. During the twelfth century the development of the pointed arch led to a new system of building throughout Europe, allowing a refinement of structure by the use of the load-bearing rib. The Gothic style in England passed through three distinct phases, Early English, Decorated and Perpendicular, and at Cambridge culminated in one of the finest examples of the Perpendicular style – King's College Chapel. In the early sixteenth century English architecture began to be influenced by the Italian Renaissance, and the slow transition began away from Gothic towards Classical architecture. During the Tudor period (1485-1603), buildings often combined both Gothic and Classical elements and this dichotomy of style can be seen in a number of interesting Cambridge buildings (figs. 84-91).

Inigo Jones introduced the classical style to England in the early years of the seventeenth century (tradition has it that the Fellows' Building at Christ's College (fig.89) was designed by Jones, this hypothesis being supported by certain internal details favoured by him, but it is now thought to be highly unlikely). Cambridge was not to receive its first wholly classical buildings until almost half a century later, the first being Pembroke College Chapel designed by the young Wren (figs 94-96).

Wren and his followers, Hawksmoor, Vanbrugh and Gibbs, proclaimed a classical baroque style (figs 95 & 96), but in the mid eighteenth century there arose a movement demanding a more 'honest' and 'correct' interpretation of ancient Greek and Roman architecture. The Classical Revival sought to throw off the 'frivolity' that the Baroque had attached to classical architecture. Cambridge did not experience this new movement until the early nineteenth century when William Wilkins designed Downing College in the Greek Revivalist manner (fig. 100). A few decades later, however, the purity of the neo-classical style gave way once again to the more flamboyant Baroque (figs. 101, 102). The eighteenth century Gothic Revival continued throughout the nineteenth (figs 103-109).

During the industrial nineteenth century, the Arts & Crafts Movement, headed by William Morris, instigated a wave of nostalgia for country life and lost medieval crafts, and although Morris & Co. did not build buildings their influence on those who did was considerable (eg figs 118, 119). The 'Revivalism' of the Victorian architects became unfashionable by the late 1800s, and 'Traditionalism' took over as the norm, giving rise to a new eclecticism, and deriving inspiration from Tudor Gothic to Georgian architecture (figs. 114-117). By the 1920s the influence of the architects of the Modern Movement in Europe began to be felt in England. Le Corbusier's *Towards A New Architecture* was translated into English in 1927, and within a few years Corbusier-inspired buildings were going up, Cambridge possessing one of the earliest examples (fig. 121 and see front cover). During the inter-war years Walter Gropius, (one of the great 'International Modern' architects, and founder of the German Bauhaus) designed a new building for Christ's College in collaboration with Maxwell Fry (figs. 126 & 127).

During the late thirties and into the fifties a number of interesting 'modern' buildings were designed (figs 129-136). Exposed brick and concrete, revealing the structure of the buildings, a number of which were designed on a modular system using pre-fabricated parts, became commonplace from the mid fifties onwards, and Cambridge has many good examples. The Erasmus Building at Queens' College (fig. 134) – a large brick and concrete cube – caused a great stir in 1959, being sited on the traditional college 'Backs', but today it lives harmoniously amongst its older historic neighbours.

The sixties saw some equally controversial projects at Cambridge, undoubtedly the most exciting being Stirling's notorious History Faculty (fig. 143 & see 36, 551). During the late seventies vernacular forms and organic materials 'softened the blow' at Robinson College, located in the 'garden suburb' of west Cambridge. And now, in the early eighties, the most exciting area of new building is by the 'high-tech' companies that have settled here, next to the University, and a few of which have commissioned equally 'high-tech' buildings (figs.153-155).

70 King's College from the west, looking across the Backs from Queens' Road – photographed in unusual light conditions just preceeding an early Spring thunderstorm. This composition illustrates a fundamental, formal contrast in architectural styles: the College Chapel, of 1446-1515, a superb example of English Perpendicular Gothic, with its strong vertical emphasis, reaching towards the heavens; and next to it the long, low form of the neo-classical Gibbs' Building of 1724-32, with its controlling line clearly being the horizontal. The chapel was built spasmodically by several medieval master masons during the reigns of six kings (see p. 120); while the Gibbs' Building was the result of an early 18th century competition to complete King's Front Court (see p. 116), designed by the London-based architect James Gibbs.

ANGLO-SAXON The Tower and Tower Arch of St Bene't's Church, **c.**1040. **71** The Tower (west face), built in three successive tapering stages, contains the characteristic Saxon constructional feature of 'long and short' work, here seen in the quoins. The upper section is the most authentic, though the round-headed openings were added in 1586. The windows in the lower part are 15th century. **72** The completely preserved Tower Arch (east face). The semi-circular arch has a moulded surround on both faces, on the east side springing from two carved lions sitting on the capitals of the simple pilaster-strips. The responds are faced with 'long and short' slabs.

71   72

NORMAN The dominant feature of the semi-circular arch in Romanesque architecture was simpler in Saxon buildings – usually of one ring of masonry with little or no decoration – whereas in Norman buildings it was built in receding tiers of two or more rings and often ornamented with geometrical carving, such as the zig-zag, crenellated, or chain patterns: **73** Doorway of the Church of St Mary Magdalene **74** Doorway of the Round Church of the Holy Sepulchre (restored in 1841) **75** Nave arches in the Holy Sepulchre.

73

74

75

GOTHIC English Gothic progressed through three phases: Early English (late 12th – late 13th centuries), Decorated (late 13th – mid 14th centuries), and Perpendicular (mid-14th – late 16th centuries). The pointed arch was a prominent feature of Gothic buildings, in the early stages two-centred in construction, but later four-centred to create more window space and thus larger areas of fenestration to light the interiors. The design of Gothic windows and their tracery, a few examples of which are shown here, illustrate the changing phases of the Gothic style: **76** The simplest of all the Gothic windows – the lancet, seen here in this group of three original 13th century examples in the church of St Andrew The Less. **77** In the same church can be seen the next stage in window design – Plate Tracery, the grouping together of two or more lancets separated by a mullion and with a simple geometric opening cut into the spandrel panel above, in this case a quatrefoil.

78 St Mary The Less, rebuilt during the mid 14th century and **79** its east window with the rather more complex flowing tracery containing characteristic ogee and dagger shapes (all windows so far of two-centred construction). **80** The east window of the 14th century church of St Michael – again flowing tracery but within a four-centred arch. **81** The late Perpendicular St Mary the Great, with many large four-centred windows, the larger, lower ones of which have a transom as a central horizontal division. **82** The interior of the magnificent Perpendicular King's College Chapel, showing the extensive fan-vault and extremely large four-centred windows allowing light to stream into the interior (see also p. 120).

78

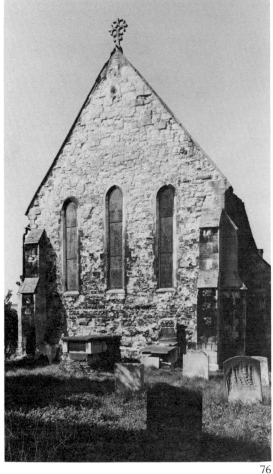

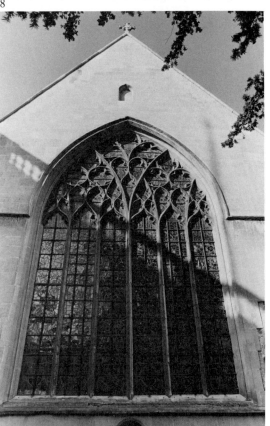

76   77   79

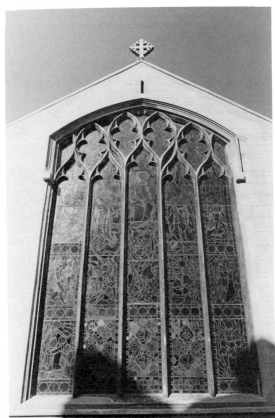

80

81

82

EARLY CLASSICAL **83** The screen and chancel stalls in King's College Chapel (c.1533-36) — the first instance of classical design at Cambridge. Here is a beautiful classical structure, the size of a small house, dividing the nave of this vast Perpendicular chapel. **84 & 85** The Gates of Virtue (1565-67) and Honour (1573-75) at Gonville and Caius College, along with the Gate of Humility (now in the Master's garden), were the first classical structures in stone to appear at Cambridge. Though far from classically correct (see Pevsner) the orders and details of both gates are no doubt derived from Roman sources, but there is still reference to traditional English forms: in Virtue although the east side arch is round-headed, the west is four-centred (*see fig. 15*); and in Honour the arch-head is wholly four-centred. **86** The fountain at Trinity College (1601-15, rebuilt 1715) – an example of early classical design from the end of the Elizabethan period. **87** The east end of Peterhouse Chapel (1628-32) – crowned with a classical pediment, yet below is a two-centred Perpendicular window, and to either side the strong Perpendicular motif of polygonal corner turrets. **88** The east range of Clare College (1638-41). The central arch is round-headed and flanked by rusticated columns, but the actual gateway is fan-vaulted inside, and the spandrels of the arch contain Gothic tracery. The gate is crowned by a segmented pediment. **89** The Fellows' Building (east) at Christ's College (1640-43, *see also figs 17 & 280*). Stylistically this was the most important building of the mid 17th century at Cambridge, as it introduced the Renaissance idea of a balanced composition – long, low and symmetrical – with almost entirely classical detailing throughout, the main exception being the four-centred arch of the central gateway. Particularly innovatory were the dormers in the roof, set behind a balustrade, with alternating triangular and semi-circular pediments; as were also the giant Ionic pilasters at each angle of the building and **90** the simple rectangular windows with a mullion-and-transom cross, the first occurrence of that motif at Cambridge. **91** The Hitcham Building, Pembroke College (1658-61), showing a mixture of late medieval and early classical features. **92 & 93** Mid 17th century influence via the Netherlands was reflected in the introduction of 'Shaped' or 'Dutch' gables; the Brick Building at Emmanuel College (1633-34) and the river elevation of St John's College Third Court (1669-72).

83

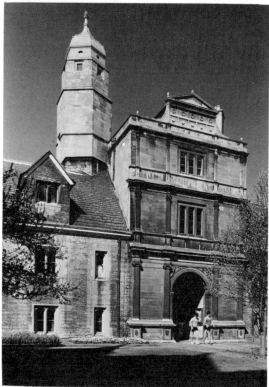

84

85

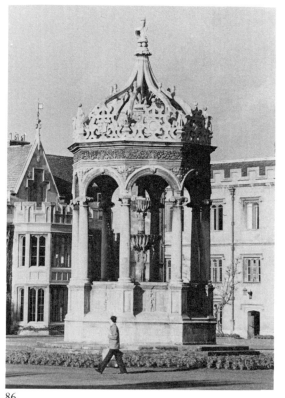

86

87

88

89

90

91

92

93

95

94   96

CLASSICAL In 1663 Christopher Wren designed his first two buildings: the Sheldonian Theatre at Oxford, and **94** the new chapel for Pembroke College, Cambridge. Being the smaller of the two buildings the Chapel was completed first in 1665. Both buildings were based on illustrations from Sebastiano Serlio's *L'Architettura,* (published 1537-51), though at Pembroke Wren deviated from Serlio in the addition of the rather dominant lantern. The Pembroke Chapel was a gift to the college from Wren's uncle, Matthew, Bishop of Ely (1638-67) and a Fellow of the College, who had been imprisoned for 17 years in the Tower and was released in 1660. **95** Wren's next building at Cambridge was the new Chapel for Emmanuel College, designed in 1666 and built 1668-74 (*see also fig. 349*). Here, the composition is more baroque, with the entablature projecting at the centre, and the pediment broken and penetrated by the base of the cupola which contains the clock. **96** Wren's Cambridge masterpiece – Trinity College Library (1676-95, see also pp. 92-94 & *figs. 210-213*). This was one of Wren's most perfect buildings, and at Cambridge set a new standard for much of the collegiate and university architecture that was to follow. Wren's influence on the local designers was considerable and his work in Cambridge was largely responsible there for the enthusiastic adoption of the new classical style. This may be illustrated, for instance, in the work of the local mason Robert Grumbold on the west range of Clare College (1669-76 & 1705-15, *see fig. 226*), St Catherine's College (1673-1704, *see fig. 317*), and the Tribune in Nevile's Court at Trinity (1682, *see fig. 208*). Grumbold was, in fact, working for Wren on the Trinity Library when he produced several of these other buildings.

97-99 Three classical buildings of the 18th century. **97** The Senate House by James Gibbs (1722-30, *see also figs 511 & 520*), summed up by Pevsner as '...a most elegant blend of the English Wren tradition with the new Palladianism (alternating window pediments) and with what Gibbs in his youth had seen in the Rome of about 1700. He was a pupil of Carlo Fontana.' **98** Burrough's Building at Peterhouse (1738-42) was also designed in the Palladian manner (ie after Andrea Palladio, 1508-80, the most influential Italian architect). This was Sir James Burrough's best building (he was an amateur architect and Master of Gonville & Caius College). **99** The West Front of Emmanuel College (1769-75) by the local architect James Essex. After Wren had introduced the classical style to Emmanuel with the building of the new chapel in 1668-74, the rest of the front court was gradually adapted to harmonize with it. The South range, or Westmoreland Building (*see fig. 350*) was the most successful outcome of that exercise, and of the west front Pevsner comments that 'The street facade is not fortunate...the centre appears crushed... between the big angle pavilions this is too prominent to appear merely as a screen, but too weak to form a real frontispiece'.

97

98

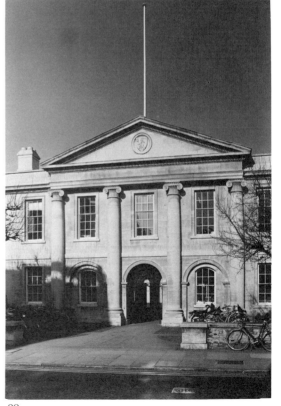

99

100

101

102

NEO-CLASSICAL   100 The Master's Lodge, Downing College (1807-13), by William Wilkins – the earliest signs of a 'pure' Classical Revival at Cambridge – in the Greek Revivalist manner.   **101 & 102** Two Cambridge buildings showing the recurrence of baroque influences: **101** The Old University Library (1837-42) by C R Cockerell; and   **102** The Fitzwilliam Museum (1837-75, *see also figs 30 & 542*) by George Basevi.

GOTHIC REVIVAL   Sir Jeffry Wyatville introduced the Gothic Revival to Cambridge when he re-designed Sidney Sussex College between 1821-33, transforming the original buildings from their authentic Elizabethan state into a comparatively unattractive neo-Elizabethan Gothic: **103** The Hall, Sidney Sussex (re-designed 1821, *see also figs 357 and 358*). The versatile William Wilkins then produced a number of neo-Gothic designs: **104** New Court at Corpus Christi College (1823-27) showing the Chapel; and   **105** King's College Gate-house and Screen (west side, 1824-28).   **106** New Court, St John's College (1826-31) by Rickman & Hutchinson — the largest and most picturesque neo-Gothic building at Cambridge, known to many as the 'wedding-cake building' (*see also fig. 346*). Although predominantly Gothic, the long, symmetrical facade with its central pedimented gateway, created a classical aura — a mixture not uncommon in other mid 19th century buildings (e.g. Houses of Parliament). The industrious Victorians built a phenomenal amount of new buildings at Cambridge, as elsewhere, though sadly often at the expense of demolishing fine historic predecessors. This can be illustrated at St John's where the prolific Gothicist Sir George Gilbert Scott built the new Chapel: **107** St John's College Chapel (1863-69) was partly inspired by early Decorated Gothic churches, and in order to build it the original medieval chapel of the ancient Hospital of St John was demolished.   **108** The layout of St John's pre Scott (from David Loggan's *Cantabrigia Illustrata*, of c.1688) showing the old chapel to the right as part of the homogenous composition of First Court — a composition that was destroyed by the addition of Scott's chapel.   **109** All Saints Church, Jesus Lane, by G.F.Bodley (1863-71) — the purest example of the Gothic Revival at Cambridge from English sources (see chapter 7, and *fig. 586*).

103

104

107

105

106

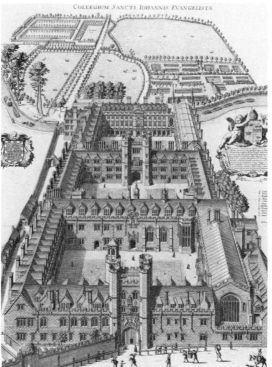

108

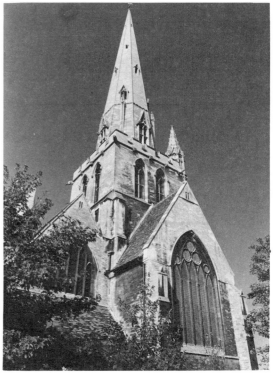

109

110

112

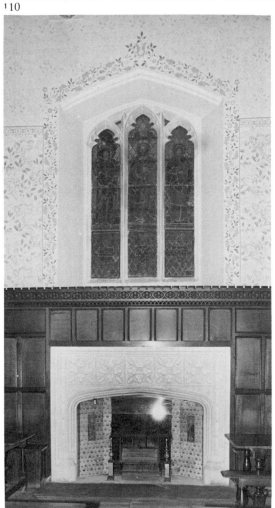

111

113

ARTS & CRAFTS and 'QUEEN ANNE' When G.F. Bodley designed All Saints Church he brought in the Arts & Crafts firm of Morris & Co. (i.e. William Morris, Edward Burne-Jones, Ford Madox Brown, and Philip Webb) to carry out most of the interior decoration and stained glass. Although collectively Morris & Co. were not architects they had an important influence on the architecture of the later 19th century. As well as All Saints they executed much other interior work in Cambridge: **110** Morris & Co. wall stencilling in characteristic organic patterns, and a stained-glass window (1870-74) in Peterhouse Hall. **111** In the same building the first Daisy-Tiled fireplace by Morris (1861) within the larger fireplace of 1501. (The influence of Morris on his contemporaries can be seen in some of the buildings opposite, particularly figs. 118 and 119). **112** In the 1870s a style nicknamed 'Queen Anne' also became extremely popular. This was a mixture of motifs, classical pediments, shaped gables, steep roofs and sash windows; in red-brick and tile, and neat white-painted woodwork — derived from a number of sources — e.g. the genuine Queen Anne (i.e. early 18th century), Dutch, Flemish and French influences, and Wren. When this architectural 'cocktail' was competently handled it produced buildings of a most attractive, strong, and rather novel character. In Cambridge this very 'feminine' style was employed by Basil Champneys, one of its most skilled advocates, at Newnham, appropriately one of the first womens colleges (begun 1875). **113** St Chad's, 48 Grange Road — a 'Queen Anne' house of 1880, possibly also designed by Champneys.

TRADITIONALIST The wave of nostalgia for country living and bygone crafts – inspired by the Arts & Crafts movement – continued into the early years of the 20th century. In England the norm in architecture – post Arts & Crafts – was 'traditionalism', and this was composed of a mixture of 'historical' styles from Tudor-Gothic to Georgian: **114** New Court, Pembroke College (1880-83) by G.G.Scott Jun., in a mixture of 16th to 18th century styles, with Dutch gables and pediments, rusticated 'Gibbs' surrounds, and Arts & Crafts details thrown in. **115** Westminster College (1899) by H.T.Hare – Tudor with some 17th century details (see p.166) **116** The Jacobean Style Hall, Selwyn College (1908-09) by Grayson & Ould. **117** North Court, Emmanuel College (1910-14) by Leonard Stokes — of Tudor Gothic and Georgian derivation. **118** 'Elmside' 49 Grange Road (c.1885) thought to be by E.S.Prior, in a strong vernacular Arts & Crafts tradition, with its tile-hung upper storey. **119** Another late Arts & Crafts house at 48 Storeys Way (1912) by Mackay Hugh Baillie Scott.

114

117

118

115

116

119

120

121

122

123

124

125

MODERN MOVEMENT Traditionalist architecture continued into the middle years of the 20th century, but in the 1920s the influence of the modern movement continental architects – in particular Le Corbusier – were felt in England. At Cambridge the first Corbusier inspired buildings came about in the early thirties, but just preceding them an interesting exercise in interior decoration took place: **120** The entrance hall of 'Finella', an early Victorian villa off Queens' Road, which was re-decorated in 1927-29 by Raymond McGrath in a mixture of unusual and wonderful materials – different types of glass, gold and silver leaf, copper — accompanied by novel colour schemes and abstract geometric patterning, all dramatically lit by concealed lighting. This was indeed innovatory for its time, and Pevsner describes it as '...a milestone in the coming of what might be called Expressionism in decoration...'.

A year or so later one of the earliest modern buildings in England was constructed at Cambridge: **121** The White House (1930-31) by George Checkley. This very simple, black and white 'prisme pure', was inspired by Le Corbusier's white Cubist houses of the 1920's in France. **122** The entrance hall of the Mond Laboratory (1931) by the local architect H.C.Hughes **123** 31 Madingley Road (1932) by Marshall Sisson. **124** 'Salix' (1933-34) – another Le Corbusier inspired house, also by H.C. Hughes. This was the first Cambridge building to employ windows turning corners as a prominent feature of its design, thus demonstrating the independence of the walls from the concrete-frame structure. **125** The south range of Gonville & Caius College, St Michael's Court to Market Hill (1934) by Murray Easton – one of the earliest modern buildings in the city centre. This building is faced in stone as opposed to the characteristic white render of its stylistic contemporaries (*see also fig. 33*). **126 & 127** A rejected scheme for Christ's College by Walter Gropius and Maxwell Fry (1936-37, reproduced by permission of the Master, Fellows and Scholars of Christ's College), and **128** what was built instead — the neo-Georgian Memorial Building (1952-53) by Professor Sir Albert Richardson, as the west range of Third Court. **129** Fen Court, Peterhouse (1939), by the local practice of Hughes & Bicknell. **130** The former Nursery School, Homerton College (1940-41 behind the glazed corridor) by Maxwell Fry.

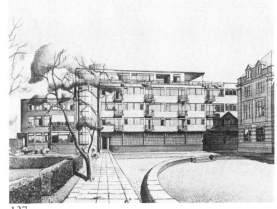

127

126

128

129

130

131

132

133

134 135

136

THE 1950s **131** 11 Wilberforce Road (1950-51, and 1957 upper storey) by David Roberts and Mrs M.M. Roberts. One of the first non-traditional buildings at Cambridge post 1945. **132** Faculty of Architecture extension (1958-59) by Colin St John Wilson and Alex Hardy. A cube of exposed brick and concrete, expressing the structure, built on a modular system. **133** Corpus Christi and Sidney Sussex Colleges Boathouse (1958-59) by David Roberts. **134** Erasmus Building, Queens' College (1959-60) by Basil Spence & Partners. Another exposed brick and concrete cube, this time raised on concrete pilotis, with characteristic alternating window patterns intended to reflect the modular building system. **135** Fitzwilliam College (designed 1958, built in the sixties) by Sir Denys Lasdun. The same policy towards materials and structure, employed also on a modular building system reflected in the regimented rows of tall floor to ceiling slit windows. **136** Churchill College (des. 1958-59: built 1959-68) by Richard Sheppard, Robson & Partners – the exposed brick and concrete forms of the boiler house, somewhat reminiscent of Le Corbusier (In the foreground is a bronze reclining figure by Henry Moore, of 1961-62).

THE 1960s **137** William Stone Building, Peterhouse (1963-64) by Sir Leslie Martin & Colin St John Wilson. **138** New Hall (1962-66) by Chamberlin, Powell & Bon – a modern womens college with its intriguing and rather curious forms. **139** George Thomson Building, Corpus Christi College (1963-64) by Philip Dowson of Arup Associates: a satisfying structure, employing a pre-cast concrete 'H' frame system as a 'hanging frame' a foot or so inside which the actual building sits. **140** The highly praised Cripps Building at St John's College (1963-67) by Powell & Moya ('a masterpiece' Pevsner). **141** The Master's Lodge, Emmanuel College (1963-64) by Tom Hancock. **142** New Court, Christ's College (1966-70) by Sir Denys Lasdun & Partners. **143** Faculty of History (1964-68, isometric view by James Stirling). Stylistically the most controversial modern building in Cambridge, referred to by Pevsner as '...aesthetically as neutral as the glazing of a tomato frame', yet praised by others as a masterpiece (*see also figs. 36 and 551*). **144** Wolfson Building, Trinity College (1968-72) by the Architects Co-Partnership – a massive building sitting right in the heart of historic Cambridge, but cleverly concealed (*see fig. 217*).

138

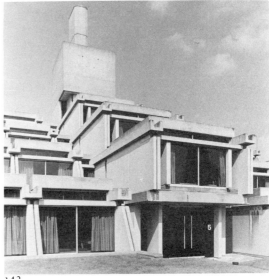

142

139

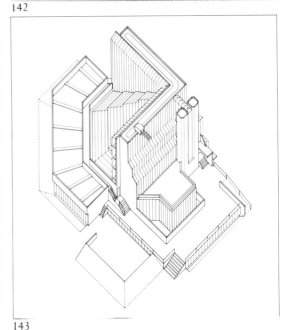

143

140

137

141

144

145

146

147

148

149

THE 1970's 145 The Senior Combination Room, Downing College (1970). 146 Science Laboratories (1971), New Museums Site, by Arup Associates. 147 Cripps Court, Queens' College (1972-79) by Powell & Moya. 148 Faculty of Music (1975-80) by Sir Leslie Martin with Colen Lumley and Ivor Richards. 149 Robinson College (1977-80), showing the use of vernacular forms and natural materials — red brick, brick paviours and even tile-hanging — on this extensive concrete — frame structure.

1980-1984 150-152 Three college hostels and commercial developments of the early eighties: 150 Trinity Hall (1980-81), Thompsons Lane, by Cambridge Design 151 Sidney Sussex (1981-83), King Street, by David Roberts (Executive Architects: Whitworth & Hall); and 152 Downing (1982-84) along Regent Street by Hughes & Bicknell. 153 The small scale 'High Tech' Sinclair Electronics H.Q. (1981-82), successfully integrated among 19th century terraces. 154 The NAPP Laboratories (1981-83) in the Science Park — for Cambridge a unique large scale industrial style of building, employing a portal frame structure and a dazzling glass and metal skin. 155 The Schlumberger Building by Michael Hopkins Limited, at present (1984) being constructed to the west of the city off Madingley Road (drawing by Michael Hopkins Limited).

150

151

152

153

154

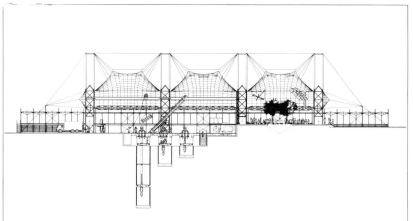

155

3 The Colleges

The evolution of the Cambridge Colleges has produced one of the most remarkable series of buildings in English architecture. Between Peterhouse Hall (fig. 157) of 1286, the first college building, and Robinson College (fig. 158), the most recent foundation, seven centuries of fascinating growth has taken place.

Introduction

Before the universities of Oxford and Cambridge were established, medieval teaching took place in schools attached to cathedrals and monasteries. These early centres of learning catered for the few who were privileged to pursue an academic, predominantly theological, career. During the twelfth and thirteenth centuries, there was a greater demand for educated administrators and specialist teachers of secular subjects as opposed to religious instruction. Out of this demand a new educational system emerged in the form of the universities and their later associated colleges, which gradually took over from the religious schools. Oxford and Cambridge began with a collection of independent teachers living in the town and offering instruction.

It was not the responsibility of the university to found colleges, and these resulted from the benefactions of wealthy individuals as places to house teachers. The early colleges did not at first contain students, who were expected to find their own lodgings in the town, and the type of institutions we know today, housing both teachers and students, did not exist until the latter years of the fourteenth century when provision was made for the unqualified students to live in the colleges under the care of graduates (which is how the term 'undergraduate' evolved).

Prior to the nineteenth century, founders of colleges, from Peterhouse to Downing, tended to be members of the Royal Family, the nobility, the clergy and the more wealthy and powerful civil servants. There is one unique exception; the college of Corpus Christi and the Blessed Virgin Mary, which was founded by two town guilds, and thus, in effect, by the people of Cambridge themselves. The reforming spirit of the later nineteenth century saw a change in the type of patronage; Girton, Newnham, and Hughes Hall, for instance, resulted directly from the fight for women's equality and the right to further education. In the same spirit, New Hall and Lucy Cavendish followed in the mid twentieth century, offering an even broader opportunity for women at Cambridge, before co-education finally infiltrated the mass of all-male colleges in the early sixties.

The university itself has played little part in the establishment of the individual colleges, though it has had a hand in three foundations: the first was University Hall, founded in 1326 by the Chancellor of the university, Richard de Badew, but then taken over by Elizabeth, Countess of Clare, later to become Clare College; the second was Fitzwilliam College, originally a nineteenth century organisation formed by the university to cater for students not attached to one of the endowed colleges, then known as the 'non-collegiates'; and, finally, University College was founded in 1965 to ease the increasing need for post-graduate accommodation in Cambridge, later to be taken over by the Wolfson Foundation and subsequently re-named Wolfson College in 1973. This need for graduate colleges in the sixties resulted in some of the senior, and more wealthy, foundations, setting up Darwin College, founded jointly by Gonville & Caius, St John's, and Trinity; and Clare Hall, founded by Clare College with help from two American benefactors.

In 1974, Robinson College was founded in a manner virtually extinct. An individual benefactor, a local millionaire, Mr David Robinson, adopted the traditional role of founder by donating in total over 20 million pounds to establish a college in his name. Although seven colleges had been founded in the two decades prior to Robinson's (eighteen in total in the previous hundred years) the last single benefactor had been Sir George Downing who died in 1749, and whose

156 The oldest college foundation at Cambridge — Peterhouse. Established in 1280 by Hugh de Balsham, Bishop of Ely, and located off Trumpington Street since 1284. **157** The first purpose-built college structure at Peterhouse was the hall of *c.*1286-90 built with the 300 marks bequeathed to his scholars by the founder on his death in 1286. Along with the rest of Old Court the hall was ashlar-faced by James Burrough in 1754-55, its present facing, however, belongs to Gilbert Scott's restoration of 1870. Thus on this (north) side the original rubble construction is hidden, but the south elevation gives a more honest impression of the building's thirteenth-century origins (*see figs 7 & 191*). **158** The newest foundation at Cambridge — the hall and residential terraces of Robinson College, built in 1977-80.

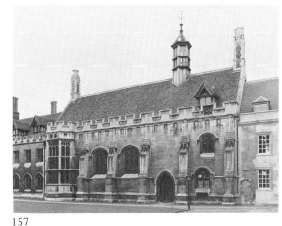
157

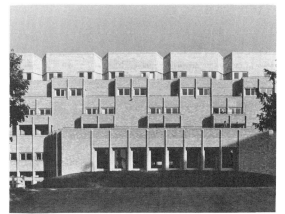
158

College was founded posthumously in 1800.

David Robinson is the latest on the list of names of those who have purchased a certain immortality by founding a Cambridge College. The medieval founders realised the need for institutions of learning, and by their wealth and good-will were able to contribute to that cause. At the same time, there was a certain prestige to be gained from such an action, and many of the early foundations were also chantries where masses were said for the founder's soul by the scholars they had endowed. In the case of Robinson College, there was no underlying necessity for another foundation at Cambridge, and arguments were strongly pressed for other uses for such a large amount of money. Nevertheless, it has been the wealth of individuals and their wish to create colleges in their own name that has at Cambridge resulted in a great heritage of institutions of learning, housed within often remarkable examples of architecture.

The word 'college' (from the Latin *collegium*) simply refers to an organised body of people incorporated together to pursue a common purpose (in this case learning) and does not necessarily refer to the buildings in which they dwell. This is the sense in which it was employed in the charters of the early foundations at Oxford and Cambridge. The words 'Hall' and 'House' were, in fact, more commonly used initially, and it was not until the collegiate system had begun to develop in the mid fourteenth century that the term 'College' became the standard reference adopted by successive foundations. The first use of the word for this purpose was made in the licence granted by King Edward II to Adam de Brom in 1324 for the founding of Oriel College, Oxford; and the first instance at Cambridge was in 1347 in a similar licence to Marie de Valence, Countess of Pembroke, for the founding of 'the college of the hall of Valence Marie', later to be called Pembroke College.

The University of Cambridge is a federation of colleges. Each college is an individual community containing the necessary buildings in which to house and feed its members, and is governed by its own statutes, electing its own fellows and admitting its own students. The college's governing body is composed of some or all of the fellows, and is presided over by the head of the college, usually called the 'Master' (though 'President' at Queens', Hughes Hall, Lucy Cavendish, New Hall, and Wolfson; 'Provost' at King's; 'Mistress' at Girton; and 'Principal' at Newnham). Each college provides its inhabitants, numbering from 100 to 700, with all necessary facilities. The colleges are not confined to specific subjects and have students in most academic fields. Membership of the university depends upon membership of one of the colleges. Today there are 31 foundations: 25 undergraduate colleges, containing also a percentage of post-graduate students; 4 graduate colleges (Hughes Hall, Darwin, Clare Hall and Wolfson); one graduate college that also admits mature undergraduates (St Edmund's House); and one college that admits mature undergraduates and affiliated female students (Lucy Cavendish). Most of the colleges are now co-educational. There are also five independent theological colleges at Cambridge (see p. 166).

The majority of the colleges are large enough to house their undergraduates within the college itself for at least two of their three years at Cambridge (usually the first and third years). Many also own hostels in and around the town. The Hall and the Junior Combination Room (JCR, the common room) form the focal points of college life, as most undergraduates have the majority of their meals in college, and use the varied facilities offered by the JCR. The MCR (Middle Combination Room) and SCR (Senior Combination Room) are the equivalents for the post-graduate students and the fellows respectively.

A student's three years in a college and the university are very organised. When an undergraduate 'comes up' to Cambridge there are three sets of people responsible for his or her curriculum and well-being: a college tutor, a director of studies, and a number of supervisors. To understand the function of these individuals one has to understand the teaching system at Cambridge. This takes place on two levels in which both the university and the colleges play their own individual parts, though intricately linked. The university organises lectures, seminars, and practical work for all students, this forming the major part of the curriculum. For these functions students from all colleges come together with the other members of their particular university faculties and meet in lecture halls, laboratories, and other buildings scattered throughout the town and around its perimeter. The second level of teaching is carried out by the colleges and is much more personal, taking the form of supervisions (tutorials). Unlike formal lectures, which can involve as many as two hundred people, the comparatively informal supervision gives the undergraduate the opportunity to discuss his work with a specialist teacher, the ratio being between one to five students per supervisor. An undergraduate would normally attend between one to four supervisions a week, which would be held in the college rooms or the home of the supervisor who is, more often than not, a member of a different college. The student's director of studies is responsible for the co-ordination of this two-tiered system, related to his individual pupils. He would usually be a fellow of the same college as his students and his academic subject would also be the same. He would advise as to what lectures to attend, books to read, etc., and would also arrange the undergraduate's supervisions. He is, thus, the student's academic guide. The role of the college tutor is more that of friend than teacher, and it is his responsibility to look after the student while at the college. The tutor's own subject is not necessarily the same as his tutorial pupils, but although his role is primarily social rather than academic, he also keeps an eye on the students' progress.

Since the mediaeval colleges did not house students, they had to seek lodging elsewhere. An alternative to rented accommodation in the homes of townspeople was offered by the monastic houses, such as the Franciscans or Dominicans, who established themselves in Cambridge in the early thirteenth century. However, the university authorities in both Oxford and Cambridge realised that the outcome of their stay with an Order was often that the students were pursuaded to become friars while too young to realise the implications of such a decision. It was a new type of student that was needed, a secular priest, rather than a friar with the commitment and restraint imposed by his Order.

As a result of such unsatisfactory conditions, the students themselves banded together to form hostels, or Literary Inns (known as Halls in Oxford). These were houses rented from townspeople, and disputes often arose between tenant and landlord over the rent. This led the university authorities in 1266 to intervene and appoint a board to regulate the rent charged for five year periods. A principal was also elected for the running of each hostel. Even though they were, in the main, small houses lacking in space for the apparently excessive number of occupants, they appear to have been extremely popular, as the remarks of Dr Caius illustrate: 'They were held in good repute by those who devoted themselves to literature and were crowded with students. Their inmates dined and supped together, as men do who have to lead a common life, and to share a common lot. Neither Inns nor Hostels were endowed with any landed property. Each student lived at his own charges, not on the charity of the community'. There were over twenty of these hostels in Cambridge in the sixteenth century but once the colleges started housing students, they either reverted back to the landlord or were incorporated into college property. Caius continued '...Now, however, [1573] they are all deserted and given back into the hands of the townspeople'.[11]

The history of the colleges properly begins at Oxford where the first foundations originated some thirty years earlier than those at Cambridge. There is, however, controversy as to which was the first Oxford College to be founded: University College commenced in 1249 but its statutes were not completed until 1280; Balliol was founded in 1260 but it did not receive its official charter until 1282; Merton (fig. 159) was established in 1263-64 and received the earliest statutes in that year and in 1270 and 1274. It was at Merton that a complete corporate body was first established and Merton is therefore regarded as the precursor of the English collegiate system. It was on the statutes of this foundation that Hugh de Balsham modelled his college in 1280, the first at Cambridge, a few years later to be called Peterhouse.

Each individual founder had different ideas concerning the running of his or her college, in respect of educational intentions and its general organisation. Walter de Merton's ideas, discussed here by Bishop Hobhouse, are of particular interest as his statutes were so influential in the formation of succeeding foundations in both universities:

> He borrowed from the monastic institutions the idea of an aggregate body living by common rule, under a common head, provided with all things needful for a corporate and perpetual life, fed by its secured endowments, fenced from all external interference, except that of its lawful patron; but, after borrowing thus much, he differenced his institution by giving his beneficiaries quite distinct employment, and keeping them free from all those perpetual obligations which constituted the essence of the religious life.
>
> His beneficiaries are from the first designated as *Scolares in scholis degentes;* their employment was study, not what was technically called the religious life. He forbad his scholars ever to take vows, they were to keep themselves free of every other institution, to enter no one else's *obsequium.* He looked forward to their going forth to labour *in seculo,* and acquiring preferment and property. Study being the function of the inmates of his house, their time was not to be taken up by ritual or ceremonial duties, for which special chaplains were appointed; neither was it to be bestowed on any handicrafts, as in some monastic orders. Voluntary poverty was not enjoined, though poor circumstances were a qualification for a fellowship. No austerity was required, though contentment with simple fare was enforced as a duty, and the system of enlarging the number of inmates according to the means of the house was framed to keep the allowance to each at the very moderate rate which the founder fixed.[12]

At Cambridge, Peterhouse was followed by Michaelhouse in 1324 (now part of Trinity), University Hall in 1326 (now Clare College), and King's Hall in 1337 (now also part of Trinity); together forming the first phase of collegiate development at Cambridge. The development of the collegiate system, though often along similar channels at Oxford and Cambridge, was not always parallel in its architectural synthesis.

159

159 Merton College, Oxford — the precursor of the English collegiate system; officially established in 1264. Mob Quad is the earliest planned quadrangle known at Oxford, built between 1304-1378.

The Development of the College Plan

There appears to have been no organised plan or system of building for the earliest colleges at Cambridge. The founder would simply purchase a site on which there would usually be adequate buildings in which to house the initial members of the college, and, as funds became available, new land and buildings would be added. The basic requirements in the earliest foundations were rooms in which the fellows could sleep and study, a kitchen, a dining hall, and an office for administration. The members' religious needs were catered for by the local parish churches, therefore a chapel was not necessary. Their library was simply a chest in the strong-room in which books would be kept; and their Master occupied an ordinary chamber. The process of growth was very slow and none of the early founders lived to see the completion of their colleges. As this somewhat random development progressed, the other components which now characterise a college, such as the chapel, library, Master's lodge, and gatehouse, were gradually introduced. The attempt to create an organised layout containing all of the required buildings, was not undertaken until long after the foundation of the earliest colleges; and in comparison to those that exist today, they would have seemed extremely humble and unimpressive.

During the mid-fourteenth century an organised college plan began to develop, based on monastic origins. From this point onwards colleges began to form self-contained communities, bearing strong resemblance to that of a monastery, the analogy being obvious in the basic plan form with its rectilinear courtyards - termed the court at Cambridge and the quadrangle at Oxford. Certain buildings used features clearly taken from monastic architecture: the cloister; the refectory, with its attached kitchen and offices; the chapel; and the Master's lodge. However, whereas a monastery would have had a dormitory in which most of the community would have slept, in the colleges the inhabitants had individual chambers.

The development of the college plan can be divided into several phases, the most important of which had taken shape by the end of the fourteenth century. Inevitably, variations on this theme followed with successive generations, in attempts to improve the system, but the basic idea has survived to the present day.

1: Random building

When the founder of Peterhouse, Hugh de Balsham, died in 1286, six years after founding the College, he left fifteen scholars 300 marks to erect new buildings. With this money they were able to do no more than enlarge the site and build the hall (see fig. 157). The main court was not begun until the second half of the fifteenth century. At Hervey de Stanton's foundation, Michaelhouse, he, and later his executors, simply acquired connecting properties over a number of years in which to house the college members, and no new buildings of importance were erected. The original buildings of Clare Hall, built by the Countess of Clare after 1338, were destroyed by fire in the early sixteenth century and, as far as is known, were not built on a quadrangular plan. The present Old Court of Clare was undertaken during the seventeenth century resurgence of building. Edward III's scholars at King's Hall lived in the house of Robert de Croyland, which was largely rebuilt in the late fourteenth century, but it was not arranged on a quadrangular plan until about 1420. Thus, the first colleges were established, but only random building was undertaken, and with no particular concept or plan in mind.

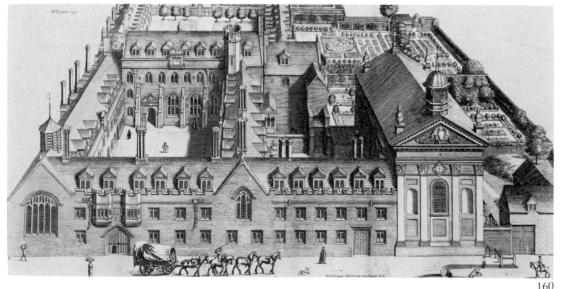

160 The former Old Court of Pembroke College (left), begun in the late 1340s but not fully completed until the 1460s, is the earliest known enclosed court to include all of the buildings required for college life: living chambers, a hall and kitchens, chapel, library and Master's lodge (print by David Loggan, c.1688). The buildings were originally of brick but were stone-faced in 1712 and 1717 (see figs 232 & 234). The Court in its entirety no longer exists as the south and east ranges were demolished in 1874-75 to make way for new buildings by the prolific Alfred Waterhouse. Interestingly, Loggan's drawing was made shortly after the completion of the new chapel by the young Christopher Wren — Cambridge's first purely classical building. Note the absence of the clockface on the present building's west front (see fig 94).

160

2: The Early Courts

In quick succession between 1347-52, a second group of colleges arose: Pembroke, Gonville Hall, Trinity Hall, and Corpus Christi. Among these are to be found the first enclosed courts at Cambridge.

The small Old Court at Pembroke College (fig. 160, now destroyed), which was no larger than 90 by 50 feet (27.4 x 15.2m), was the first enclosed court at Cambridge to include a college chapel as part of its original composition, and to contain all of the buildings required for college life. The dates of this court are uncertain, but it was begun in the late 1340s and continued into the fifteenth century. Unfortunately, the court no longer exists in its entirety as its south and east ranges were demolished in the nineteenth century (this whole court, originally built of brick, was ashlared in the early eighteenth century).

Little remains of the original architecture of Gonville Hall (now Gonville Court in Gonville & Caius College), though this was also an early quadrangular composition. At Trinity Hall the founder, William Bateman, probably built the hall in the south half of the west range, and the east range next to the street (re-built in 1852). The remainder of the west range and the north range were added in the 1370s thereby completing the court (see fig. 249). This was larger than any other court to that date, measuring 115 by 80 feet (35 x 24.3m), and it also had an unusual entrance court between itself and the street to the south (re-built in the nineteenth century as South Court).

The most intact example of the medieval court surviving in Cambridge is the Old Court at Corpus Christi (fig. 161). This was built between 1352-77, and, with its simple, carefully planned arrangement of parts, is regarded as the first completely enclosed composition on the court plan (see fig. 258). Apart from the west half of the south range, which was rebuilt in 1823-27, the buildings remain virtually untouched but for the buttresses, which were added for support in the late fifteenth and early sixteenth centuries. The court originally consisted of hall, kitchens, and Master's Lodge in the south range, with chambers in the other three sides. St Bene't's Church, to the immediate north-east, served as the college chapel.

Thus, in the third quarter of the fourteenth century the very gradual synthesis of the basic college plan began to resemble the standard form that exists today. The next important step was taken at Oxford by William of Wykeham, Bishop of Winchester, in his innovatory designs for New College in 1379. Here, for the first time, students were to live in the college in the care of graduates (their teachers), and the college community thus became an educational establishment rather than a brotherhood of fellows.

161 The Old Court of Corpus Christi College, built between 1352-1377, was the first enclosed collegiate composition to be conceived and built on the court plan; consisting of chambers, hall and kitchens, library and Master's Lodge, with the neighbouring church of St Bene't acting as the college chapel (see figs 260 & 262). Although the buttresses and garrets were added in the sixteenth century, this court provides an almost intact picture of the typical medieval Cambridge college (only the south-west corner was rebuilt in the nineteenth century as part of the neo-Gothic New Court by William Wilkins).

161

3: The Organised Quadrangle after Wykeham at Oxford (1380-86)

Wykeham possessed considerable knowledge of building as he had been Clerk of Works to Edward III, and he himself undertook the design of his college, using the examples of his predecessors as a guide. He completed the college in six years without interruption (1380-86), and in so doing produced the first example of an organised plan containing all the principal elements of collegiate architecture: chapel, hall, library, Master's lodge, chambers, and a towered gatehouse (the first occurrence of the latter in collegiate building: see chapter 4).

Great Quad at New College (fig. 162) was built to a clear and logically worked-out plan (fig. 163), and measured 150 by 125 feet (45.7 x 38.1m). It is entered via the gatehouse in the west range, and in the layout and arrangement of its buildings is divided neatly into two halves along its central east-west axis. The north half contains mainly buildings for communal use, while the south half consists almost entirely of chambers. An interesting feature of this composition is the chapel and hall which form the north side of the quad as a continuous range; the ante-chapel is placed transversally across the west end of the chapel,

forming the transepts. This layout, which denies the chapel an east window, was used many times thereafter at Oxford but rarely at Cambridge, where the chapel and hall are almost always located in separate ranges.

After his university foundation, Wykeham built Winchester College (at Winchester), in 1387-1393, as a school from which the scholars would proceed to New College (Cardinal Wolsey later established a similar dual foundation when he set up Cardinals College in 1525, now Christ Church, linking it with the Grammar School at Ipswich). Wykeham's ideas provided either the model or the inspiration for most of the succeeding foundations at Oxford, new colleges being planned or existing ones converted on his principles. It is from this point that organised collegiate architecture begins.

At first, Cambridge was little affected by Wykeham's innovations, and during the first half of the fifteenth century progressed along its own lines. It was not until more than fifty years later that the influence of Wykeham was felt in Cambridge when Henry VI founded King's College in 1441, after founding Eton, at Windsor, the previous year, on the same basis as New College and Winchester. Henry's own design for King's,

162

164

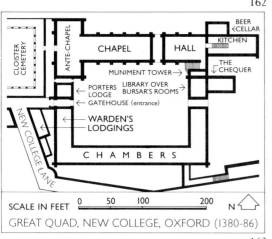

163

162 & 163 Great Quad of the innovatory New College, Oxford, built by William of Wykeham without interruption between 1380-86: a predetermined composition containing all of the principal elements of the traditional college plan to accommodate not only teachers but also students for the first time at either Oxford or Cambridge university. **164** Old Court, Queens' College (1448-49) — the first complete Cambridge court to be built as a whole without interruption — inspired both by Wykeham and the planning of fifteenth century manor houses.

Plan labels (fig. 163): CLOISTER CEMETERY · ANTE-CHAPEL · CHAPEL · HALL · BEER CELLAR · KITCHEN · MUNIMENT TOWER → · THE CHEQUER · PORTERS LODGE · LIBRARY OVER BURSAR'S ROOMS → · ← GATEHOUSE (entrance) · ← WARDEN'S LODGINGS · C H A M B E R S · NEW COLLEGE LANE · SCALE IN FEET 0 50 100 200 N · GREAT QUAD, NEW COLLEGE, OXFORD (1380-86)

from his 'wille and entent' of 1448, was based upon Wykeham's large enclosed quad, but his deposition and death during the Wars of the Roses, meant that he was unable to pursue his ideas, and only the famous chapel was built as the intended north side of the plan (see King's College).

4: The College Court as a derivative of the Medieval Manor House

The Old Court at Queens' College (fig. 164), was designed and built in 1448-49 by Reginald Ely, the King's mason. This was the first example in Cambridge of the complete college court, which contained all the principal elements, and was built without interruption, as with Wykeham at Oxford seven decades earlier. It is interesting to note here the similarity pointed out by Professor Willis between the ground-plan of Queens' two oldest courts and that of Haddon Hall, near Bakewell, Derbyshire. Haddon Hall is predominantly fifteenth century, Queens' two courts fifteenth and sixteenth century, and, with the exception of a few minor points, the overall arrangement of the buildings in the two is almost identical. This, and other similar examples, led Willis to put forward a theory that the great country manor houses of the fifteenth century also played an important role in the planning of the medieval college.[13]

Layout of the typical Medieval Cambridge College

The majority of the medieval colleges were located outside the town. The main courts of the colleges had one side ranged along the street in which would be the entrance, though Peterhouse and Corpus were entered via the yards of their attached parish churches. This layout, where the court is entered from the public street, has given rise to one of the most notable characteristics of the Cambridge townscape – small entrances opening into the domestic atmosphere of quiet courtyards (see fig. 165).

In the typical college plan of this period (fig. 166) one would enter the court via a turreted GATEHOUSE in the east or west wall, usually asymmetrically placed just off centre (normally centred at Oxford). The HALL would then be in front of you, in the opposite range, thus remote from the street. The BUTTERY would be part of the hall range, and also

165

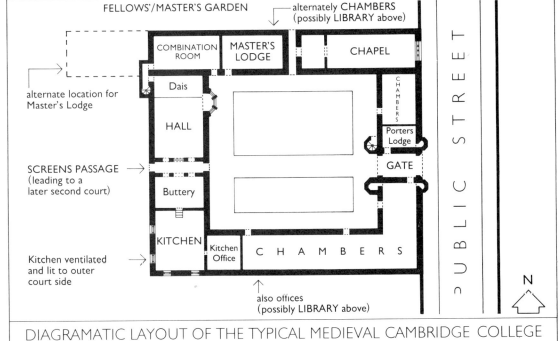

DIAGRAMATIC LAYOUT OF THE TYPICAL MEDIEVAL CAMBRIDGE COLLEGE

166

165 A typical Cambridge feature — an archway from the public street leading into the quiet domesticity of a college courtyard (Magdalene). **166** The typical college plan of the early foundations, consisting of only one primary court. The orientation of the plan would depend on the location of the public street from which the court was entered (here along the east side), the position of certain buildings being dictated by set criteria, such as the chapel requiring an east west axis so that the altar was at the east end.

the KITCHEN, which would be placed in the corner of the court so that it did not look inward but was lit and ventilated from outside. The buttery and kitchen would later be separated from the hall by the SCREENS PASSAGE, providing access to a second court (the first colleges had only a single primary court, Queens' being the first to start building a second court). The MASTER'S LODGE would normally connect with the opposite end of the hall range, providing the Master with direct access for dining etc. The CHAPEL at this time was generally in the north range of the court. Apart from the usual requirement that the chapel should be on an east-west axis, and that it had thus to be in either the north or south range, Professor Willis believed that the north range was chosen for the chapel so that the warmer south range could be used for chambers. CHAMBERS would thus occupy most of the south and east sides, and whatever remained in the other ranges. The chambers themselves would be located off a vertical stack from a staircase, a tradition which still predominates. The LIBRARY was randomly located and would often be at first floor level.

The college precinct was not restricted solely to the buildings of the court and, once the collegiate system had been established, it was intended that all the academic and recreational needs of the members of each foundation should be met within the confines of the college grounds. In particular, the gardens became of paramount importance as a most desirable adjunct to intellectual college life.

The younger members, or undergraduates, were not allowed to leave the college unless accompanied by an older person, their conduct being strictly controlled. They were forbidden to take part in the pastimes of the young townsmen, and their main forms of exercise were tennis, bowls, and archery, for which provision was made within the colleges. The use of these facilities was, in turn, also strictly controlled and it is amusing to note an incident which took place in 1719 when four Bachelors of Arts were suspended from their degrees by the Vice-Chancellor 'for being caught at a tumultuous and disorderly meeting at the Tennis Court'. Furthermore, regulations of 1750 included tennis courts among the places of 'diversion' at which undergraduates were likely to assemble, and: 'Every person in statu pupillari who shall be found at any coffee-house, tennis-court, cricket-ground, or other place of publick diversion and entertainment, betwixt the hours of nine and twelve in the morning, shall forfeit the sum of ten shillings for each offence.'[14] Thus, these places of recreation within the college played a very important social role and formed an integral part of the college plan.

Tennis and bowls were the most popular sports and up to 1594 and the foundation of Sidney Sussex College, out of the sixteen colleges in existence, nine had tennis courts, thirteen had bowling greens, and eight had both. The earliest reference to a tennis court was in the late fifteenth century when a court upon which to play 'hand-tennis' was built at Corpus Christi. The earliest mention of a bowling green was at Queens' in 1609, and, like tennis, it was very popular during the first half of the

seventeenth century. The topography of the old bowling green at Pembroke College is still quite noticeable today in the college gardens to the west of Orchard building.

During the fifteenth century six new foundations arose at Cambridge. The Monks' Hostel, founded in 1428, was planned as an enclosed court but it was not completed until the late sixteenth century after its re-foundation as Magdalene College in 1542. The small grammar college of God's House was originally located in the area of what is now the west half of King's College chapel, although little is known of its buildings, as it was re-located to its present site only a few years later. It was refounded as Christ's College by Lady Margaret Beaufort, in 1505, and its old court was completed by 1511 as an enclosed composition. King's, founded in 1441, in its original location (see p. 116) soon formed a small enclosed court, though shortly afterwards Henry VI extended the site southwards intending to develop the college on a spacious quadrangular plan. Queens' Old Court was built in mid century, with its innovatory Second Court following some decades later. The original buildings of St Catherine's Hall, founded in 1473, were based on a quadrangular plan, but all were demolished in 1673 when the present buildings were begun, later forming the large open-ended court that exists today as St Catherine's College. In 1496, Bishop Alcock founded Jesus College, taking over the buildings of the Benedictine nunnery of St Radegund and converting them to college use. They survive as a fascinating architectural composition, now forming the nucleus of the enlarged college, but as they were simply adapted from the buildings of the nunnery, they play no part in the development of the college plan.

In the sixteenth century four new colleges were established: like Christ's College, St John's was founded by Lady Margaret Beaufort and received its first, completely enclosed, court only a few years after foundation. Trinity, although founded in mid-century, was made up of a combination of existing foundations dating back to the early fourteenth century, to the beginnings of King's Hall and Michaelhouse. When Henry VIII founded the college in 1546, its site was occupied by an array of individual establishments, and it was not until Dr Thomas Nevile became Master, in 1593, that the organised composition that exists today began to take shape. Between 1597-1605 Nevile completely re-organised the site of Trinity to form the magnificent Great Court (see Trinity College). Emmanuel and Sidney Sussex Colleges, the two Elizabethan foundations at Cambridge (1584 and 1594), are both located on the sites of dissolved monastic houses; at Emmanuel some of the original monastic buildings remain, but at Sidney very little survived. The architect responsible for the conversion of both colleges was Ralph Symons, and each consisted originally of three-sided courts with walls closing off the open fourth side.

5: The three-sided, or 'sanitary' plan, after Dr Caius (1565-69)

The effect of the Reformation on college architecture is more marked in elevation than plan, because of the stylistic changes which accompanied it as English art and architecture began to be influenced by the Italian Renaissance. However, during this period a new plan form was also introduced, by an eminent physician and amateur architect, Dr John Caius (pronounced 'Keys'). In 1557 Caius refounded his old college of Gonville Hall as Gonville & Caius College, and in 1565 he set about adding a second court, Caius Court (fig. 167), to the original foundation. This composition is interesting in that it has buildings only on three sides: the existing south range of Gonville Hall provided the north side; Caius's two new ranges formed the east and west sides; but only a wall with an elaborate, though most noticeable gate, closed off the south side. This new three-sided plan has also been termed the 'sanitary arrangement' because it was designed for reasons of health and hygiene, as a clause in Caius's refoundation statutes illustrates:'We decree that no building be constructed which shall shut in the entire south side of the college of our foundation, lest for lack of free ventilation the air should become foul, the health of our college, and still more the health of Gonville's college, should become impaired, and disease and death be thereby rendered more frequent in both.'[15]

Caius was not completely innovatory in this arrangement, for it was a scheme often used in French country houses, and he had travelled widely through Europe in the 1540s. Nevertheless, this new plan became commonly adopted at Cambridge in place of the completey enclosed court characteristic before the Reformation. It was employed, for example, at Emmanuel (originally a collection of three-sided courts which were retained after the conversion of the monastery to the college, fig. 168), Sidney Sussex (Hall and Chapel Courts), Trinity (Nevile's Court in its original form before the addition of the Wren library as the west range), Trinity Hall (Library Court), Peterhouse (Entrance Court), Pembroke (Ivy Court), and Jesus (First Court). The idea has also continued to be used, though more for reasons of composition than for the alleviation of 'disease and death'; for example the main court at King's (1824-28); Gisborne Court at Peterhouse (1825-26) New Court at St John's (1826-31) Memorial Court at Clare (1923-24) North Court at Jesus (1963-64) and the Wolfson Flats at Churchill (1965-68)

It is curious that while these new three-sided courts were being built at Cambridge in the latter half of the sixteenth century, the idea did not find favour at Oxford, where many new, completely enclosed, quads were being built at about the same time.The only exceptions to the three-sided plan at Cambridge at this time, were at Magdalene (the completion of the old court in the late sixteenth century); Clare (Old Court was begun in 1635); Trinity (the reorganisation of the site to form

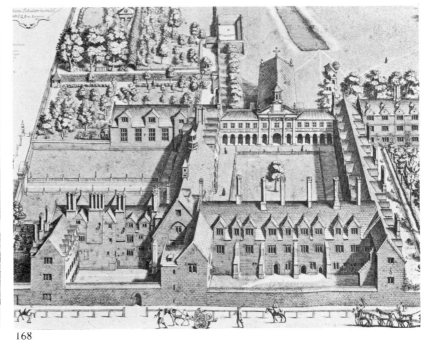

167

168

167 Caius Court, at Gonville & Caius College, designed by Dr John Caius and built between 1565-69 as the first three-sided court at Cambridge. Also termed the 'sanitary arrangement', the court was left open on one side in order to aid hygiene by allowing 'ventilation' to take place. **168** The original composition of Emmanuel College, as a collection of mainly three-sided courts, after its conversion from the Dominican Friars' Priory (both prints by David Loggan, c.1688).

Great Court at the turn of the sixteenth century); and St John's (Second Court in 1598-1602). Oxford did later respond to the influence of Caius, however, and his three-sided plan was taken up by Wren and his followers there, from the mid seventeenth to the early eighteenth century.

In the early seventeenth century a modification was made to the three-sided plan at Cambridge when the chapel at Peterhouse was placed in the centre of the open east end of Old Court (fig. 169). The chapel was joined to the north and south ranges by an open arcade with a gallery above, thereby still providing good 'ventilation' to the court. The same device was employed at Emmanuel by Wren in the late 1660s.

The idea of the three-sided plan thus broke with the medieval tradition of the completely enclosed court, and it introduced a new concept of space into college planning, creating a relationship between the inner court and the outer surroundings — between private and public — and yet boundaries were still retained. Caius Court illustrates this idea best, where the beautiful collection of buildings to its south becomes an integral part of its still intimate composition (fig. 170).

In terms of the development of the college plan, the period between the Restoration (1660) and the nineteenth century saw a return to the enclosed quadrangular plan; for example at St John's Third Court (1669-72); Trinity's Nevile's Court (by the addition of the Wren Library in 1676-84; though this building is raised on columns still allowing free passage of air); and St Catherine's, which was originally planned as an enclosed composition (1673-1704) although it is three-sided today. During the eighteenth century the Old Court of Clare was finally completed with the building of the north half of the west range (1705-15), and perhaps the most interesting event was the competition for the completion of King's Front Court. Schemes were put forward by some of the most eminent architects of the day: Nicholas Hawksmoor, in consultation with Sir Christopher Wren; James Gibbs; Robert Adam and James Wyatt, but only Gibbs's Fellows Building came to fruition in 1724-32. William Wilkins finally completed the court one hundred years later, in 1824-28, when he resumed the Caiusian principle to conclude the composition, with his new buildings providing the south range, and the Gothic screen and gatehouse as the 'open' east range (the famous chapel forms the north side, and Gibbs's Fellows Building the west). Wilkins choice of the three-sided plan in this location at King's is interesting, as at the same time he was building additional courts at Trinity (New Court, 1823-25), and Corpus Christi (New Court, 1823-27) both on the enclosed plan.

William Wilkins was one of the most important architects of the early nineteenth century, and it was he who introduced the next major development in the college plan, with the building of Downing College between 1807-20.

169

170

169 The east range of Old Court, Peterhouse, showing the location of the chapel and its attached arcades; built between 1628-33 (arcades rebuilt 1709-11) under the direction of the Master, Matthew Wren. Although breaking with tradition by its location in the east side of the court *(see fig. 166)*, the chapel was placed transversely, its west end facing into the court, so that its own axis remained east-west, and was connected to the parallel north and south ranges by open arcades. This arrangement allowed Caius's principles of hygiene to be adhered to by allowing 'ventilation' to the court via the arcades.   **170** Caius Court, Gonville & Caius College, looking south out through the 'open' side of the court, showing the relationship created by the three-sided plan between the college and the town outside. There is only a wall as the south range, interrupted by the ornate Gate of Honour, beyond which can be seen the neighbouring buildings: the tower of Great St Mary's Church, the Senate House, a glimpse of King's College Chapel, and the north-east corner of the old University library.

6: Downing College and the Campus Plan (1807-20)

Downing was founded in 1800, although its origins go back to 1749 and the death of its founder, the third Sir George Downing. The founding history of the college is complex as is the story of its proposed design, the earliest submissions for which were made by James Wyatt in 1784. Wyatt submitted further designs in 1804, after being confirmed as the college's architect in 1800, and his ideas were based upon those of James Gibbs for the completion of King's Front Court, for which they had been competitors. (Gibbs's designs for King's in 1723-24, were for a quadrangle 240 by 282 feet (72.1 x 95.9m), with each range separated at the corner). However, Wyatt's plans were never executed and the college was eventually designed by Wilkins in the fashionable Greek Revivalist style, employing the Doric and Ionic Orders.

In plan, Downing was completely innovatory, as it was designed on a spacious campus layout (fig. 171) and was the first example of this type of composition in collegiate architecture, preceding Thomas Jefferson's University of Virginia, at Charlottesville, USA, by ten years. Wilkins intended plan (fig. 172) had the buildings dispersed around a large expanse of grass, forming a court 300 feet square (91.4m), roughly equal in area to the Great Court at Trinity. The college was entered from Downing Street through a Greek Doric propylaeum (fig. 173). The east

and west ranges of the actual court were each composed of two separated blocks of chambers to north and south with a house disposed between them; on the east side was the house of the professor of medicine, and on the west the professor of law. At the south end of the east range was the independent Master's lodge, and of the west range the similarly free-standing hall, both with Ionic porticos facing to the south and into the court and intended to match those of the south range which was never built (see fig. 365).

The building of Downing made a complete break with the traditional monastic court. The whole feeling of Wilkins's college was to be one of space with buildings set in a landscape, and the most notable difference in the plan to that of previous foundations, quite apart from the immense scale, was that all of the buildings were designed as individual and separate units, joined in places by low screen walls. Sadly, however, Wilkins's plan was never fully completed and those buildings that were, only the east and west sides, were later adapted to form continuous ranges, thus changing the original concept of the designer. Nevertheless, enough was built to give an impression of the desired effect and, regardless of the changes, Downing remains a surprise to the visitor to Cambridge who, upon completion of the standard tour of the central nucleus of colleges, may find themselves in the midst of this extensive open court surrounded by low classical ranges (see title page).

171

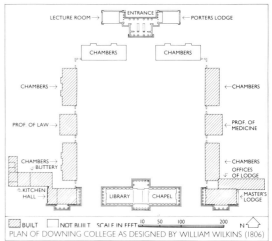

172

171 Downing College as built. **172** Downing College as intended and designed by William Wilkins in 1806 on the spacious campus plan. In the aerial view (from the east) one can see the components of Wilkins's design that were executed; the individual blocks of the east and west sides (later joined together to form continuous ranges). Wilkins's elaborate south range was never built *(see fig 365)*, and the buildings in the north range are twentieth century. **173** The intended entrance to the college from Downing Street in the north (drawn by R. Harraden, 1808).

173

The Nineteenth and Twentieth Centuries

The nineteenth century saw a considerable amount of buiding activity in Cambridge, though no attempt was made to follow Wilkins in either plan or style. New buildings were added to existing colleges, and in many cases new courts were created, both on the enclosed and the three-sided plan. Examples of enclosed courts from this period are to be found at New Court in Corpus Christi and New Court and Whewell's Courts at Trinity. More examples of the three-sided plan include New Court at Pembroke; Second Court at Christ's; Second Court at Jesus; and New Court at St John's.

Unfortunately, during the nineteenth century many old buildings were demolished to make way for new Victorian structures. For instance, the south and east ranges of Pembroke's early medieval Old Court were cleared and the new hall, by Alfred Waterhouse, inserted in place of the east range. To make room for the new chapel at St John's, built by Sir George Gilbert Scott, its thirteenth century predecessor was pulled down, sacrificing the medieval plan and intimate character of that college's First Court (see figs. 107 & 108). This was, perhaps, the saddest instance of Victorian 'vandalism' at Cambridge.

The latter half of the nineteenth century saw the foundation of three women's colleges at Cambridge: Newnham (1871); Girton (1873); and the Women's Training College (1885, now Hughes Hall). Alfred Waterhouse was the first architect at Girton (followed, as it happens, by his son and grandson) and although he followed tradition elsewhere in his design, he broke with the established pattern of rooms arranged on a vertical stack accessible from staircases, and instead introduced the corridor plan, which was also adopted at Newnham and the Women's Training College. (It is interesting to note here that in almost all of the residential buildings of the women's colleges founded at Oxford, a few years after those of Cambridge, the corridor plan was also employed in place of staircases). Both Girton and Newnham at Cambridge were

located on extensive sites and their buildings planned in a free manner, allowing for easy future addition. Girton is composed of both enclosed and open-sided courts, while Newnham could be regarded as one large three-sided composition (see fig. 376), its buildings following the site perimeter and looking inwards (south) to beautiful gardens with playing fields beyond.

The twentieth century has been a time of much expansion in most of the colleges, and, as in the nineteenth century, this has until recently been along traditional lines. By the 1950s several new courts had been created: on the enclosed plan at St Catherine's (Sherlock Court); St John's (Chapel Court), and Trinity Hall (North Court): and on the three-sided composition at Magdalene (Second Court); Emmanuel (North Court); Clare (Memorial Court); King's (Bodley's Court); Downing (where the north range was added, turning the spacious composition into a vast three-sided court); Jesus (Chapel Court); Gonville & Caius (St Michael's Court); Peterhouse (Fen Court); and Christ's (Third Court, consisting of three blocks of buildings separated at their corners). One of the most extensive development schemes was undertaken at Magdalene, where, in 1925, the college began to adapt the site to the west of its old court on the opposite side of Magdalene Street. The result is one of the most succesful urban developments in Cambridge, creating an enclosed area of courts and open-sided spaces by the addition of new buildings connecting the older medieval cottages of Magdalene and Northampton Streets.

In 1935-36, the Fisher Building extended Queens' College's site on to the west bank of the Cam. This was an unusual building as it was on a curvilinear plan, perhaps appropriate in that it followed the natural contours of the site boundary (the small tributary of the river to the south-west, and Silver Street to the south-east), but difficult for any future addition as it was unsympathetic to the formation of a later court and, indeed, the recently completed Cripps Court sits with some awkwardness to its immediate north (fig. 174). This was something that

174 175

would normally be taken into consideration when planning a new building in a college; it was a fundamental principle to design a building that could lend itself to future addition.

During the 1960s and 1970s an acceleration in college building took place unprecedented in the history of Cambridge. In this period ten new colleges were founded (see p. 87) and many extensions were added to existing colleges creating more courts. Those on the totally enclosed plan include Wolfson Court at Girton (Clarkson Road); and of the three-sided type Kenny Court at Downing; North Court at Jesus; South Court at Emmanuel; Cripps Court at Selwyn; and both courts at Wolfson College. Several 'satellite' sites also sprang-up around the town's perimeter, as some colleges ran out of space in their cramped city-centre locations: for example, King's Garden Hostel off West Road; Corpus Christi's Leckhampton House site off Grange Road; Trinity Hall's Wychfield House site off Huntingdon Road; Trinity's Dryden House in Newton Road; and St Catherine's recently completed St Chad's Hostel in Grange Road.

In planning terms the most interesting of the sixties additions were

Harvey Court, for Gonville & Caius College (West Road), with its raised inner plinth over communal rooms, surrounded by tiered inward-looking living quarters fronted with terraces (fig. 175); the meandering plan of the Cripps Building at St John's, which tied together the two halves of that college's west-bank site (fig. 176); the joint undertaking of King's and St Catherine's Colleges in the King's Lane Courts, a clever piece of jigsaw-puzzle planning creating several new courts on the cramped urban site of the two colleges' adjoining south-east and north-east borders; and Newnham College's Strachey Building, the first example in Cambridge of a 'Y' shaped plan (fig. 177).

Of the completely new foundations two, in particular, are important with regard to the development of the college plan: Churchill and Robinson, though New Hall, Fitzwilliam, and Clare Hall, are also interesting.

176

174 Fisher Building, Queens' College, of 1935-36 by Norman Drinkwater. An unsual curvilinear plan unsympathetic to future expansion, as shown here by the awkward juxtaposition of the recently completed Cripps Court to its north. **175-177** Three interesting planning exercises of the 1960s: **175** Harvey Court, Gonville and Caius College (West Road site) of 1960-62 by Martin and Wilson. Here, the architects re-interpreted the traditional courtyard by having three sides of tiered terraces facing inward on to a formal, raised court, but the fouth side turns its back on the enclosure and looks

outward into the gardens to its south. **176** Cripps Building, St John's College, of 1963-67, by Powell and Moya. One of the largest modern complexes in Cambridge, this meandering structure successfully unified this fragmented site by bridging the Bin Brook, a tributary of the Cam, and created two new three-sided courts. **177** Strachey Building, Newnham College, of 1966-68 by Lyster & Grillet. The first example of a 'Y' shaped plan at Cambridge, strongly suggesting new directions for future expansion via its projecting arms.

177

7: Churchill College: Courts within a Campus (1959-68)

At Churchill, Richard Sheppard's fascinating plan (fig. 178 & see fig. 419) consists of a main primary court formed by surrounding secondary courts, the whole of which is set in a campus-like environment; thus in effect combining the traditional monastic origins of Cambridge planning with the innovatory concept of space used by Wilkins at Downing at the beginning of the last century.

The ten outer, secondary, courts at Churchill are set in clusters within the landscape, and, with the main block of public rooms in the north-east form the perimeter boundary of a main central court, the whole being set in an extensive campus. Here, instead of the traditional ranges of buildings forming each side of a court, a series of 'satellites' revolve around the main space, and the landscape, which flows freely between the individual elements, also becomes an integral part of the

whole composition. Although this is a most imaginative reinterpretation of traditional ideas, opinions differ nevertheless as to whether such an open composition succeeds in representing the college as a corporate institution. The most recent college, Robinson, certainly adopts a completely different strategy.

Peter Chamberlin's ingenious handling of internal space at New Hall (fig. 179 & see p. 154) and his strong vistas in which water, gardens, and sunken courts interact with the architecture, almost compensates for the curious and strongly criticised style of those buildings. The plan of Denys Lasdun's Fitzwilliam College, next door to New Hall, is based upon the spiral, or 'snail shell', idea with capacity for future growth as funds become available (fig. 180 and see p. 150). Collectively, these three colleges; that is Churchill, New Hall and Fitzwilliam, provided a great opportunity for their development as parts of a whole, as they were all

178

located in close proximity to one another on the north-west outskirts of the city. Some link between the colleges themselves, and the area of modern university expansion to the south between Madingley Road and Sidgwick Avenue, might have been instigated. The late Peter Chamberlin's ideas along these lines, were disappointingly never taken up.

It became increasingly apparent during the sixties that there was a need for graduate communities at Cambridge to house the growing number of research students wanting to use the facilities offered by the university. Of the five graduate colleges that were founded (Darwin, Clare Hall, Wolfson, Hughes Hall, and St Edmund's House) the most interesting architecturally is Clare Hall, designed by the Anglo Swedish architect Ralph Erskine. The college is a collection of individual houses and flats with accompanying communal rooms, and was designed to accommodate visiting academics and their families. The character of the buildings, with their attached courtyards and walkways, is very domestic (see fig. 183), the court in this instance being used more as a yard for each of the houses, and as a pleasant atrium to the studies in the south east corner. Here, the enclosed plan is employed on a completely different scale, even more intimate than the smallest of its Cambridge ancestors (e.g. fig. 181).

181

179

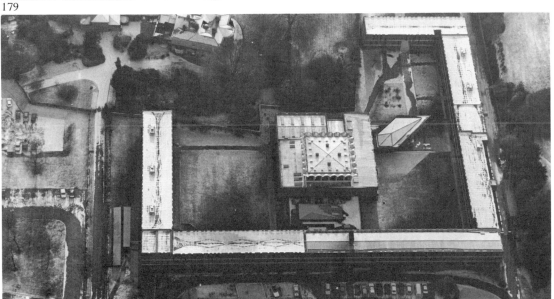

180

178 Churchill College from the west, 1959-68 by Richard Sheppard, Robson & Partners. Here, the planning concept of a series of 'satellite' courts surrounding and forming the main primary court in effect combines the traditional monastic origins of Cambridge college planning with the innovatory idea of landscape interreacting with the buildings (as intended by Wilkins at Downing College in the early 1800s). **179** New Hall from the north-east, 1962-66, by Chamberlin, Powell & Bon (the college is incomplete as a third court and chapel were also designed, *see fig 413*). All three courts are connected by the central circulation spine. In the foreground is the main residential court, with the sunken water court beyond containing the 'orange-peel' dome of the hall and the barrel-vaulted roof of the library. **180** Fitzwilliam College from the north-east, 1961-67, by Sir Denys Lasdun & Partners. Another, as yet, incomplete composition which will eventually consist of one large court, formed by the mainly residential perimeter ranges, enclosing the central block of communal rooms, such as the hall. **181** The main courtyard of Clare Hall, 1966-69, by Ralph Erskine. A Cambridge court on a very small, intimate scale (*see also fig. 183*).

8: Robinson College: The Court as the Castle Bailey (1977-80)

Robinson College was a project which excited much controversy and has been the subject of mixed criticism. From the point of view of this survey it is an important exercise in the continuing development of the college plan, and it is an interesting addition to collegiate building at Cambridge.

Of the initial ten architectural practices that were invited to submit proposals for the new college, four schemes were short-listed for further development, and of these Gillespie, Kidd & Coia were the winning partnership. It is interesting to note the different approaches of the three runners-up and the winning architects to the planning of the college. The 12 1/2 acre site in residential west Cambridge is crossed by the Bin Brook, a small tributary of the river Cam, and comprised several gardens with many trees which had belonged to some of the large nineteenth

century houses in the area. The site was the main dictating factor, and the three runners-up treated it in a very similar way; buildings dispersed widely throughout the whole site and arranged within the landscape. In particular, MacCormac & Jamieson (fig. 182) proposed a series of 21 linked cruciform pavilions between which courts and partial courts were formed, the planning grid being so designed that it related well to the pattern of the existing trees, creating a collection of buildings as an integral part of the landscape. All the buildings were of two or three storeys, and the domestic atmosphere created would have been in sympathy with the local environment. This scheme was clearly designed in response to the location in this residential district, and, like the neighbouring Clare Hall and nearby Wolfson Court, would have been an appropriate solution to college expansion in west Cambridge. The other two schemes (see Robinson College) were of a similar domestic character.

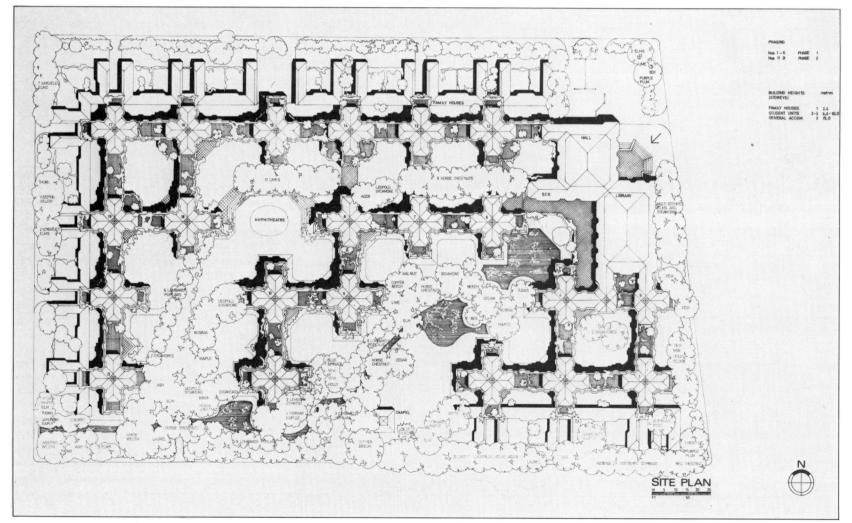

SITE PLAN

182

In contrast, the winning plan (fig. 183 and see fig. 440) concentrated the buildings around the eastern perimeter of the site, forming a massive double wall which presents the lower of its ranges towards Grange Road, and a cliff-like face to the undisturbed garden area to the west. Between the two 'layers' are the so-called 'courts' of the college. Upon completion of the college, in years to come, it will take the form of an enormous three-sided court open towards the gardens (see fig. 440), with the perimeter formed by a series of smaller subsidiary 'courts', joined to create a long and narrow continuous space.

At Robinson the designers have drawn on traditional sources in the placing of the main facade to the public street, whilst behind this the college gardens remain calm and private. The buildings are dispersed about courts, all the necessary component parts of a college being present with, in addition, the impressive theatre, and student rooms are laid out on the traditional staircase plan. At this point tradition ends and the architects' attempts to re-interpret the 'generic college image' have clearly resulted in quite a different animal. The fortress-like monumentality throughout, reminiscent of a castle; the entrance at the corner, with its ramp approach and gatehouse with portcullis-like screen; and, perhaps the most noticeable innovation of all, the rather undefined inner spaces, which resemble streets rather than courts (e.g. fig. 184), are alien to the established form.

182 One of the unsuccessful runners-up in the Robinson College design competition — MacCormac & Jamieson's site plan. In the same way that other college developments in this 'garden-suburb' district of west Cambridge had been designed to fit in with the local, residential, environment (eg Clare Hall and Wolfson Court), so this scheme was most sympathetic to the landscaped site and the scale of the surrounding houses. A planning grid, which related to the pattern of the existing trees, formed a campus of domestic-scale pavilions creating courts and partial courts with the landscape flowing freely between all of the individual components. Undoubtedly one of the most adventurous and exciting ideas for a modern Cambridge college, designed with much sensitivity to a beautiful site and its suburban location. **183** Robinson College as built (from the south-west, with Clare Hall to its south), 1977-80, by Gillespie, Kidd & Coia. The college is concentrated in a massive, double-walled building which displays an impenetrable, castle-like momumentality both to the public street and to its own back garden. **184** The 'courts' of the college, contained between the continuous double wall, are long and narrow, hard and claustrophobic spaces — more like streets and alleyways than the traditional welcoming enclosure. (The college is not yet complete, and will eventually form a large three-sided composition once the north range has been built).

183

184

In the desire to create a barrier between the town and the college's inner sanctum, an extreme overstatement has been achieved at Robinson, on the street-side almost offensive to the public in its defensive nature (fig. 185), and on the private side the buildings fail to relate to the landscape but rather compete with, and dominate it (fig. 186). The massive six-storey block of the main building forms a barrier making access to the gardens from the inner 'bailey' (the courts) of the 'castle' most awkward. Incredibly, the only room designed with doors opening directly into the gardens is the cafeteria in the north-west. Though some critics praised this plan as being 'a sympathetic response' to the site, it can also be seen as a rather drastic solution, resulting in the subordination of the gardens to the gigantic 'wall'. Here, the buildings and gardens have become two totally separate elements whereas traditionally they have been treated integrally.

A certain relationship with their surroundings has evolved in both plan and scale in the Cambridge colleges, and in most instances the buildings of the often divided factions of 'Town' and 'Gown' sit harmoniously side by side. This homogeneity has led, in part, to the unique quality of Cambridge townscape. Superb architecture has often resulted from imperiousness, and where this has occurred at Cambridge, for instance King's College Chapel, or even St John's College Chapel, the buildings today play an important role in the townscape. In contemporary building, however, this same attitude has led to some highly controversial projects at Cambridge; such as Stirling's History Faculty, or Lasdun's New Court for Christ's College, with its vastly overscaled public elevation to King Street. In the same way that Christ's New Court was a most desirable building from the college's point of view, but not from that of King Street onto which it backs, so Robinson was equally regarded as an appropriate solution by its commissioning panel. It is interesting that the type of idea proposed by all three of the runners-up at Robinson, was considered to be 'inappropriate' to Cambridge. Clearly a certain monumentality was desired for Robinson, and it over-ruled other criteria regarded as equally important by the residents of West Cambridge.

186

185

185 The monumental, defensive character of Robinson College to the public street, with its ramp approach and portcullis-like screens — a harsh statement in this friendly area of suburban west Cambridge. **186** The same, impenetrable facade to its own back gardens, creates a barrier between what has traditionally been a sought-after aspect of college life, with buildings giving onto beautiful gardens to provide a therapeutic haven for the academic. Here, the two elements are totally separate and access between the two has been made most awkward.

Chronological Summary of the founding of the Cambridge University Colleges

	DATE	FOUNDATION	FOUNDER	LOCATION (Grid Ref. see p. 8)	PAGE
	(1264	Merton College, Oxford	*Walter de Merton*	*Merton Street, Oxford*)	
1	1280	Scholars of the Bishop of Ely	*Hugh de Balsham, Bishop of Ely*	*Hospital of St John*	
	1284	**Peterhouse**		Trumpington Street (E/F5)	88
2	1317	Edwards II's 'King's Childer'	*King Edward II*	*King's Childer Lane (demolished)*	
	1324	Michaelhouse	*Hervey de Stanton*	*(St Michael's Lane) Trinity Lane*	
	1337	King's Hall	*King Edward III*	*(High Street) Trinity Street*	
	1546	**Trinity College**	King Henry VIII	Trinity Street (E3/4)	90
3	1326	University Hall	*Richard de Badew*	*(Milne Street) Trinity Lane*	
	1338	Clare (House) Hall	Elizabeth de Burgo, the		
	1856	**Clare College**	Countess of Clare	Trinity Lane (E4)	99
4	1347	**Pembroke College**	Mary, Countess of Pembroke	Trumpington Street (F5)	102
5	1348	Gonville Hall	Edmund Gonville	*(Luthburne Lane) Free School Lane*	
	1557	**Gonville & Caius College**	Dr John Caius	Trinity Street (E4)	104
6	1350	**Trinity Hall**	William Bateman, *Bishop of Norwich*	*(Milne Street)* Trinity Lane (E4)	106
7	1352	**Corpus Christi**	Gilds of Corpus Christi and St Mary	Trumpington Street (F4/5)	108
8	1428	Benedictine Monks Hostel	*Abbot Litlyngton*	*(Bridge Street)*	
	1542	**Magdalene College**	Thomas, Lord Audley of Walden	Magdalene Street (E2)	110
9	1437	God's House	*William Bingham*	*(Milne Street) Trinity Lane*	
	1505	**Christ's College**	Lady Margaret Beaufort	St Andrew's Street (F4)	113
10	1441	**King's College**	King Henry VI	King's Parade (E4)	116
11	1446	College of St Bernard	*Andrew Docket*	*(Milne Street) Queens' Lane*	
	1448	The Queen's College of St Margaret & St Bernard	Margaret of Anjou *(Q of Henry VI)*		
	1465	**Queens' College**	Elizabeth Woodville *(Q of Edward IV)*	Queens' Lane/Silver Street (E5)	124
12	1473	**St Catherine's College** (St Catherine's Hall, pre 1860)	Robert Woodlark	Trumpington Street (E4/5)	126
13	1496	**Jesus College** ('College of the Blessed Virgin Mary, St John the Evangelist, and the Glorious Virgin St Radegund')	John Alcock, *Bishop of Ely*	Jesus' Lane (G3)	128
14	1511	**St John's College**	Lady Margaret Beaufort	St John's Street (E3)	131
15	1584	**Emmanuel College**	Sir Walter Mildmay	St Andrew's Street (G4)	136
16	1594	**Sidney Sussex College**	Lady Frances Sidney	Sidney Street (F3)	138
17	1800	**Downing College**	Sir George Downing III	Regent Street (G5)	140
18	1869	Non-Collegiate Body established	Cambridge University		
	1874	Fitzwilliam Hall ('House' from 1922)		31 Trumpington Street	
	1966	**Fitzwilliam College**		Huntingdon Road (C1)	150
19	1871	**Newnham College** (first womens College)	Council for Higher Education of Women	Sidgwick Avenue (C/D 5/6)	144
20	1873	**Girton College** (previously Benslow House, Herts: 1869)	Emily Davies	Huntingdon Road *(N-W Cambridge)*	146
21	1879	**Selwyn College**	*via Committee (after Bishop Selwyn)*	Grange Road (C5)	148
22	1885	Cambridge Womens Training College	Miss Clough *and committee*	*Newnham*	
	1949	**Hughes Hall**	*(named after Miss E. P. Hughes)*	Wollaston Road *(off Mill Road)*	151
23	1894	**Homerton College** (Teachers Training: affil. to CU 1976)	Congregational Churches *(London 1695)*	Hills Road *(S-E Cambridge)*	152
24	1896	**St Edmund's House** (originated in Flanders, 1568)	Baron Anatole von Hugel	Mount Pleasant (C2)	153
25	1951	Ladies Dining Society formed	Dr Anna Bidder, Mrs Margaret		
	1965	**Lucy Cavendish College**	Braithwaite, Dr Kathleen Wood-Legh	Lady Margaret Road (C/D2)	158
26	1954	**New Hall**	Association for Women in Cambridge	Huntingdon Road (C1)	154
27	1958	**Churchill College**	*via Committee* (after Sir Winston)	Storey's Way (B2)	156
28	1965	**Darwin College**	*Gonville & Caius, St John's and Trinity*	*Silver Street (E5)*	159
29	1965	**Clare Hall**	Clare College and Benefactors	Herschell Road (B/C4)	161
30	1965	University College	Cambridge University	*Bredon House, Selwyn Gardens*	
	1973	**Wolfson College**	Wolfson Foundation *(after Sir Isaac)*	Barton Road *(S-W Cambridge)*	162
31	1974	**Robinson College**	David Robinson	Grange Road (B/C4)	163

Peterhouse

This first Cambridge College was established by Hugh de Balsham, l0th Bishop of Ely, in 1280, and was based upon the statutes of Walter de Merton's College at Oxford of 1264. Initially, de Balsham's scholars were housed in the Hospital of St John the Evangelist in the north part of the town (later to become St John's College), but in 1284 they moved south to two hostels next to the church of St Peter-without-Trumpington-Gate (now St Mary the Less) on which site the college has expanded over the last seven centuries.

The main area of building is along the north boundary of the site, on the west side of Trumpington Street, where there are four courts: First, Old, Gisborne, and Fen Courts. Further development has recently taken place in the south-east corner of the site where the William Stone Building was erected in 1963-64. The two areas are connected by a footpath through the gardens and former deer park, which runs behind the Fitzwilliam Museum. The Master's Lodge and Cosin Court are situated on the east side of Trumpington Street.

The first college building to be completed was the Hall, in 1286, which now forms part of the south side of Old Court (fig. 191). It has been much altered and to obtain an impression closest to its original form, it is best viewed from the south (see figs 7 & 157). George Gilbert Scott Jun. carried out major restoration work on the hall in 1870, around which time the Arts & Crafts firm of Morris & Co. executed much interior work in both the hall and the Combination Room. There are tiled fireplaces by William Morris (see fig. 111) and some fine examples of pre-Raphaelite stained-glass by Ford Madox Brown, Edward Burne-Jones, Morris and Philip Webb (see fig. 110)

Dr Matthew Wren, uncle of Christopher, was Master between 1625-35 and was responsible for much building activity. His main achievement was the Chapel (fig. 189 & see 87), one of the finest buildings of its date in Cambridge and certainly the most striking at Peterhouse. The designer of the chapel is unknown, but the mason was George Thomson. The cloisters flanking the west end are later additions in the classical manner. The Palladian range of chambers to the north of the chapel was designed by Sir James Burrough and built between 1732-43. Burrough's Building (fig. 188 & see 98) is one of the best examples of the period in Cambridge and was the last major building at Peterhouse until the early nineteenth century neo-Gothic Gisborne Court (fig. 192). To the west of Gisborne is Fen Court, built at the beginning of the Second World War, and one of the earliest 'modern' buildings for a Cambridge college (fig. 192 & see 129).

One of the most successful examples of 'Sixties' architecture in Cambridge is the William Stone Building at Peterhouse (fig. 193 & see 137). Designed by Sir Leslie Martin & Colin St John Wilson, past and present Cambridge Professors of Architecture, this was the first attempt at Cambridge to house students in a high-rise building. It is an eight storey block of loadbearing brick. Comparisons have been drawn with the work of the Finnish architect Alvar Aalto, and, indeed, it is particularly reminiscent of his 'Neue Vahr' apartment building in Bremen, West Germany, of 1958-62.

See also figs: 7, 87, 98, 110, 111, 129, 137, 156, 157, 169, 482

Chronological Summary of Buildings

Date	Building/Occurrence	Location/Details
1286	Hall (heightened in C15)	Old Ct., S range, middle
1450	Kitchens	Old Ct., W end, S
1460-66	Master's Chambers and Combination Room	Old Ct., E of Hall
1590-95	Dr Perne's Library	First Ct., S range, W
C17	Original hostels demolished	First Ct., street side
1628-32	Chapel (Master: Matthew Wren)	First Ct., centre
1633	Chapel, S and N cloisters	W end of chapel (rebuilt)
	Perne Library extended E	First Ct., S range, E
1709-11	Chapel cloisters rebuilt	(by Robert Grumbold)
1725	House donated for use as a Master's Lodge	Trumpington St., E side (house built in 1702)
1738-42	Burrough's Building (Burrough)	First Ct., N range
1754	Old Court ashlared (Burrough)	(W side restored in 1981)
1825-26	Gisborne Court (McIntosh Brooks)	W of Old Court
1868-74	Rest. of Hall and Comb. Room (Morris & Co. interior work)	Old Court, S range (fireplaces, glass etc)
1926	New Court begun (incomplete)	SW of Old Court
1939	Fen Court (Hughes & Bicknell)	W of Gisborne Court
1963-64	William Stone Building	Far SE corner of site
1969	Cosin Court (Roberts & Clarke)	Trumpington St., E side

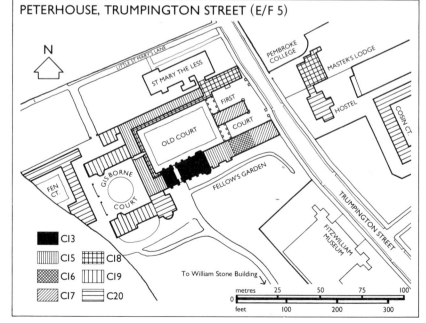

PETERHOUSE, TRUMPINGTON STREET (E/F 5)

■ C13
▦ C15 ▦ C18
▨ C16 ▥ C19
▧ C17 ▤ C20

To William Stone Building

metres 0 25 50 75 100
feet 100 200 300

188

189

190

194

191

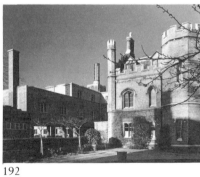

192

193

195

187 Peterhouse site plan.   188 The college front to Trumpington Street with the Perne library, the east end of the chapel, and Burrough's Building beyond.   189 The east side of Old Court comprising the west end of the chapel and its arcades.   190 The north and west ranges of Old Court — brick buildings which were fashionably stone-faced in the eighteenth century.   191 The outer, south side of Old Court reveals the original rubble construction of the Hall and Combination Room.   192 The Gothic-Revival Gisborne Court contrasts to the sternly functional 'Modern Movement' form of Fen Court *(see also fig. 129)*.   193 William Stone Building from the east.   194 The Master's Lodge — an elegant Queen Anne house of 1704.   195 A portion of the modern, residential Cosin Court.

Trinity College

Trinity, the largest Cambridge college, was founded in 1546 by Henry VIII on the sites of two older foundations, King's Hall and Michaelhouse, and of several academic houses, the most important of which was the Physwick Hostel. In characteristic Henrician manner, it was intended to surpass all the existing establishments in both Oxford and Cambridge, and in particular Cardinal College, Oxford (now Christ Church), founded in 1525 by Cardinal Thomas Wolsey.

Trinity's antecedents can be traced back to the early fourteenth century and the Plantagenet Edward II, who in 1317 granted royal funds to support certain scholars at Cambridge (the 'King's Childer'); and in 1337 his son, Edward III, converted the grant into a college proper by purchasing the house of Robert de Croyland and founding King's Hall. Meanwhile, Hervey de Stanton, Edward II's Chancellor of the Exchequer, founded Michaelhouse in 1324 in the same vicinity. Thus, possibly because of its royal connections, King's Hall was chosen by Henry VIII to form the nucleus of his great foundation.

Henry VIII granted the foundation charter for Trinity on 19 December 1546, and died on 28 January 1547. It is an interesting thought that had he lived longer he might have produced a plan for the layout of his new college, in the same way as Henry VI had done at King's. However, this was not to be, and the gradual shaping of the college was undertaken by three prominent Masters: Nevile (1593-1615), Bentley (1700-42), and Whewell (1841-66).

The original site was complex, the area being dissected by several lanes, now no longer in existence, and also by the King's Ditch, which was filled in in the early seventeenth century. The present-day site is very large, stretching from Sidney Street in the east to Grange Road in the west, a distance of almost one mile. The main concentration of building is in the eastern part, between the river and Sidney Street. The more spacious western area contains the Backs, the Fellows' Garden, and the Burrells Field Hostels bordering on Grange Road. The site of Trinity can be divided into four sections: the old site, between the river and Trinity Street; the new site, between Trinity and Sidney Streets; the garden site, between the river and Grange Road; and, from 1949 onwards, various satellite sites situated throughout the town (see chronology).

The old site contains four courts and the Bishop's and King's Hostels. The magnificent Great Court (figs 197-206) fills half of this site and is a jigsaw-puzzle of buildings, lacking in any of the formal qualities of the traditional court plan, yet aesthetically very pleasing. It has no symmetry either in plan or elevation, yet the whole is successful, its charm being partly due to this lack of uniformity aided by its sheer size; were it smaller, this diversity might well cause conflict. The layout of this vast court is the work of Dr Thomas Nevile, who, at the turn of the sixteenth century, reorganised the site to provide a sense of order within the newly founded college. The north-east area, around the main gateway and the King's Hostel, dates back to King's Hall, and it is also likely that remnants of Michaelhouse and the Physwick Hostel survive in some of the walls in the south-west corner of the site. The south and east ranges are domestic in character, consisting mainly of student accommodation (figs 201 & 202), while the north and west sides contain buildings such as the Hall, Master's Lodge and Chapel.

The late Gothic Chapel (fig. 200) is the product of the patronage of Queen Mary and Elizabeth I. The screen (fig. 203), added during Dr Bentley's eighteenth century redecoration, is Wren in style with large corinthian columns flanking the central doorway leading from ante-

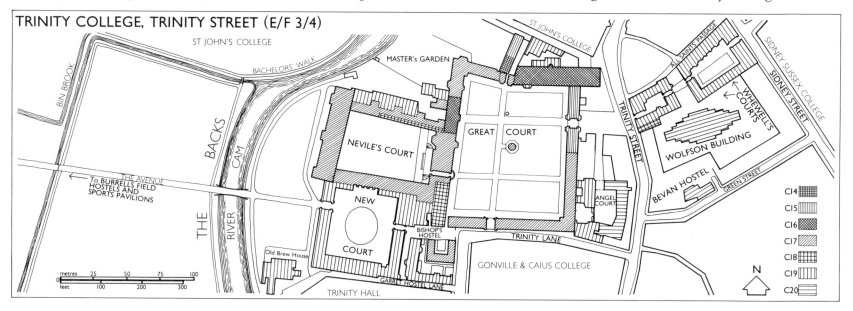

198

199

196 Trinity site plan. **197** The north and north-east sides of Great Court. The old library range to the west (one of the earliest three-storey college buildings at Cambridge, *c.*1600), King Edward's Tower, the chapel, the gatehouse, and the fountain in the foreground. The north-east corner was previously the site of King's Hall, but Dr Nevile's reorganization created Great Court as the largest Oxbridge composition, measuring: 257 ft(N) x 288(S) x 325(E) x 340(W). **198** The fountain and King Edward's Tower *(see also figs 86 & 460).* **199** The north-west corner of Great Court showing the Master's Lodge between the old library and Nevile's Hall. **200** The Chapel was built mainly with re-used stone from the dissolved Franciscan Priory at Cambridge (now Sidney Sussex College) and Ramsey Abbey in Huntingdonshire, the mason was a Mr Perse.

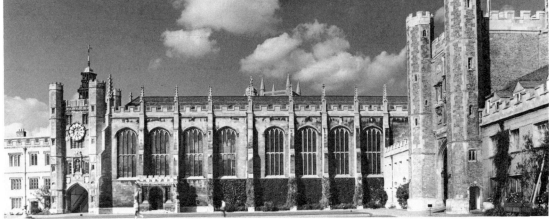

200

chapel to chapel. The superb standing statue of Newton (fig. 204) in the antechapel, is by Roubiliac, and is among his finest work (there is also sculpture by Roubiliac in the library).

The oldest surviving building in the college is King Edward's Tower (figs 198, 200 & see 460) situated at the west end of the chapel. This gate tower originally stood about 23 yards (21 metres) south of its present position, where the sundial stands today. Nevile moved the tower in 1600 to fit in with his plans (for the gatehouses of Trinity see pp. 170-3).

To the west of King Edward's Tower is a three storey range of chambers, the original library. Abutting these is the Master's Lodge (fig. 199). Begun in the mid sixteenth century, but built mainly by Nevile around 1600, the Lodge contains rooms of great architectural interest. Much has been added to the original building; first by Bentley who had the interior refitted and built the grand staircase; secondly, by Salvin in the nineteenth century, when he restored and rebuilt the porch and east and west bay windows; and, finally, by Blomfield, who added the west extension in 1892.

Continuing south down the west range, is Nevile's Hall (figs 205-207), a great Elizabethan structure with hammer-beam roof and minstrels' gallery. Modelled upon the hall of the same proportions at Middle Temple, London, (103ft x 40ft x 50ft high), it was built by Ralph Symons, who two years earlier had completed St John's Second Court only a short distance away. To the east of the Hall and near the centre of the court, is the superb octagonal fountain (fig. 198 & see 86), built in the early seventeenth century, although extensively rebuilt in 1716 by Robert Grumbold.

On completing Great Court, Nevile began another court to the west of the Hall, which he himself financed. Nevile's Court (fig. 209), built in the classical manner, was originally three-sided and only just over half its present length, the west end bounded only by a wall and a gate. In 1676 the Master, Isaac Barrow, asked his friend Sir Christopher Wren, to design a new library for the college, which he generously did free of charge. The library was placed some distance west towards the river, and on completion, the north and south ranges of Nevile's Court were extended to connect with it (the initial, and rejected, design that Wren put forward was totally different to that executed; it consisted of a free-standing rotunda linked to the west end of Nevile's north and south ranges by low walls and railings; the idea was used by Hawksmoor in his designs for the Radcliffe Camera at Oxford, which was eventually executed by Gibbs some sixty years later between 1737-49).

Wren had already provided Cambridge with its first purely classical buildings in the 1660s, the Pembroke and Emmanuel College Chapels. The Trinity Library (figs 210-213) continued to exert an influence on the local designers and, indeed, set a new precedent for much of the collegiate architecture to follow. The building is faced in Ketton stone, the library being on the upper floor above an open undercroft and supported along its centre by a single row of Tuscan columns with an open arcade along the court side. The external appearance of the library from the east (court) side belies the internal arrangement; because it was desirable to have windows starting well above the bookcases in the library, Wren employed an ingenious device to give the necessary depth between the level of the windowsill and the floor. He achieved this by filling in the tympana of the arcade and having the floor at the level of the springing of the arches and not at the level of the Doric frieze, as the exterior implies. Wren also designed the interior fittings for the library, where there are some superb examples of the work of Grinling Gibbons, in particular the wood carvings on the north and south walls (fig. 212), as well as busts by Roubiliac and Pieter Scheemakers.

On completion of the library, Nevile's Court became a four-sided composition, but the older, Tudor Gothic Hall (fig. 207) was now at odds with the new classical ranges. In an attempt to provide some sort of harmony between the Hall and the rest of the court, Grumbold, probably under the direction of Wren, attached the classical rostrum, or Tribune (fig. 208), to the west side of the Hall, providing an appropriate platform from which to view the library upon entering the court via the screens passage.

Because of the deterioration of the facades, the north and south ranges of Nevile's Court (fig. 209) were rebuilt by James Essex in the mid eighteenth century, certain original Jacobean detailing being omitted. Essex raised the height of the original, attic storey, replacing tall gabled dormers with larger windows and a balustraded parapet above, to match that of the library. Apart from this, little building activity of any importance took place at Trinity during the eighteenth century, the next major project being William Wilkins's neo-Gothic New Court (fig. 214) in 1823-25.

The new site, to the east of Trinity Street, was purchased by William Whewell in the nineteenth century. Whewell's Courts (fig. 220), designed in a Tudor style by Anthony Salvin, but with early twentieth century Arts & Crafts decorative bay windows added by Caroe, consist of two courts, with an adjoining central area known as the 'Garden of Eden'. To the south of this is the modern Wolfson Building (fig. 217), by the Architects Co-Partnership. This little-known building, completed in the early 1970s, was potentially controversial, but owing to its very concealed site it appears to have escaped largely unnoticed (see fig. 144).

A massive building for its location, the constructional idea behind the Wolfson Building was based upon the use of an enormous podium set 12ft above street level and slotting into the backs of the shops along Trinity and Sidney Streets, thus creating space for commercial development. A centrally placed, vertical circulation core, contains a lift and east and west staircase which are top-lit by pyramidal rooflights designed to throw light as far down into the building as possible, and also to add interest to the city skyline (see fig. 51) From the podium rise five storeys of rooms on the east side of the circulation core, and four on the west, each floor being connected by glazed corridors. Large open terraces are created on the external podium level.

201

202

203

204

205

206

201 Eastern half of Great Court's south range with the Queen's Gate *(see also fig 468)*.
202 Southern half of Great Court's east range. **203** Chapel interior showing the Wren-style screen dividing ante-chapel and chapel. **204** Statue of Sir Isaac Newton in the ante-chapel. **205** The hammerbeam roof of Nevile's Hall. **206** Nevile's Hall from the east.

The Wolfson Building is reminiscent of nautical shapes and, indeed, various analogies have been drawn with ocean liners, whales, etc. The form is, in fact, modelled upon the Assyrian or Babylonian Ziggurat (a truncated pyramid built in successively receding stories) and was chosen for two very appropriate reasons. Firstly, for maximum daylight within the building itself, and so as not to block daylight from the neighbouring buildings, and, secondly, the choice of this very geometric form was a deliberate attempt by the architects to establish 'order' within an area of 'romantic chaos'. However, the building as executed was not exactly as the architects intended, because of the college's insistence upon the use of externally clad, brick panels. The architects' wish to create an effect of 'soaring verticality', with the use of vertically ribbed concrete creating a monolithic impression much more in keeping with the ziggurat form was therefore lost. The brick panels, separated at each floor level by concrete 'string courses', severely compartmentalises the facade, giving the unintended impression of a pile of stacked boxes.

Owing to lack of space prior to the Wolfson development, several new buildings were located away from the main college. Bevan Hostel was the first to be built in 1949 and simply takes the form of a large, traditional town house with a mansard roof and much decorative brickwork. Dryden House (fig. 219), on the southern outskirts of town, comprises nine graduate flats and was built by Eric Lyons in the late Sixties. Also at this time the Sports Pavilions (fig. 216) were built in Grange Road by Lyster & Grillet. Consisting of two cubes in light grey brick with pyramidal roofs, there is a strong similarity between these pavilions and the contemporaneous buildings for Homerton College by the same practice (see p. 153). More recently, Trinity have developed their Burrells Field site on the opposite side of Grange Road to the sports pavilions. Roberts & Clarke were the architects of the Burrells Field Hostels (fig. 215) which are located on the western edge of this pretty garden site, through which flows the Bin Brook.

See also figs: 14, 51, 86, 96, 144, 460, 463, 468, 486, 502

Chronological Summary of Buildings

Date	Building/Occurrence	Location/Details
1317	Edward II's endowment of scholars	(the 'King's Childer')
1324	Michaelhouse est. by Stanton	SW area of site
1337	King's Hall founded by Edward III	NE area of site
1427-32	King Edward's Gate Tower (see p. 170)	Great Ct., N range, centre
1490-92	Porter's Lodge	Great Ct., E range, N
1518-35	Great Gate (see p. 171)	S of Porter's Lodge
1546	Trinity College founded	(by Henry VIII)
1554	Master's Lodge, S half	Great Ct., W range, N
1554-55	N range of Great Court (W)	W of Edward's Tower
1555-57	E range of Great Court N1/4	N of Porter's Lodge
1555-67	Chapel	Great Ct., N range, E
1593-1615	Master: Thomas Nevile	
1597-1605	Nevile's reorganization	(forms Great Court)
1598-99	Great Gate heightened.	E and S
	sides of Great Court completed	
1599-1600	Library (old) range completed	Great Ct., N range, W
	King Edward's Tower relocated	(to present position)
1600-01	Master's Lodge, N Half. Battlements added to Great Court chambers	
1601-15	Fountain	Great Ct., centre
1604-05	Nevile's Hall	Great Ct., W range, centre
1605-06	King's Ditch filled in	W area of site
1611-12	Original bridge over river (wood)	SW of Nevile's Court
1612-14	Nevile's Ct., N & S ranges, E halves	W of Great Court
1669-71	Garret Host. rebuilt as Bishop's Host.	SW of Great Court
1676-95	Wren Library (fabric: 1676-84)	Nevile's Ct., W range
1676-81	W extension of Nevile's Court	N & S ranges, W halves
1682	The Tribune by Robert Grumbold	Nevile's Ct., E end
1691-93	Grinling Gibbons wood carvings	Library
1700-42	Master: Richard Bentley	
1704	Sundial set up in Great Court	S of Edward's Tower
1706-17	Chapel restoration, screen made	(E window blocked)
1715-16	Fountain re-built by Grumbold	
1733	Iron gates at W end of avenue	W of bridge
1750-51	Great Court stuccoed by Denston	
1752-53	King Edward's Gate 'beautified'	
1755	Roubiliac's statue of Newton	Chapel, antechapel
1755-58	Reconstr. of Nevile's Ct by Essex	
1764-65	Bridge rebuilt in stone by Essex	
1770-75	Combination Rooms re-built by Essex	Gt. Ct., W. range, S
1795	Sundial renewed	
1810-13	E. side of Great Court, King's gate	and Old Library stuccoed
1823-25	King's, or New Court, by Wilkins	S of Nevile's Court
1831-32	Chapel restored by Blore	
1833	New Lecture Rooms by Humphrey	W of Great Court (S)
1841-43	Alterations to Master's Lodge by Salvin	
1841-66	Master: William Whewell	
1845	Oak vault of Gatehouse	
1856	E front (N) rebuilt by Salvin	N of Gatehouse
1859-68	Whewell's Courts (A. Salvin)	E side of Trinity Street
1867-75	Chapel interior decorated	(by Blomfield)
1876-78	Two new ranges by Blomfield	SW of Bishop's Hostel
1892	N range of Nevile's Court and Lodge	extended to W, by Blomfield
1905-06	Restor. of King's Hostel by Caroe	N of Great Court
1908	Remod. of Whewell's Courts by Caroe	(external decor etc)
1949	Bevan Hostel (Ian Forbes)	Green Street
1957-59	Angel Court	W of Great Court (S)
1967-68	Dryden House by Eric Lyons & Ptnrs	Newton Road (S Camb)
	Sports Pavilion by Lyster & Grillet	Grange Road
1968-72	Wolfson Building by Archit. Co-Ptnrshp	E side of Trinity St
1978-79	Burrells Field Hostels (Roberts & Clarke)	Grange Road (W Camb)
1981-84	Restoration of Whewell's Courts	
1983-84	Restoration of Chapel and Gatehouse	

207

208

207 Nevile's Court: Nevile's Hall from the west. **208** The Tribune, a classical rostrum from which to view the Wren library at the opposite end of Nevile's Court, built by Robert Grumbold, Wren's mason on the library **209** The north range of Nevile's Court from the south cloister.

209

210

211

212

213

210 Sir Christopher Wren's library (1676-95) - the east elevation to Nevile's Court. The building is 150 feet long constructed of Ketton stone in a subtle mixture of cream and pink hues. The four standing statues on the balus- trade represent *Divinity, Law, Physic* and *Mathematics,* and were executed in 1681 by Gabriel Cibber, a sculptor often employed by Wren, who charged £80 for the work. **211** The library interior looking north. **212** One of the many beautiful wood carvings in the library by Grinling Gibbons, executed in lime wood between 1691-93. **213** The west elevation of the library as seen from the Backs.

214

214 The east range of the Gothic Revival New Court (officially christened 'Kings Court' in honour of George IV who donated £1000 towards its construction) by William Wilkins; designed in 1821 and built 1823-25. Interestingly, the versatile Wilkins also put forward an alternative design, in the classical style, to harmonise with the west elevation of the Wren Library, to the south of which New Court's west range continues *(see fig 213)*. **215** Trinity Sports Pavilions and Groundsman's House, Grange Road, 1967-68, by Lyster & Grillet. **216** Burrell's Field graduate hostels - Adrian and Butler Houses off Grange Road - 1978-79, by Roberts & Clarke.

217

218

217 The Wolfson Building, of 1968-72, by the Architects Co-Partnership *(see also fig 144).* **218** Angel Court. **219** Dryden House, Newton Road. **220** Whewell's Courts from Trinity Street, 1859-60 & 1865-68, by Anthony Salvin but with remodelling of the facades by W.D. Caroe in 1908.

220

221

Clare College (main essay overleaf)

221 This composition is quite unusual amongst the Cambridge colleges in that the buildings appear to be of one foundation whereas they are, in fact, of two: the south range of Clare seen from the lawns of King's, with King's Chapel and the Gibbs Building to its south-east (see p. 116) – a distance of only 11 metres separates the north-west angle of the chapel from the south-east angle of Clare. None of the original buildings of the fourteenth century Clare 'Hall' have survived and the south range dates to 1640-42 (the entire court behind it to 1638-

1715) The east range was started first in 1638 *(see fig. 223)* and the south continued along roughly the same pattern before building activity was interrupted by the outbreak of Civil War in 1642. These two earlier ranges are described in the Royal Commission's survey as being "... exceptional for the formality of their calculated design, depending for effect more upon repetition than upon symmetry, although the latter is observed, and for the fusion of classical divisions and details with the traditional medieval features of stone mullions and, before they were removed in 1762, arched windows and

battlements". Indeed, this was an interesting period at Cambridge when classicism was slowly starting to make an appearance alongside the traditional medieval styles *(see pp. 54-57)*. The south range is particularly pleasing, with its three storeys topped by attics lit by the long row of dormer windows with their individual hipped roofs. Also attractive are the materials; the walls being of Ketton and Weldon stone ashlar (facing an inner core of brick and clunch) with roofs of Collyweston slates. Professor Willis calculated from the accounts that the total cost of building between 1638-1715 was £15,340.

Clare College

University Hall was founded in 1326 by Richard de Badew, Chancellor of the University. In 1338, Elizabeth de Burgh, Countess of Clare, re-founded it as Clare House, later to be called Clare Hall, and supplied the necessary endowments which it had previously lacked. It finally became Clare College in 1856.

Nothing remains of the original buildings, but present-day Clare is divided into three sites: the Old Court, situated between Trinity Lane and the river; Memorial and Thirkhill Courts, on the west side of Queens' Road; and the Castle Hill Hostel in north Cambridge.

The Old Court of Clare is the product of a seventeenth century rebuilding scheme, and is one of the most beautiful compositions in the university, particularly the south range viewed from the lawns of King's (fig. 221), and the west range seen from the river (fig. 226). This court is significant in that it embodies seventeenth century Cambridge architecture, its homogeneous appearance being the result of 77 years of continuous building activity, from 1638-1715. The east range (fig. 223 & see 88) was the first to be built, and set the pattern for the rest of the court — three storeys with dormer windows in the roof. The details above the gateway of the two-storey oriel window, with niches and crocketted ogee gables on either side, were probably copied from Peterhouse Chapel, completed only six years earlier. By the time building had commenced on the west range, in 1669, Christopher Wren had made his debut in Cambridge with Pembroke College Chapel (1663-5) and had just started on the Chapel at Emmanuel College . Wren's considerable influence on local designers can be seen in the west range, where the design was changed to include a giant Ionic order to the river front. It is not known who produced this new design, but it is possible that it was one of the local master masons, Robert Grumbold or George Jackson, the latter having worked for Wren as a bricklayer at Pembroke and was also employed at Clare as 'Surveyor' (a title then denoting architect). The later north range (fig. 225) is even more strongly influenced by Wren, and can be attributed to Robert Grumbold, who was at this time working not only at Clare but also on the Trinity Library.

The Chapel (1763-69, fig. 224), was designed in the classical style by James Burrough, though completed after his death in 1764 by James Essex. Once again Wren's influence can be seen in the east front, which is modelled on Pembroke College Chapel.

In the early years of the twentieth century Clare took the unprecedented step of building to the west of Queens' Road. The neo-Georgian Memorial Court (fig. 227), by Sir Giles Gilbert Scott, was later enlarged to the south with the addition of Thirkhill Court, also by Scott.

Further expansion by Clare meant leaving the town centre and moving north to build in Castle Drive, off Chesterton Lane. Castle Hill Hostel (fig. 230) by David Roberts, is set in a pretty garden environment with other houses, one red-brick Gothic and another whitewashed neo-Georgian, also Clare hostels. The informal and relaxed atmosphere here is domestic rather than collegiate, created perhaps by the combination of the unusual hillside site with unpretentious and colourful buildings. The Roberts hostel is described by Booth and Taylor as 'one of Cambridge's best post-war buildings. Its principal qualities are freedom and simplicity...freedom from the gloom of academic introversion...'

See also figs: 9, 49, 64, 68, 88, 492, 505, 506

Chronological Summary of Buildings

Date	Building/Occurrence	Location Details
1326	University Hall founded	Area of Old Court
1338	Clare House founded	(later called 'Hall')
1635	Rebuilding scheme starts	(subscriptions begin)
1638-41	Old Court, E range	(Master mason J. Westley)
1638-40	Bridge (T. Grumbold, see p. 184)	W of Old Court
1640	W range, S half begun	Old Court
1640-42	S range, (J. Westley)	Old Court
1642-52	Civil War stops building	
1669-76	W range, S half completed	Old Ct.
1673	Gates and walls to Trinity La.	Old Ct., E boundary
1683-90	N range (R. Grumbold)	Old Court
1690	Stone gate piers built	W end of avenue
1691	Avenue laid out and planted	W of bridge
1705-15	W range, N half (R. Grumbold)	Old Court
1713-15	Iron gates at E & W entrances	(Warren)
1762	Balustrades added, S&E ranges	(replacing battlements)
1763-69	Chapel (J. Burrough & J. Essex)	Range NE of Old Court
1856	Name changed to Clare College	(from Clare Hall)
1923-34	Memorial Court (G.G. Scott)	W side of Queens' Rd.
1953-55	Thirkhill Court (G.G. Scott)	SW ext. to Memorial Ct.
1957-58	Castle Hill Hostel (D. Roberts)	Chesterton Lane

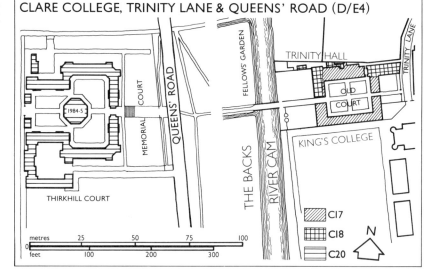

CLARE COLLEGE, TRINITY LANE & QUEENS' ROAD (D/E4)

223

224

225

226

227

228

229

230

222 Clare site plan.   **223** The east front of Old Court to Trinity Lane, of 1638-41, by John Westley *(see also fig. 88)*.   **224** The Chapel of 1763-69 designed by Sir James Burrough though completed after his death by James Essex.   **225** The north range, 1683-90, by Robert Grumbold.   **226** The west range facing the river, 1669-76 & 1705-15, also by Grumbold. Both the north and west ranges show the influence of Wren on a local designer *(see p. 57)*.   **227** The east front of Memorial Court - west of the river - of 1923-34, by Sir Giles Gilbert Scott. The sculpture in the foreground is *Divided Form* by Barbara Hepworth.   **228** The west range of Old Court, east side.   **229** A glimpse of Clare through the trees across the Backs from Queens' Road. **230** Castle Hill Hostel, 1957-58, by David Roberts.

Pembroke College

Pembroke was founded in 1347 by Mary de St Pol, widow of Aymer de Valence, Earl of Pembroke, who died in 1324, and daughter of Guy de St Pol, Count of Chatillon.

The site is fairly spacious, with a concentrated line of perimeter building to the north and west, creating a pleasant open area including gardens and the old bowling green. There are four courts: Old, Ivy, Library, and New. The far north corner of Old Court (fig. 234) contains the oldest buildings of the college, dating back to the latter half of the fourteenth century, the east end of the Pembroke Street facade giving the impression closest to the original Old Court was originally divided in two by a range running east-west across its centre, the earlier north court being one of the best examples of the typical collegiate plan at Cambridge (see p. 72, fig. 160). The early eighteenth century saw the ashlaring of the whole court but even more destructive was the demolition by the Victorians of the entire south and east ranges.

Ivy Court (fig. 237) was created in the seventeenth century by extending eastwards the north and south ranges of Old Court. The Hitcham Building, or south range, is interesting in that the three west bays differ in detail to the rest of the range. Instead of the dormer windows in the roof being contained within the traditional gables, they are here topped with pediments, the centre one segmental and those on either side triangular (see fig. 91). This change heralded, in a small way, the arrival of the classical style in Cambridge, and four years later Cambridge achieved its first truly classical building in Wren's Pembroke College Chapel (see pp. 56, 57).

The Chapel (see figs. 18, 94) was a gift to the college from Bishop Matthew Wren, the architect's uncle. Built between 1663-65, the Chapel was Wren's first completed building, although designed slightly later than his Sheldonian Theatre at Oxford of 1663-69. It was extended to the east in 1880 by George Gilbert Scott Jun (fig. 233).

Nineteenth and twentieth century development at Pembroke has been considerable, more than doubling the area of the college buildings. Work began in 1871 with the Master's Lodge (fig. 239) by Alfred Waterhouse, to the north-east of Ivy Court (now the JCR). After this, Waterhouse added Red Buildings (fig. 236) in a strong, French Renaissance style, to the south west of the Chapel, whilst the Library (fig. 235) followed a few years later, its polygonal spire providing a suitable foil to the picturesque pavilion roof of Red Buildings. It was at this time that the south and east ranges of Old Court were demolished, the east range being replaced by a new Hall (fig. 237), also by Waterhouse, and the south range being omitted altogether to open up the court towards the chapel. Building continued in the north-east part of the site with the younger G.G. Scott's north and east ranges of New Court (see fig. 114), designed in a mixture of styles, with Arts & Crafts decoration on the street facades and in the entrance arch. The neo-Georgian Orchard Building (fig. 238) with its strong 'Gibbsian'

detailing, was built in the late 1950s. Since then no new building has taken place, though much restoration has been carried out.

See also figs. 18, 58, 91, 94, 114, 160, 493.

Chronological Summary of Buildings

Date	Building/Occurrence	Location/Details
1346-51	Purchase of Old & Ivy Ct. site	NW area of site
1347	Foundation of College	(Countess of Pembroke)
1351-98	Old Court, N and W sides	NW street ranges
C15	S and E side of Old Court	(demolished: 1874-75)
1610-34	Ivy Court, N range, W2/3	NE of Old Court
1658-61	Hitcham Building (J. Young)	Ivy Court, S side
1663-65	New Chapel (C.Wren)	Old Court, S side, W
1664-66	Hitcham's Cloister (Christmas)	Old Court, SW corner
1670-71	Ivy Court, N range, finished	(R. Grumbold)
1690	Old chapel conv. into library	Old Court, N range, W
1712&17	Outer and inner Old Ct. ashlared	(including gatehouse)
1871-73	Master's Lodge (A. Waterhouse)	E of Ivy Ct. (now JCR)
1871-72	Red Buildings (A. Waterhouse)	SW range of site
1874	S range of Old Ct. demolished	N of chapel
1875	E range of Old Ct. demolished	Rebuilt as Hall (A.W.)
1875-77	Library range (A. Waterhouse)	S of Ivy Court
1880	Chapel extended E by one bay	(G. G. Scott Jun.)
1880-83	New Court (G. G. Scott Jun.)	NE corner of site
1907	Buildings by W. D. Caroe	E of Ivy Ct.
1932-33	New Master's Lodge (M. Webb)	Far SE corner of site
1957-58	Orchard Building (M. Sisson)	S of New Court
1961	Old library restored (D. Croghan)	Old Court. N range, W
1962-64	Hitcham Building reconstructed	(D. Roberts)
1970	Ivy Bld. restored (Roberts & Clarke)	Ivy Court, N range

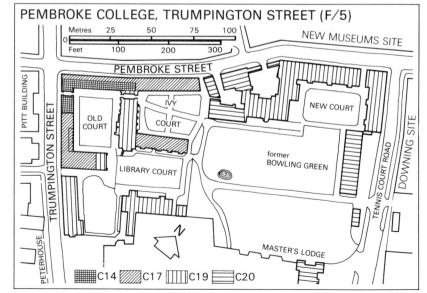

PEMBROKE COLLEGE, TRUMPINGTON STREET (F/5)

232

233

234

235

236

238

239

237

231 Pembroke site plan.　**232** Northern half of the college front to Trumpington Street *(see fig 18)*. **233** East end of Wren's Chapel *(see fig. 94)* and south end of the Hall.　**234** Old Court, showing the surviving gable which marks the line of the demolished south range of the original small court *(see fig. 160)*.　**235** The west end of the Library by A. Waterhouse.　**236** Red Buildings along Trumpington Street, also by Waterhouse.　**237** Ivy Court from the east.　**238** The neo-Georgian Orchard Building, 1957-58, by Marshall Sisson. **239** The former Master's Lodge by Alfred Waterhouse (now the JCR).

Gonville and Caius College

Gonville Hall was founded in 1348 by a Norfolk clergyman, Edmund Gonville, and was situated roughly in the area of what is now the Master's Garden of Corpus Christi College Gonville died in 1351, leaving as his executor William Bateman, Bishop of Norwich, who had founded Trinity Hall in the previous year. In 1353 Bateman aquired a new site for Gonville Hall, opposite his own college in Milne Street, now Trinity Lane. Almost two centuries later, in 1529, the young John Keys entered the Hall as a scholar, to become a fellow in 1533-45. In the fashionable manner of the day, Keys Latinized his name to 'Caius', and from 1539-45 he studied medicine in Padua and travelled widely in Europe. Upon his return to England he became an eminent physician, serving both Edward VI and Queen Mary. In 1557 he refounded the Hall, and enjoyed the unique position in the history of Cambridge colleges of being founder and Master of the new college of 'Gonville and Caius'.

There are three courts on the old site west of Trinity Street; Gonville, Caius, and Tree Court. St Michael Court is on the east side of Trinity Street, and Harvey Court some distance away, to the west of the Backs.

Gonville Court (fig. 245) is the original site of Bateman's relocated Gonville Hall, though the old medieval buildings were considerably altered and rebuilt in the eighteenth and nineteenth centuries. After his travels in Italy and France, Dr Caius acquired a certain taste for architecture which he was able to put into practice with the design of Caius Court (fig. 244) and the three famous gates, the original arrangement of which romantically symbolised the students journey through the college (the student would enter the college through the Gate of Humility in his first year - since rebuilt and relocated in the Master's garden - he would later progress through the Gate of Virtue (see figs 15, 84), between Tree and Caius Court, and eventually proceed at the end of his third year, to the neighbouring Senate House, via the Gate of Honour (see fig. 85) to receive his degree). In designing this court, Caius introduced the novel, three-sided plan to Cambridge.

As at Pembroke, much Victorian building activity took place at Caius. Anthony Salvin built the new Hall and Library (fig. 247) in 1853 to be followed, in 1870, by Waterhouse's complete rebuilding of Tree Court in his characteristic French Renaissance style (figs 243, 246). Building then continued on the other side of Trinity Street where Aston Webb built St Michael's Court (fig. 242) at the very beginning of this century. Murray Easton's south range of St Michael's Court, added 1934, was the first 'modern' addition to the Cambridge colleges (see fig. 125).

Harvey Court (fig. 248 & see 175), by Sir Leslie Martin & Colin St John Wilson, is situated in West Road, its vast monolithic appearance being a surprise in the context of suburban west Cambridge. It is a building of much architectural and aesthetic note, and particularly interesting is the sculptural use of the brickwork on the outer facades; it has, however, proved inappropriate to its suburban location. The idea of the stepped terrace and raised inner piazza arose from an earlier idea of

Sir Leslie Martin's for King's Market Court in 1957 (never built) where the buzz of city life in the town centre, with a regular flow of pedestrian traffic, would bring alive a building of this type. However, Harvey Court's introversion, inward to its piazza, has dictated a self-imposed isolation - so much so that the piazza, the intended hub of community life, remains secluded and empty.

See also figs 15, 24, 33, 41, 42, 84, 85, 125, 167, 170, 175, 481.

Chronological Summary of Buildings

Date	Building/Occurrence	Location/Details
1348	Gonville Hall founded	Luthburne Lane
1353	Hall Moved to present site	NW area of Old Site
1393	Chapel completed, Gonville Ct.	NW court, S range
1426-54	Gonville Court, W range	(hall, library, lodge)
1490	Gonville Court, E range	(demolished: 1868)
1557	Dr Caius refounds college	(Royal charter obtained)
1565-69	Caius Court (J. Caius)	SW court of Old Site
1565	Gate of Humility (J. Caius)	S wall, Master's garden
1565-67	Gate of Virtue (J. Caius)	Caius Court, E range N
1573-75	Gate of Honour (J. Caius)	Caius Court, S wall
1637	Chapel extended E	(J. Westley)
1717-26	Chapel ashlared (J. James)	(buttresses built)
1751-55	Gon. Ct. ashlared (J. Burrough)	(N side partly rebuilt)
1853	New Hall & Library (A. Salvin)	Far NW corner of site
1868-70	NW, N, and E sides of Tree Court demolished and rebuilt	E court of Old Site. (A. Waterhouse)
1870	Chapel restored & apse added	(A. Waterhouse)
1883	Lecture Rooms (A. Waterhouse)	Far SW corner of site
1901-03	St Michael's Court (A. Webb)	Trinity Street, E side
1934	St Michael's Court, S range	(M. Easton)
1960-62	Harvey Court (Martin & Wilson)	West Road

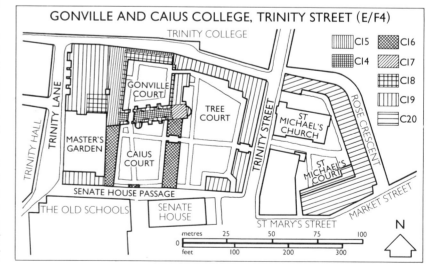

GONVILLE AND CAIUS COLLEGE, TRINITY STREET (E/F4)

241

247

243

244

245

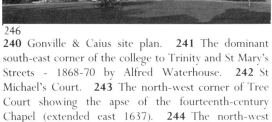

246

248

240 Gonville & Caius site plan. **241** The dominant south-east corner of the college to Trinity and St Mary's Streets - 1868-70 by Alfred Waterhouse. **242** St Michael's Court. **243** The north-west corner of Tree Court showing the apse of the fourteenth-century Chapel (extended east 1637). **244** The north-west

247

corner of Caius Court *(see figs 167 & 170).* **245** The original Gonville Court (much altered; ashlared 1751-55). **246** The north-east corner of Tree Court by Waterhouse. **247** The Library and Hall from Trinity Lane, by Anthony Salvin. **248** Harvey Court, West Road, by Martin & Wilson *(see fig. 175).*

Trinity Hall

Trinity Hall was founded in 1350 by William Bateman, Bishop of Norwich, with the specific intention of providing both the church and crown with clergy and lawyers. The Bishop, himself a doctor of Canon and Civil Law, may well have been prompted by the shortage of clergy arising from the severe outbreak of bubonic plague, the 'black death', during the summer of 1347. The initial growth of the college was delayed by the death of Bateman in 1355, who left as his executor Simon Sudbury, Bishop of London.

The college consists of five courts: Principal, Library, North, South, and Cherry Tree Courts, and other buildings forming a particularly intimate community atmosphere. The college garden is in the north-west area of the site and the Fellows' garden in the south-west, with the Backs and river providing a pleasant western boundary to the site. 'Wychfield' and Bolton House are situated in north Cambridge, and a new hostel in Thompson's Lane/New Park Street.

Principal Court (fig. 250) was built in the latter half of the fourteenth century but, unfortunately, like so many other medieval college courts, its appearance was disguised in the eighteenth century when it was ashlared and other fashionable changes were made. The nearest impression one can get to the original is from the north wall (fig. 252) where the old clunch remains exposed and some interesting details exist.

The Elizabethan north range of the Library Court (fig. 251) contained the Combination Room below and Library above (now entirely library), and is important in that it has remained almost completely unaltered. The south range had the Master's Gallery on the first floor (now entirely Master's Lodge) and has undergone numerous changes, the only surviving sixteenth century feature being the two-storeyed gable in the west front (fig. 254). Another interesting feature of this court is the small wooden door set in the library's south facade at first-floor height (fig. 251); the original function of this door was to provide direct access for the Master via a walkway at this level around the east side of the court, from his gallery in the south to the library and Combination Room in the north range.

Once again, those industrious Victorians Waterhouse and Salvin added to, or rather re-built, much of this college. Waterhouse in the east ranges of both Principal and South Courts, and Salvin with the Master's Lodge and chapel extension. Also in this area, though a hundred years later, Trevor Dannatt incorporated the New Combination Room, ingeniously handling the very cramped space south of the hall and east of the Master's Lodge.

More twentieth century expansion took place further away, in Huntingdon Road, where Philip Dowson, of Arup Associates, built Bolton House (fig. 257) in the late sixties, using a similar pre-cast concrete 'H' frame system to that he had employed in his earlier building for Corpus Christi (see fig. 139). In the early seventies David Roberts & Geoffrey Clarke added the new bar and theatre on the north side of

Cherry Tree Court (fig. 255). Trinity Hall's New Hostel, by Cambridge Design, has some interesting details, characteristic of this firm's work, which have added a touch of excitement to this quiet little backstreet (see fig. 150).

See also figs 45, 150, 490

Chronological Summary of Buildings

Date	Building/Occurrence	Location/Details
1321-41	Prior Crawden's 'Ely Hostel'	Area of Pricipal Ct.
1350	Foundation of college	(Purchase of 'Ely Host.')
1350-74	Principal Court	Central E court of site
1366	Chapel built by now	Prin. Ct., S range, W
Late C14	Master's Lodge (much rebuilt)	SW of Principal Ct.
1545	Garret Hostel Lane built	N boundary of site
C16	Master's Lodge extended SW	(further altered:C19)
1600?	Library (Library Court)	W of Principal Ct.
1728&29	Parapets added to Pricipal Ct.	N and S sides
1742-45	Prin. Ct. ashlared (J.Burrough)	N, S and W, sides
1823	South Ct, W range (A. Waterhouse)	SE court of site
1852	Principal Ct. E range, rebuilt	(A. Salvin)
	Master's Lodge rebuilt	(A. Salvin)
1864	Chapel ext. to E (A. Salvin)	Prin. Ct., S range, W
1872-73	South Court, E range, rebuilt	(A. Waterhouse)
1876	Chapel decorated	(stained-glass added)
1889-90	Latham Bldg. (Grayson & Ould)	N range of garden, E
1890	Master's Lodge rebuilt	(Grayson & Ould)
1909-1910	Thornton Bldg. (Grayson & Ould)	N range of garden, W
1926	Gatehouse Building (heightened 1950-51)	N range of gdn., mid.
1934	N Ct., E & W ranges (G. G. Scott)	NE court of site
1949-51	North Court, Central range	(A. E. Richardson)
1963-65	New Comb.Room (T. Dannatt)	E of Master's Lodge
1967-68	Bolton House (Arup Assoc.)	Huntingdon Rd.
1973-75	Central Site dev. (Roberts & Clarke)	Cherry Tree Ct., N side
1980-81	New Hostel (Cambridge Design)	New Park Street

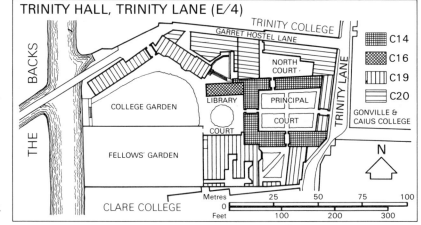

TRINITY HALL, TRINITY LANE (E/4)

C14 / C16 / C19 / C20

250

251

252

253

254

255

256

257

249 Trinity Hall site plan. **250** The west range of Principal Court. **251** The Elizabethan Library. **252** The north wall of Principal Court (North Court) showing the original fourteenth-century clunch rubble and red brick construction. **253** Library Court from the west showing the crow-stepped gables of the Library, *c.* 1600. **254** The Master's Lodge from the Fellows' Gardens. The gable and chimney (left) are all that remains of the original Elizabethan Lodge, as it was rebuilt in 1852 (Salvin) and again in 1890 (Grayson & Ould). **255** Cherry Tree Court by Roberts & Clark. **256** Latham Building by Grayson & Ould. **257** Bolton House, Huntingdon Road, by Sir Philip Dowson of Arup Associates.

Corpus Christi College

Amongst the colleges of both Cambridge and Oxford, that of Corpus Christi and the Blessed Virgin Mary is unique because it was founded, in 1352, by two town guilds (as its full name implies), and so became the first college to be founded by the townspeople, as opposed to the aristocracy or clergy.

There are two main courts: Old Court to the north, and New Court to the south-west. The Anglo-Saxon church of St Bene't', which forms the northern boundary of the site, has been connected with the college since 1353 and is the oldest building in Cambridge (see p. 11). The original entrance to the site was from Bene't Street, along the west side of the church, and until 1827, when the present entrance in Trumpington Street was built, the college was commonly known as 'Bene't College'. Modern expansion has taken place to the west of the Backs in a cul-de-sac off Grange Road, where the Leckhampton House site forms a small and intimate graduate community.

Built between 1352-77 of stone rubble with clunch dressings, Old Court (fig. 262 & see 161) was the first complete court at Cambridge (see p. 73), and is a good example of how a medieval college looked, if one can imagine it without the buttresses and garrets added in the sixteenth century. The court was designed without a chapel, because of the close proximity of St Bene't's, and consisted of Hall and kitchens, Master's Lodge, Library, and chambers. The north side, towards St Bene't's churchyard, is the best preserved, and the gallery here which connects the court to the church (fig. 260), was added in about 1500. In 1597 a separate and more spacious chapel was built to the south of Old Court (demolished in 1823), Queen Elizabeth I and Sir Francis Drake being amongst those who contributed to the cost of its construction.

The neo-Gothic New Court (figs 259, 263 & 264), an important example of Gothic Revivalism, was built between 1823-27 by William Wilkins (architect of Downing College, Cambridge). When work commenced here the intention was to preserve as many of the existing, older buildings as possible: however, this was soon found to be impracticable and the college sadly decided to demolish the old chapel and to convert the hall into kitchens. The new buildings are of Ketton stone with some white brick, symmetrically composed, and with a centrally placed gatehouse (see fig. 469) falling directly in line with the new Chapel opposite (see fig. 104). The Library (fig. 264), with its eight large neo-Tudor windows, is in the south range and contains Matthew Parker's great collection of medieval manuscripts. New Court also provided a new Hall and Master's Lodge (fig. 265). Apparently this was Wilkins's favourite work in the Gothic style, and he was buried in the chapel.

In the early 1960s Corpus developed the Leckhampton House site with the George Thomson Building (see fig. 139) by Philip Dowson of Arup Associates, in the gardens of this red brick Victorian villa (fig. 266). The pre-cast concrete structure uses an 'H' frame system, also employed in Arup's later building for Trinity Hall (see fig. 257), and consists of two separate blocks, linked by a red-brick service core. It is placed near the villa, taking full advantage of the picturesque garden site. On the croquet lawn to the east is Henry Moore's *Seated Figure*.

See also figs: 8, 104, 133, 139, 161, 469, 491

Chronological Summary of Buildings

Date	Building/Occurrence	Location/Details
1342-46	Guild of Corpus C. acquire site for Old Ct. in Luthburne Lane	NE area of site (now Free School Lane)
1352	The two guilds unite and building commences	NE area of site
1353	Site of Gonville Hall acq.	SE area of site
1377	Old court complete	NE area of site.
1411	Purchase of ground from town	completes main site W area of site
1487-1515	Buttresses added to Old Court. Connection to church made	(Duchess of Norfolk) NE side of Old Court
1578+	Chapel (demolished in 1823)	SE of Old Court
1823-27	New Court: chapel, Master's lodge, library, hall, etc.	S area of site (W. Wilkins)
1870	Chapel ext. E (A. Blomfield)	To Free School Lane
1930	Hostel and Stable Yards developed (G. Dawbarn)	NW corner of site to Trumpington Street
1963-64	Leckhampton House site dev. (1881: Leckhampton House) George Thomson Building	Grange Road (W.C. Marshall) P. Dowson of Arup Ass.).

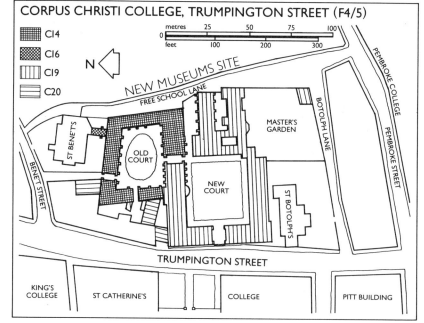

CORPUS CHRISTI COLLEGE, TRUMPINGTON STREET (F4/5)

C14
C16
C19
C20

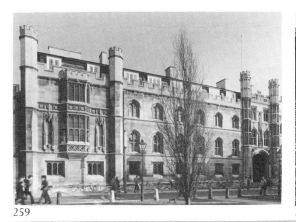

259

260

261

262

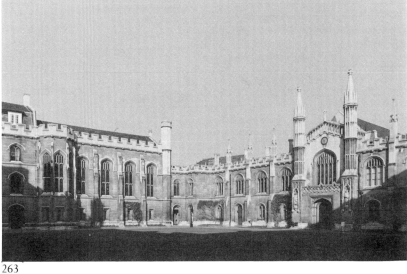

263

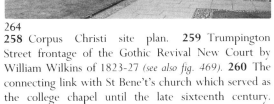

264

265

266

258 Corpus Christi site plan. **259** Trumpington Street frontage of the Gothic Revival New Court by William Wilkins of 1823-27 *(see also fig. 469)*. **260** The connecting link with St Bene't's church which served as the college chapel until the late sixteenth century.

261 The east side of Old Court to Free School Lane. **262** The north range of Old Court with the Saxon tower of St Bene't's beyond. **263** The north-east corner of New Court with the chapel in which Wilkins is buried. **264** The south range of New Court containing

the Library. **265** Wilkins's Gothic Revival Master's Lodge. **266** Leckhampton House, off Grange Road, a neo-Tudor villa of 1881 by W.C. Marshall *(see also fig. 139)*.

Magdalene College

See also figs: 48, 165, 476, 480

In 1428, Abbott Litlyngton of the Benedictine monastery at Crowland received a grant from Henry VI to establish a hostel for his monks studying at the university. Monks from the monasteries of Ely, Ramsey, and Walden were also included. The hostel became known as 'Buckingham College' from about 1483 as a result of benefactions from Henry and Edward, second and third Dukes of Buckingham. However, as the college was a monastic institution, it suffered during the latter years of Henry VIII's reign, and after the final dissolution of the monasteries in 1539, it had virtually ceased to exist; but, in 1542, Thomas, Lord Audley of Walden, the Lord Chancellor, was granted permission to re-found it under the new dedication to St Mary Magdalene.

The present-day site is divided in two by Magdalene Street: the old site to the east, with the spacious Fellows' Garden occupying half of it; and the new site to the west, bordering on St John's College.

On the old site, First Court (figs 268 & 270) contains the original buildings of the college, some of which were constructed under Abbot Wisbech, Litlyngton's successor, in around 1476. The Chapel is attributed to the 2nd Duke of Buckingham, and the Hall to the 3rd. The staircases were built by the various orders housed therein, although it is not clear who was responsible for which. The south range is interesting in that it retains almost intact the arrangement of medieval student rooms (staircase E particularly, fig. 270).

The Second Court was formed by the construction of the Pepys Building (fig. 276) for which neither the architect nor the exact dates are known, though the dichotomy between front and back suggests that it is not of one period alone. Pevsner postulates a history of the building: begun circa 1587, central portion facing west 1640-79, ornamental embellishments added in the eighteenth century. It was completed sometime in the early 1700s as Samuel Pepys, the seventeenth century diarist, bequeathed his library to the college at that time. The recent Master's Lodge (fig. 271), to the north of Second Court, is by Roberts & Clarke and was initially flat-roofed, the pitched-roof being added in 1979.

The new site contains the majority of the college's twentieth century development within and around the older buildings of Mallory Court (fig. 274), Benson Court (fig. 269) with its west range (fig. 272) by Sir Edwin Lutyens, and Buckingham Court with the Tan Yard cottages. In 1952, Roberts & his associates were commissioned to develop this site, the intention being to bring some cohesion to the area and to provide more accommodation. Many of the surrounding 16th century buildings were converted into undergraduate sets (eg fig. 269), and two new buildings were added (1954 and 1958, fig. 273), successfully pulling together the whole area and creating an atmosphere of domesticity. Roberts & Clarke were also the architects of the west range of Buckingham Court (1970, fig. 275), Magdalene's most recent addition.

Chronological Summary of Buildings

Date	Building/Occurrence	Location/Details
1428	Benedictine Hostel established	Old site, First Court
1430-1587	First Court	Old site, W centre
1430-75?	Chapel (Henry, Duke of Buck.)	First Ct., N range, E
1519	Hall (Edward, Duke of Buck.)	First Ct., E range, N
(1539	Dissolution of Monasteries	under Henry VIII)
1542	Foundation charter: Magd. Coll.	(granted by Henry VIII)
1586-88	Louvre over Hall and Belfry	(replaced in C18?)
1587-1703?	Pepys Building	Second Court, E range
1724	Arrival of Pepys Library	(S. Pepys: 1633-1703)
1733-55	Chapel renovated	(also in 1847-51)
1759-60	First Court stuccoed	(also in 1812-15)
1876	Pinnacle with statue on chapel	
1908-09	Bright's Bldg. (Webb & Bell)	Second Court, S range
1925-26	Mallory Court (H. Redfern)	New Site, NE area
1930-32	Lutyens Building, Benson Court	New site, SW range
1952-58	Dev. and conv. in Benson and	Inner courts and E
	Mallory Cts. (D. Roberts & Ass.)	ranges to Magdalene St.
1959-66	Restoration of First Court	(S. Dykes Bower)
1966-68	New Lodge (Roberts & Clarke)	Old site, NW area
1967	Tan Yard conversion	New site, NE corner
1968	New Kitchens (Roberts & Clarke)	SW end of Bright's Bldg.
1968-70	Buckingham Ct (Roberts & Clarke)	New site, NW range
1979	Pitched-roof added to lodge	(previously flat)

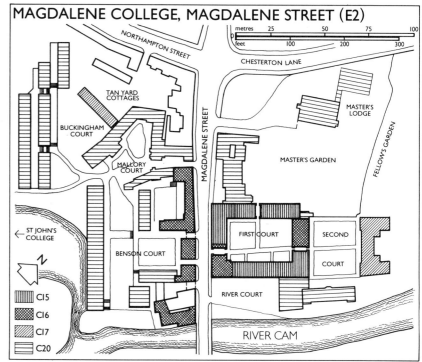

MAGDALENE COLLEGE, MAGDALENE STREET (E2)

268

269

270

271

272

273

275

274

267 Magdalene site plan.   268 The east range of Old Court containing the Hall of 1519.   269 Medieval cottages in Benson Court - converted into under-graduate sets in the 1950s.   270 The south-east corner of Old Court.   271 The new Master's Lodge by Roberts & Clarke.   272 The west range of the incomplete Benson Court, 1930-32, by Sir Edwin Lutyens.   273 A 1950s residential block in Benson Court by David Roberts.   274 The old vinegar factory, now student sets, in Mallory Court.   275 The west range of Buckingham Court by Roberts & Clarke.

276 The attractive Pepys Building at Magdalene of which the architect and precise dates of construction are unknown. The inscription over the central arch of the colonnade 'BIBLIOTHECA PEPYSIANA. 1724' refers to the date when Samuel Pepys's library was installed (bequeathed to the College in his will of 1703); it is now housed on the first floor in the centre. The building was probably completed in three phases. Pevsner points out the similarity in layout to Elizabethan houses and suggests that the main block, with its two flanking three-storey wings, was begun c. 1585. Interestingly, however, the windows are not Elizabethan but later - the larger ones are of the mullion and transom cross type and the smaller have a single mullion, forms which only appeared

in Cambridge after 1640 having been introduced in the Fellows' Building at Christ's College *(see pp 54 & 55)*. The RCHM suggest that the fabric was completed by 1679 when John Maulyverer, a Fellow, wrote to Pepys (29 Nov.) stating that 'We have not yet finished the inside, and I know not when we shall'. There is a possibility that the architect of the west front was Robert Hooke, who submitted a 'draught' (design) to the college in 1677 when he may have re-designed the facade of the older structure which might explain the curious dichotomy between front and rear (the rear consists of a recessed centre with wings projecting in two 'steps' and is of brick with stone quoins). Of Hooke's possible facade Pevsner comments that the

rhythm created by the pedimented and straight-headed windows creates '. . . a characteristic clash between Tudor tradition and the new oncoming classical fashion. But those clashes were over at Cambridge by 1675 at the latest'. It can be seen from Loggan's engraving of the college of 1688, that it was still incomplete as certain embellishments are absent; as, for example, the two busts above the windows immediately flanking the central bay, the cartouche ornamentation below the central windows, and the elaborate decoration of the spandrels of the arches, all of which were probably added during the eighteenth century.

Christ's College

277 The front of Christ's College to St Andrew's Street. This range forms the west side of the original court of the college, which was built between 1505-11 after its re-foundation by Lady Margaret Beaufort (previously it was called 'God's House', see overleaf). The building is actually constructed of clunch and red brick, but like so many other college buildings it was re-faced with stone in the eighteenth century, in this instance with Ketton stone ashlar. When re-facing this outer court side, mainly between 1714-16, Robert Grumbold adhered fairly closely to the existing design, though the fenestration has been altered and sash windows incorporated. (James Essex was not as sympathetic when he re-faced the inner court to a classical design between 1758-69, changing its character by 'Italianising' certain features - he inserted an elliptical entrance arch in place of the pointed, four-centered arch as in the west front; topped-off the two battlemented, octagonal corner turrets; inserted a Venetian window in the gatehouse; and placed pediments above all of the doors). The elaborate armorial work on the gatehouse represents Lady Margaret's coat of arms (Countess of Richmond and Derby, and mother of Henry Tudor) and should be compared with her other Cambridge foundation, of 1511, St John's College *(see p. 131 & figs 457, 466)*. A statue of the foundress stands within the niche above the main entrance and is flanked by the Rose of Lancaster and a coroneted portcullis. The gate itself dates from the late sixteenth century and is of oak, with characteristic linenfold panels within a moulded frame. Interestingly, if one looks at David Loggan's print of the College of 1688, it can be seen that the lower panels have at some time been cut short to accommodate a rise in the level of the pavement. Apart from its 'cosmetic' re-facing and other alterations, this college front represents well the typical medieval Cambridge court facade to the public street with its sturdy, battlemented gatehouse placed asymmetrically just off centre *(see p. 75, fig. 166).*

277

Christ's College

The small grammar college of God's House was established by William Byngham, a London parish priest, in the late 1430s. It was originally situated on the east side of the ancient Milne Street (now Queens' and Trinity Lanes) roughly in the area of what is now the antechapel of King's College chapel. In 1446 Henry VI requested that Byngham vacate his site in order to allow the King's college to expand, and it was thus relocated to its present position. The college was refounded by Lady Margaret Beaufort in 1505, at which time her son – Henry VII – granted a new foundation charter and the dedication was changed to that of Jesus Christ. Lady Margaret also founded St John's College in 1511 (posthumously, see p. 131).

The homogeneity of First Court quickly disintegrates as one progresses through Second and Third Courts. This is because of the siting of the Fellows' Building in the mid seventeenth century which, although an important building in its own right, did not lend itself to becoming part of a further composition (ie of a complete second court) and in the nineteenth and twentieth centuries led to the erection of a chain of separate buildings. The modern New Court slopes towards one with its pleasant, south facing grassed terraces, whilst it turns its monolithic grey back on King Street. Although a building with a seductive, sectional design (fig. 285) it is, nevertheless, a harsh expression of the line drawn between 'Gown' and 'Town'. The Fellows' Garden occupies the north-east quarter of the site with Christ's Pieces to its east.

In First Court (figs 279, 281) part of the north-west range dates back to the time of God's House, whilst the remainder was built between 1505-11 under the auspices of Lady Margaret. The court was ashlar-faced by James Essex in 1758-69, although the north wall of the north range retains the original exposed masonry of clunch and red brick. The most striking feature of this court is the main entrance gatehouse (fig. 277 & see 465) from St Andrew's Street, which bears the arms of Lady Margaret (see also fig. 457).

The Fellows' Building (fig. 280 & see pp 54-5) is one of the most original examples of mid-seventeenth century architecture in England. It was innovatory in its detached, symmetrical composition, as well as in certain new details, particularly the mullion and transom cross windows, the first occurrence of this motif in Cambridge. The extremely competent designer is unknown, though tradition attributes the building to Inigo Jones (see p. 49) because of certain interior details such as the bunched hanging garland decoration on a fireplace, but this is now thought to be unlikely.

Third Court (fig. 283) comprises three detached buildings: J. J. Stevenson's north range, and Professor Sir Albert Richardson and Eric Houfe's east and west ranges. Richardson's scheme for the latter was chosen in preference to one put forward by Walter Gropius who was briefly in practice in England with Maxwell Fry in the mid thirties (see pp. 62-3). The modern New Court (figs 284, 285) is by Sir Denys Lasdun and is the first stage of a three-part development plan for the whole north-west part of the site, providing the college with sixteen shops to King Street (when fully completed) with a new college car park above, residential accommodation for 220 students and 25 Fellows, additional public rooms, squash courts and a porter's lodge.

See also figs: 17, 46, 89, 90, 126-8, 142, 465, 478

Chronological Summary of Buildings

Date	Building/Occurrence	Location/Details
1437?	God's House established	Area of King's chapel
1446	God's House relocated	St Andrew's Street
1448	Foundation charter	(granted by Henry VI)
late C15	First Court, N range	S area of site
1505	Refounded: Christ's College	(Lady Margaret Beaufort)
1505-11	First Court completed	S area of site
1640-43	Fellows' Building	Second Court, NE range
1758-69	First Court ashlared	(J.Essex)
1823	Second Court, S range	S of Fellows' Building
1875-79	Hall rebuilt (G. G. Scott)	First Ct., NE range, S
1876	Lecture Room rebuilt	SE of First Court
1888-89	Third Court, N range	Centre of site
1895-97	Library extended S	First Ct., SW range, S
1936-37	Gropius & Fry's rejected project to Hobson Street	(see pp. 62-3)
1948-50	Chancellors Building	Third Ct., E range
1952-53	Memorial Building	Third Ct., W range
1966-70+	New Court (D. Lasdun)	N of Third Court

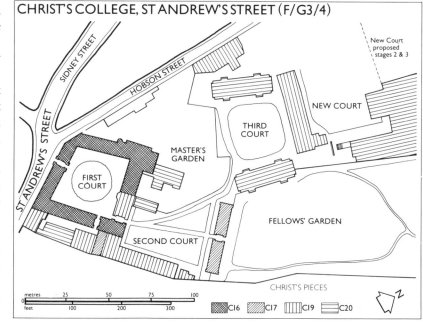

CHRIST'S COLLEGE, ST ANDREW'S STREET (F/G3/4)

279

280

281

282

283

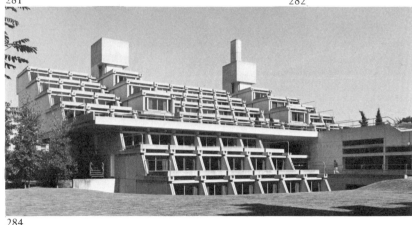
284

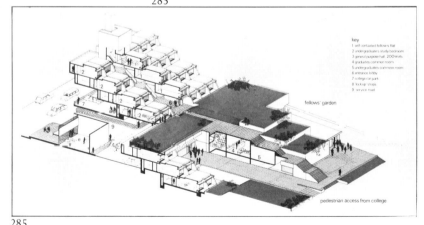
285

278 Christ's site plan.   **279** The Master's Lodge and the Hall in First Court, built 1505-11.   **280** The north half of the west front of the innovatory Fellows' Building of 1640-43, the first almost purely classical building at Cambridge *(see p. 54 & figs 17, 89, 90).*   **281** The north-west range of First Court consisting of chambers and the Chapel.   **282** The south range of Second Court, 1823-25.   **283** The north range of Third Court, 1888-89, by J.J. Stevenson - Victorian repetition of the Fellows' Building.   **284** New Court from the south-west, 1966-70, by Sir Denys Lasdun.   **285** An isometric section of New Court (drawing by Denys Lasdun & Partners).

King's College

In 1441 King Henry VI founded his College of St Nicholas at Cambridge only a few months after founding Eton College, Windsor. In 1443, Henry enlarged the site and started to develop the college on a scale unprecedented at Cambridge. At this time the name was altered to 'the King's College of the Blessed Mary and St Nicholas' and a definite link established with Eton, the intention being that Eton Scholars would proceed to King's for their university education. It is more than probable that Henry was using as his model the dual foundations of William of Wykeham, Bishop of Winchester, who had similarly founded New College, Oxford, in 1379, and Winchester College in 1382 (see p. 74).

Henry himself specified the first plan for his college in his 'wille and entent' of 1448, though the only building to be completed to his design was the famous Chapel. The whole work was to be financed by an annual grant of £1000 from the revenues of the Duchy of Lancaster. However, 1455 saw the beginning of the Wars of the Roses and Henry was deposed, first in 1461 and then finally in 1471. The revenues of the college were ordered to be paid into the Exchequer and the foundation, though maintained, was considerably reduced under Edward IV, and it took until the middle of the following century to really re-establish itself.

The site is very spacious, with the meadow called Scholars Piece to the west of the river, and the main college to the east. The original site, Old Court, is now occupied by the University Old Schools (see p. 190) to the north of the Chapel. Great, or Front Court is entered from King's Parade, with the concentration of buildings along the south boundary and within which there are three subsidiary courts: Chetwynd, Webb's and Bodley's Courts. The most remarkable aspect of the site is the view looking north-east from the bridge (fig. 291) as, prior to Henry VI, this was the busy industrial heart of Cambridge; Henry's scheme completely transformed the townscape, removing warehouses, streets and shops, to create extensive lawns and the Backs (see p. 22).

After the completion of the Chapel in 1515, major building work ceased for over two hundred years, until in 1714 the Provost, Dr John Adams, set up a building fund with the aim of completing Front Court. During the eighteenth century schemes were submitted by some of the most eminent architects of the day; among them Nicholas Hawksmoor in consultation with Sir Christopher Wren, James Gibbs, Robert Adam, and James Wyatt. However, the only building that came to fruition was the Fellows', or Gibbs' Building (fig. 288). Finally, William Wilkins was given the opportunity of completing Front Court between 1824-28 with a neo-Gothic screen and gatehouse (fig. 287) along the east side, and the south range (figs 289, 290) containing the Hall, Combination Room, Chambers, Library, and old Provost's Lodge.

For modern expansion King's went just outside its boundaries to build two hostels: Garden Hostel (fig. 295), and Peas Hill or Market Hostel (fig. 294). In the late 1960s they undertook a unique joint development in conjunction with St Catherine's, building the King's

Lane Courts on a site which bordered both colleges (see p. 126).

See also figs: 10, 21, 22, 28, 47, 52, 63, 70, 82, 83, 105, 461, 470, 496, 507

Chronological Summary of Buildings

Date	Building/Occurrence	Location/Details
1440	Eton College founded	(11th October)
1441	King's College founded	(12th February)
1441	Site of Old Court acquired	N of chapel (see p. 190)
1443-49	Enlarged site acquired	E and W sides of river
1446-1515	Chapel built (see p. 120)	NE corner of site
1448	Henry VI's will made	(plan for college)
(1455-85	Wars of the Roses)	
1461 & 71	Deposition & death of Henry VI	
1714	Building fund set-up (Dr Adams)	(to complete Front Ct.)
1724-32	Gibbs' Building (J. Gibbs)	Front Court, W range
1818-20	Bridge (W. Wilkins, see fig. 507)	SW corner of site
1824-28	Front Ct. completed (W. Wilkins)	SE and S of chapel
1829	Old Ct. sold to university	N of chapel
1871-85	Chetwynd Court (G.G. Scott)	SE corner of site
1874-79	Fountain (figures: H.H. Armstead)	Front Court, centre
1889-1927	Bodley's Court (G.F. Bodley)	SW corner to river
1908-27	Webb's Court (A. Webb)	S of Gibbs' Building
1948-50	Garden Hostel (G. Hyslop)	West Rd, W of site
1954-55	Bodley's Ct., SW extension	(W. Holford & Ptnrs)
1960-62	Market Hostel (Arch. Co Ptnrshp)	SW of Market Place
1965-68	King's Lane Courts (see p. 126)	W of Chetwynd Court

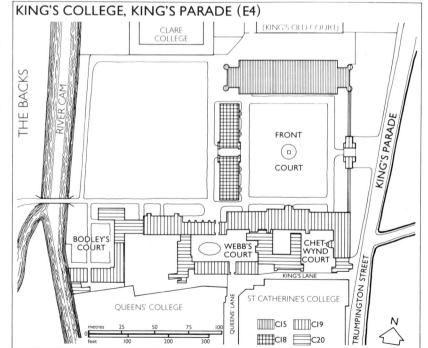

KING'S COLLEGE, KING'S PARADE (E4)

286 King's site plan.   **287** The college front to King's Parade - although homogeneous in appearance a period of more than 300 years separates the superb Perpendicular chapel from the Gothic Revival screen and gatehouse. A number of medieval master masons built the chapel between 1446-1515, and then it was not until the eighteenth century that any further building was undertaken, and a building fund set up with the intention of completing Front Court *(see caption 296)*. The first step was the construction of   **288** The Gibbs' Building (east elevation), 1724-32, by James Gibbs, which forms the west range of the court. By 1822 sufficient funds had been accumulated to proceed with the rest of the court. The scheme was put out to competition and won by William Wilkins, who designed the east screen and south range, all in Tudor Gothic. It was also intended at this time to 'Gothicise' Gibbs's building, under the direction of Wilkins, but as the cost of the new buildings considerably exceeded the tender this was never carried out. Thus, this predominantly Gothic/Gothic Revival Court has as its west range a neo-classical building by one of the most competent eighteenth century architects

287

288

289

290

289 The east half of the south range to Front Court (north elevation), 1824-28, by William Wilkins. The Hall is in the centre, with its two timber lanterns which were rebuilt in 1950-51 by W.F. Haslop of the local builders Rattee & Kett. **290** The west half of the south range showing Wilkins's two-storeyed Library and old Provost's Lodge. The ground floor of the Library was opened up in 1934-35, by Kennedy & Nightingale, with arches providing access to the later Webb's Court. The south end of the Gibbs Building is to the left, and the east end of Bodley's Court (1889, 1927 & 1954-55) is connected to the Provost's Lodge by an infill of 1927. **291** A view of the Gibbs Building, King's Chapel, and the Old Court of Clare College, from Bodley's Court next to Wilkins's bridge (see fig. 507).

291

292

293

292 An impression of scale: Wilkins's Gothic Revival gatehouse seen between the neighbouring angles of the chapel and the Gibbs Building. 293 The neo-Tudor Bodley's Court from the west side of the river - the gable is of 1889-93 by G.F. Bodley (east and south ranges), while the north-east angle beyond is by Kennedy & Nightingale, of 1927. 294 Market Hostel, 1960-62, by Kenneth Capon of the Architects' Co-partnership-student accommodation above a bank. 295 Garden Hostel, off West Road, 1947-50, by Geddes Hyslop, hints at Georgian derivation in windows, doors, stone balls above a cornice - a missed opportunity to build something contemporary in this modern area of college and university expansion west of the Backs.

294

295

King's College Chapel

One of the most important examples of English medieval architecture, and the most famous building in Cambridge, the Chapel was modelled not on previous college chapels, but on the cathedral choir, and created an internal space that can only really be fully appreciated at first-hand, as reproduction cannot do it justice.

The chapel was begun by the Founder of the college, Henry VI, and building continued through the reigns of the five following monarchs to reach final completion under Henry VIII. It is the only building to be completed to Henry VI's own specifications of 1448, the final dimensions relating almost exactly to the original design: 289ft (88m) long, 94ft (28.6m) high, 80ft (24.4m) internal height and 40ft (12.2m) wide.

Owing to the turbulent political state of the country at this time, construction was constantly held up and there are three main periods of building: 1446-61, 1477-85, 1508-15 (see fig. 296). White magnesium limestone from Yorkshire was used during the first phase, and a buff limestone from Northamptonshire in the later periods, this change in the stonework being particularly visible on the north and south elevations (fig. 298).

The magnificent nave (figs 300, 303) is a single, vaulted space, of twelve bays, the beautifully elegant fan-vault being the largest in existence. This massive Perpendicular structure (the vault is estimated to weigh 1,875 tons) creates an impression of almost unbelievable weightlessness, the stresses being transferred via the cones of the vaulting to the eleven buttresses on either side of the nave, and to the four corner towers. Research by George Gilbert Scott Junior in 1881 indicated, however, that a complex lierne-vault was originally intended, possibly derived from the vault of the earlier Lady Chapel (1321-49) at Ely Cathedral, and that the idea of a fan vault came about sometime during the second phase of building, c.1480. Furthermore, Pevsner points out that it would have been inconceivable during the first phase of building to construct a fan vault on such a large scale, Sherborne Abbey in Dorset of 1475 or later being the first example of this technique. The most recent research on the subject, by Walter C. Leedy Jr., suggests that the decision to build a fan vault was probably made at a very late stage, during the final phase of construction. The north and south side chapels are vaulted as follows (see fig. 297): fan vaults in A B C D Q R S; simpler vaults with tiercerons in E F G K L M N O P; lierne vaults in H and J.

The outstanding interior fittings of the chapel provide superb examples of the art of their day; the screen and chancel stalls, thought to be the work of the Florentine sculptor Benedetto da Rovezzano (1474-1552), being one of the finest works in the early Classical style in England. The exact dates of the screen are unknown although the coving bears the initials of Henry VIII and Anne Boleyn ('H&A'), suggesting that it was built between 1533-36. The 26 huge stained-glass windows of the nave are mainly the work of Flemish glaziers between 1517-31. The list below is a brief guide to some of the scenes portrayed and is based upon the Royal Commission on Historical Monuments where a fully detailed description is given. The iconography is taken from the Old and the New Testament. The windows are numbered in fig. 297 and the position of the scenes is indicated by (a) for upper left, (b) lower left, (c) upper right, (d) lower right.

Guide to stained-glass windows

Window	Subject
1	The birth of the Virgin
2d	Marriage of Mary and Joseph
3a	Temptation of Eve
4d	Adoration of the Magi
5b	Presentation of Christ in the Temple
6d	Massacre of the Innocents by Herod
7b	Baptism of Christ
8c	Triumph of David over Goliath
9b	The Last Supper
10b	Betrayal of Christ
11d	Christ before Herod
12d	Christ crowned with thorns
13	Trial and Crucifixion of Christ
14a,c	Moses and the Brazen Serpent
15d	Harrowing of Hell
16a	Jonah cast forth from the whale
17d	Christ appearing to Mary Magdalene
18d	Supper at Emmaus
19d	Christ appearing to the Apostles
20b	The Ascension
21d	Death of Ananias
22d	Paul stoned at Lystra
23b	Harbour of Samothrace (or Troas)
24b	Death of the Virgin
25d	Coronation of the Virgin
26	Last Judgement (inserted 1879)

Chronological Summary of Building

Date	Occurrence
1446	Foundation stone laid at altar by Henry VI (July 25)
1446-71	Master Mason: Reginald Ely
1448	Henry's will, spec. of buildings
1461 & 71	Deposition & death of Henry VI
1471-77	Master Mason: John Wolrich
1477-84	Master Mason: Simon Clerk
1480	Edward IV donates 1000 marks
1484	Work resumed by Richard III
1506-12	Henry VII's donation (£14,100)
1508	Master Mason: John Wastell
1508-1509	Master Masons: Wastell and Lee
1512	Timber roof completed
	Wastell and Harry Semark contracted to built stone vault
1515	Fabric completed
1515-31	Windows inserted (Henry VIII)
1533-36?	Screen built under Henry VIII
1535	Chapel paved
1614-15	West door made
1702	Choir paved with b&w marble
1879	New (coloured) W window
1961	Donation of Ruben's *Adoration of the Magi*
1967-68	Restoration of the interior
1974-84	External restoration

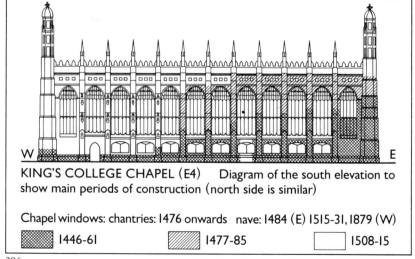

KING'S COLLEGE CHAPEL (E4)   Diagram of the south elevation to show main periods of construction (north side is similar)

Chapel windows: chantries: 1476 onwards   nave: 1484 (E) 1515-31, 1879 (W)

1446-61   1477-85   1508-15

296

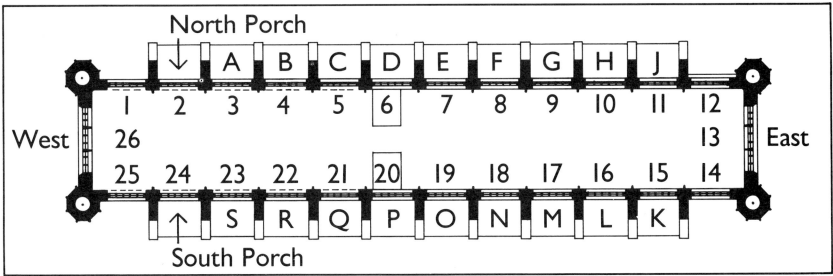

297

298

296 Diagrammatic sketch of the chapel to show the main periods of construction (based upon the research of the RCHM). In his will of 1448, Henry VI set out in detail his plans for both King's and Eton. At King's the chapel was to form the north side of the main court, as it now does, but with a cloistered cemetery to its west; the east and south ranges were to be composed of blocks of chambers, with a gatehouse in the middle of the east range and the Provost's Lodge at the west end of the south. The west range was to comprise the Hall in the southern part and the library in the northern, with a smaller court to the west of the Hall. **297** Plan of the chapel as a guide to the vaulting of the side-chapels and the stained-glass windows (see main text). **298** South elevation of the chapel to Front Court

299 300

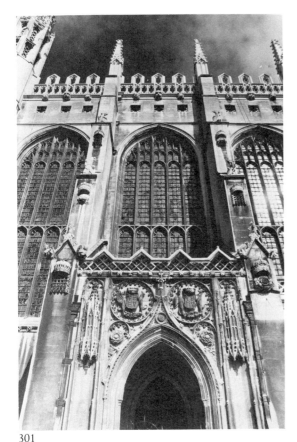

301

302

303

304

299 The west elevation of the chapel towards the river and the Backs, with the church of St Mary the Great in the distance. The west door was made in 1614-15, a century after the completion of the main fabric. The porch was restored by Sir George Gilbert Scott in 1875. The coloured west window, depicting the *Last Judgement*, was inserted in 1879 at the expense of F.E. Stacey, a former Fellow of the college, and was made by Clayton & Bell.　**300** The nave interior looking east, showing the superb fan-vault (estimated to weigh 1875 tons) and the classical screen *(see also figs 82, 83)*.　**301** The south porch.　**302** The lead-covered wooden roof of the chapel above the vault (looking east).　**303** The nave interior looking west.　**304** A stonemason of the old-established local firm of Rattee & Kett installing new sculptural figures on a south buttress.　**305** North elevation of the chapel from the tower of St John's College Chapel. The rooftops of the old University Library and the Old Schools precinct are in the foreground.

305

Queens' College

Queens' was founded three times over: first in 1446 by Andrew Dockett, Rector of St Botolph's, as the College of St Bernard; then in 1448 Henry VI's Queen, Margaret of Anjou, followed her husband's example at King's and re-founded St Bernard's as 'the Queen's College of St Margaret and St Bernard'. No statutes were drawn up by Margaret, and about 1465 Dockett, the first President of the College, appealed to Elizabeth Woodville, Queen of Edward IV, to perfect the foundation, and the first statutes were granted in 1475. Thus, the plural spelling of Queens' takes account of both royal ladies, and a tradition grew that the Queens of England became successive patronesses of the college. This tradition ceased in the sixteenth century and was only recently revived by Her Majesty Queen Elizabeth the Queen Mother in 1948.

The river divides the college site in two; the east bank comprises mainly the older buildings, and there are five courts: Old, Cloister, Pump, Walnut Tree, and Friars', with the President's and Fellows' Gardens in the north-west along the river. The north half of this site originally contained the monastery of the Carmelite Friars, and was acquired at the time of the Dissolution (see p. 24). The west bank site has the Fisher Building as its southern boundary, with the new Cripps Court and The Grove to the north. The two sites are connected by the Mathematical Bridge (see figs 508, 509).

Old Court (figs 307, 309) is the most complete and one of the best preserved examples of a medieval Cambridge college. Professor Willis points out that certain features, particularly the square corner towers, suggest a strong link in design with the other two royal foundations of this period, King's and Eton, and that the architect was probably the same for all three - the King's mason, Reginald Ely. Queens' was the first Cambridge college to employ cloister walks, and Cloister Court (fig. 308 & see 13), with its half-timbered President's Lodge and Gallery, is one of the most picturesque of all the Cambridge courts.

The Erasmus Building (fig. 311 & see 134) by Sir Basil Spence, forms the west range of the Victorian Friars' Court. Supported on concrete pilotis and brick piers to provide an uninterrupted flow of space from court to river, this was a highly controversial building of the late 1950s (see p. 49), which, nevertheless, now fits comfortably with its historic neighbours.

On the west bank site is the Tudor-style Fisher Building (fig. 312 & see 174) of 1936, and to its north the new Cripps Court (fig. 313 & see 147) by Powell & Moya, which relates disappointingly to its surroundings, especially in the awkward spaces created between it and the Fisher Building (see fig. 174). A completely enclosed court seems inappropriate here, and it is unfortunate that a more fluid and landscaped environment, similar to that of the same architects' work at St John's College at the opposite end of the Backs (see fig. 176), could not have been achieved on this similar site, making use of the whole area including The Grove. A meandering, snaking plan, involving the existing

trees could have resulted in a fascinating composition, enclosed by water on three sides and reflecting the strongly defined pattern dictated by the small western tributary of the Cam - an idea already taken up by the curvilinear Fisher Building.

See also figs: 11, 13, 134, 147, 164, 174, 462, 476, 480, 508, 509

Chronological Summary of Buildings

Date	Building/Occurrence	Location/Details
1446	College of St Bernard	Queens' Lane, SE corner
1448-49	Old Court (R. Ely)	E bank site, SE corner
1448 & 65	Queens' College founded	(Statutes: 1475)
1475	W bank site acquired from town	W of river
mid C15	Cloister Court, W range	W of Old Court to river
c.1494-95	N and S cloisters built	Cloister Court
c.1540	President's Gallery	Cloister Court, N range
1544	Carmelite Monastery acquired	E bank, N (est. C13)
1616-19	Walnut Tree Court, E range	E bank, centre, E
1733	Sun/Moon dial in Old Court	N range, upper S front
1749-50	Mathematical Bridge (see p. 185)	(rebuilt: 1867 & 1902)
1756-60	Pump Court rebuilt (J. Essex)	E bank, SW corner
1861	Rest. of hall (Bodley & Morris)	Old Court, W range, N
1886	Friars' Building (W. M. Fawcett)	E bank, NE Ct., N range
1889-91	New Chapel (G.F. Bodley)	Walnut Tree Ct., N range
1912	Dockett Building. Rest. of Pres. lodge & gal. (E.T. Hare)	Friars' Court, E range / Cloister Court, N range
1935-36	Fisher Building (N. Drinkwater)	W bank site, S range
1959-60	Erasmus Building (B. Spence)	Friars' Court, W range
1972-80	Cripps Court (Powell & Moya)	W bank site, centre

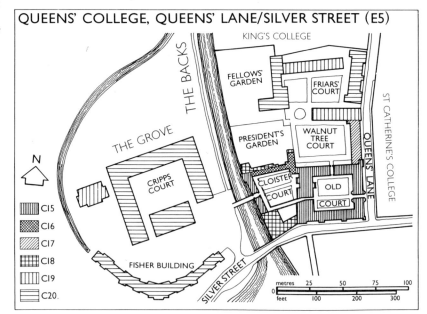

QUEENS' COLLEGE, QUEENS' LANE/SILVER STREET (E5)

KING'S COLLEGE
THE BACKS
FELLOWS' GARDEN
FRIARS' COURT
THE GROVE
PRESIDENT'S GARDEN
WALNUT TREE COURT
ST CATHERINE'S COLLEGE
CRIPPS COURT
CLOISTER COURT
OLD COURT
QUEENS' LANE
FISHER BUILDING
SILVER STREET
N

C15
C16
C17
C18
C19
C20

metres 0 25 50 75 100
feet 100 200 300

307

308

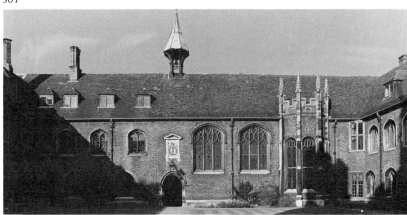

309

310

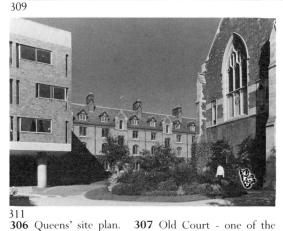

311

312

313

306 Queens' site plan. **307** Old Court - one of the best preserved medieval college courts at Cambridge *(see p. 74)* laid out on the typical plan of the early foundations *(see p. 75 & fig. 166)*. **308** The President's Gallery of *c.* 1540 *(see also fig. 13)*. **309** The west range of Old Court consisting of Hall, buttery and kitchens *(see fig. 166)*. The Hall contains much interior decoration by the Arts & Crafts firm of Morris & Co (roof and stencilled walls). **310** Walnut Tree Court. **311** Friars' Court from the corner of Erasmus Building *(see p. 49 &* *fig. 134)*. **312** Fisher Building and Cripps Court from Silver Street *(see also fig. 174)*. **313** Cripps Court, 1972-80, by Powell & Moya *(see also fig. 147)*.

125

St Catherine's College

In 1473, Dr Robert Woodlark, third Provost of King's College, founded St Catherine's Hall, dedicated to the honour of God, the most blessed Virgin Mary, and St Catherine. His intention in founding it was nearer that of a chantry than a college, the priests' duties being to pray for their benefactor and to study theology and philosophy. However, with the Reformation the society was forced to become a teaching body in order to survive.

Principal Court (fig. 316) forms the nucleus of the college and is straightforward and simple in its three-sided plan (though it was not originally intended as such, fig. 315). In contrast, to the north and south the cramped layout is less formal, a muddle of individual buildings rather than a collection of ordered courts, which do nevertheless create an atmosphere of comfortable domesticity. This is particularly so in the south-east area of the site around Sherlock Court (fig. 319); but the modern development to the north competes with its older neighbours. Recent expansion has taken place in west Cambridge with the newly completed St Chad's Hostel.

The original buildings of the college were situated in the north-west part of the site, however, probably owing to poor materials and methods of construction they fell into decay. During the mastership of Dr John Eachard (1675-97) a complete rebuilding scheme was executed and the majority of Principal Court was built. Robert Grumbold was the mason, and it is clearly a continuation of his work on the Old Court of Clare, which had been started earlier and was still under construction (see pp. 57, 100). The ranges are of three storeys with bold details, such as the dormers alternating with steep triangular and nearly semi-circular pediments, as in Clare's north and west ranges. The Chapel (fig. 317) is also very similar to Clare's north range, and the influence of Wren on Grumbold (he also worked on Wren's Trinity Library, 1676-95) is apparent in the east front which should be compared to that of Pembroke College Chapel (fig. 94). Buried within this fine example of the Queen Anne style is the renowned Dr John Addenbrooke, fellow of the college and founder of the famous Cambridge hospital bearing his name.

The original entrance to the college was from the west, in Queens' Lane, but in the mid-eighteenth century the orientation was completely reversed when Principal Court was opened up to Trumpington Street. The twentieth century Hobson's and Woodlark Buildings (fig. 316) by Kennedy & Nightingale, flank the entrance to north and south.

In 1965, St Catherine's and King's united to develop their confined sites bordering on King's Lane. The King's Lane Courts (fig. 318) by Fello Atkinson of James Cubitt & Partners, are divided in area almost equally between the two colleges, and, apart from providing accommodation and other facilities, gave St Catherine's a large new dining hall and underground car park, and King's a new concert hall, the Keynes Hall. The architects should be complimented on having developed this small site without exceeding the surrounding skyline, but the relationship between new and old has in places been criticised, and the draughty, dreary King's Lane passage remains an unpleasant byway separating 'Cat's and King's'. The extensive St Chad's Hostel (fig. 321) in west Cambridge by the same architects, was completed in the spring of 1981.

See also figs: 113, 487

Chronological Summary of Buildings

Date	Building/Occurrence	Location/Details
1473	St Catherine's Hall founded	NW area of site
By 1673	Original buildings cleared	
1673-1704:	Principal Court rebuilt (except SE range & E front)	Centre of site (Master: Dr J Eachard)
1673-75	N range, W half (Old Hall)	(note: design for Princ.
1678-83	S range, W half (Old Lodge)	Ct. probably by a Mr
1679-87	W range (chambers)	Elder of London)
1694-97	Chapel (Talman & Grumbold)	Princ. Ct., N range, E
1704	Chapel interior & consecration	
1743	Mrs Ramsden's bequest	
1757	Ramsden Building (J. Essex)	Princ. Ct., S range, E
	E front open to street	To Trumpington Street
1779	Gate and railings to Trump St.	Princ. Ct., E side
1860	St Catherine's 'College'	
1868-69	Hall windows gothicised	(W. M. Fawcett)
1875	New Master's Lodge (Fawcett)	SW corner to Queens' La.
1930	Hobson's Bldg. (Kennedy & Night.)	N of entrance front
1935-36	John's Building (H.L. Mullett)	Sherlock Ct., W range
1948	Bull Inn converted for coll.	NE range to street
1949-51	Woodlark Bldg. (Kennedy & Night.)	S of entrance front
1965-68	King's Lane Courts (joint venture with King's College)	N area of site (James Cubitt & Ptnrs)
1976-81	St Chad's Hostel (Cubitt & Ptnrs)	Grange Road

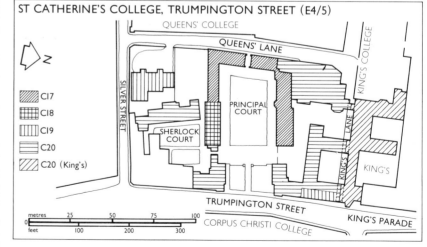

ST CATHERINE'S COLLEGE, TRUMPINGTON STREET (E4/5)

QUEENS' COLLEGE

QUEENS' LANE

KING'S COLLEGE

SILVER STREET

PRINCIPAL COURT

KING'S LANE

SHERLOCK COURT

KING'S

C17
C18
C19
C20
C20 (King's)

N

TRUMPINGTON STREET

CORPUS CHRISTI COLLEGE

KING'S PARADE

metres 0 25 50 75 100
feet 100 200 300

315

316

317

318

319

320

321

314 St Catherine's site plan. **315** David Loggan's print of the proposed college, drawn in 1688, with the library and gatehouse as the un-executed east range. **316** Principal Court as built. **317** The Chapel of 1694-

97. **318** King's Lane Courts - a joint venture by James Cubitt & Partners with the neighbouring King's College, 1965-68. **319** John's Building, Sherlock Court. **320** The Master's Lodge in Queens' Lane, 1875, by

W.M. Fawcett. **321** St Chad's Hostel, Grange Road, 1976-81, by James Cubitt & Partners *(see also fig. 113).*

127

Jesus College

See also figs: 464, 489

The College of the Blessed Virgin Mary, St John the Evangelist, and the Glorious Virgin St Radegund, commonly known as Jesus College, was founded in 1496 by John Alcock, 28th Bishop of Ely. It occupies the site and buildings of the earlier Benedictine Priory of St Radegund which was taken over by Alcock, with permission from Henry Tudor, the convent only housing two nuns at the time.

The site is very spacious, the five courts being completely surrounded by gardens and playing fields. The college is entered via the 'chimney' from Jesus Lane, through the Tudor gatehouse (see fig. 464) and into First Court (fig. 324). The ranges of this three-sided court are uniform in style, although they differ in date quite considerably. Access to Cloister Court (fig. 326) is through the central archway in the east range, above which are the arms of Alcock and the See of Ely. Alcock's rebus (three cock heads) is depicted frequently throughout the college buildings.

The college developed around the existing buildings of the Priory – the Chapel and Cloister Court – after alterations were carried out in and around the Nuns' Church converting it to college chapel, Master's Lodge, and student accommodation. The cruciform plan is still apparent (fig. 322) though the long nave was foreshortened to house the lodge and now forms the south range of Cloister Court. Part of the former Chapter House, in the east range, was converted into chambers, and the Refectory, in the north range, became the college hall (fig. 326). Particularly fine are the Early English arches in the west front of the east range which once formed the entrance to the Chapter House (fig. 327). The chapel itself contains interesting restoration work by A.W.N. Pugin, the great nineteenth century Gothicist (woodwork and glass in the chancel) and the Arts & Crafts firm of Morris & Co. (glass and ceilings in the nave and transepts).

A strong Victorian flavour was added to the college with Second Court's north range (fig. 330), unmistakably by Waterhouse, and then in the later nineteenth century with the east range of Chapel Court (fig. 329) by Carpenter & Ingelow. Morley Horder built the south range of Chapel Court in 1931, the coat of arms above the archway being added by the renowned designer/sculptor Eric Gill.

To the west of the Waterhouse building is the modern North Court (fig. 325) by David Roberts. This employs an interesting plan with square, double-banked rooms set at an angle of 45 degrees to the facade and terminating in triangular, oriel windows, the external spaces between rooms being filled by large, inverted triangular balconies. A straight facade is created by the dominant balcony fronts, yet the diagonally orientated plan is emphasised by the loadbearing brick cross-walls which project above the roofline. The advantages of natural lighting and privacy obtained by placing rooms diagonally in echelon are here carried one step further than at Mr Roberts' Castle Hill Hostel, for Clare College, of a few years earlier (see fig. 230).

Chronological Summary of Buildings

Date	Building/Occurrence	Location/Details
1133–38?	Benedictine Priory established	Chapel and Cloisters Ct.
1150–1245	Priory Church built	S & SE of Cloister Ct.
1495+	Alcock adapts Priory buildings	Chapel and Cloister Ct.
1497	Foundation charter granted	(by Henry VII)
early C16	First Court, S range	SW court of site
1608–09	Wall around Fellows' Garden	SW of First Court
1638–42	First Court, N range	
1681–82	Wall around Master's Garden	S of chapel
1703 & 25	Piers and gate to Jesus Lane	(R.Grumbold)
1718–20	First Ct., S range, heightened	Top storey added
1762–65	Open arches added to Clstr.Ct.	S, mid. Ct. (J.Essex)
1815	Chapel cased in Roman cement	Exterior
1822	Second Court, E range	N of First Court
1846–49	Rest. of chapel (A.W.N. Pugin)	Chancel
1864–67	Repairs to chapel structure	(G.F. Bodley)
	New ceilings: nave, cross, tower	Plus chancel (W. Morris)
1869–70	Second Court, North Range	(A. Waterhouse)
1873–77	Chapel windows (Morris & Co.)	(+ armorial gl. in hall)
1884–85	Chapel Court, E range	E Ct. (Carp. & Ingelow)
1886	Two bay windows added to lodge	SW side of chapel nave
1922–23	Second Court, NE corner range	(M. Horder)
1931	Chapel Court, S range	(M. Horder)
1962–64	Hall ext. W and gallery added	Cl.Ct.N (D. Roberts)
1963–66	North Court (D. Roberts)	NW court of site
1966–67	Garages, bicycle sheds and new vehicular entrance	S middle to Jesus La. (Roberts & Clarke)

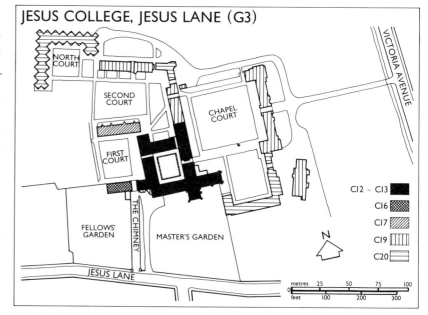

JESUS COLLEGE, JESUS LANE (G3)

128

323

326

324

327

325

322 Jesus College site plan. **323** The south front of the College towards Jesus Lane - the Gatehouse, Master's Lodge, and the Chapel, originally the church of St Radegund's Nunnery. **324** First, or Outer Court from the west. The east side was the west range of the nunnery and was heightened to three storeys in the late fifteenth century. The gatehouse range, along the south side of the court, is early sixteenth century, and the north range was built to match in 1638-42. **325** North Court, 1963-66, by David Roberts. An interesting planning exercise employing both the traditional stair-case and the corridor layout, with student rooms set diagonally in echelon to catch the sun. **326** The north range of the original Cloister Court - initially the refectory of the nunnery but then converted into the College Hall. **327** An arcaded entrance in the east side of Cloister Court, all that remains of the nunnery's Chapter House, *c.* 1230.

328

329

328 The west range of Chapel Court, the south half of which is the original east range of the nunnery; the duplicate northern part was built in 1822 in a lighter coloured brick. **329** The east range of Chapel Court, 1884-85, by Carpenter & Ingelow, in red brick with stone dressings, and the northern end of a 'U'-shaped range of 1931 by Morley Horder built to form the southern end of the court *(see fig. 322)*. The large coat of arms above the south-east archway is by Eric Gill. In 1922-23 Horder also created another court by building a small 'dog-legged' range connecting the north-west end of Chapel Court and the east end of **330** the Water-house Building, which then became the north range of second, or New Court. Built in 1869-70 by Alfred Waterhouse this building, with its asymmetrically placed tower and spire, is reminiscent of the same architect's contemporaneous work at Gonville & Caius *(see figs 241, 246)* and the slightly later Pembroke College Library.

330

St John's College

The Hospital of St John the Evangelist at Cambridge was established about 1208. In 1280, Hugh de Balsham, Bishop of Ely, attempted to house scholars with the monks at the hospital. After a few years this proved unsatisfactory and resulted in the scholars' moving to the other end of the town and the foundation of Peterhouse, the first of the Cambridge colleges. Over two centuries later, in 1511, the College of St John the Evangelist was founded on the dilapidated site of the hospital, by Lady Margaret Beaufort, the mother of Henry VII. The main impetus behind Lady Margaret to found the college was her confessor, John Fisher, Bishop of Rochester, and an eminent figure within the university (Master of Queens' 1505-08). It appears that the idea of a College of St John was first discussed by Fisher and Lady Margaret as early as 1505, at which time she founded her other Cambridge college, Christ's, for which Fisher was, once again, the inaugural influence. During the formative years of St John's, Fisher's role was all-important as Lady Margaret died in 1509 and he became the driving force among her executors, gaining the necessary licences for the dissolving of the hospital, and the charter of foundation, from Henry VIII.

The site of St John's is very large and it houses the second largest number of students of all the Cambridge colleges (after Trinity). The river divides the site in two, the east and west banks. The east bank site contains six courts and the Master's Lodge, with its large garden down to the river. The west bank site is less crowded, with three courts, including the 'School of Pythagoras' and Merton Hall. The Bin Brook, a tributary of the Cam, enters the college grounds in the spacious gardens towards Queens' Road, and flows to the river sub-dividing the west bank site also in two. The east and west banks of the Cam are connected by two bridges, the Kitchen Bridge, and the Bridge of Sighs (see p. 183).

On the east bank site, the buildings of First Court (figs. 334-336) are those of the original college with the exception of the Chapel (fig. 335) and the north quarter of the east range. This court contained all of the necessary component parts of a college, adapting the old hospital chapel and infirmary for collegiate purposes (demolished in 1869). The plan of the old chapel can still be seen on the grass in the northern part of the court. The new chapel was built by Sir George Gilbert Scott in the nineteenth century, employing a late thirteenth century plan frequently used at Oxford, the model being the chapel of Merton College, with a transverse antechapel forming a 'T' plan. However, if one looks at Loggan's print of St John's (see p. 59 & figs 107 & 108) made in about 1688, when the old hospital chapel was still in existence, there is a marvellous sense of unity within the court, today quite lacking as a result of Scott's chapel which is on a vast and unsuitable scale. Also, the form

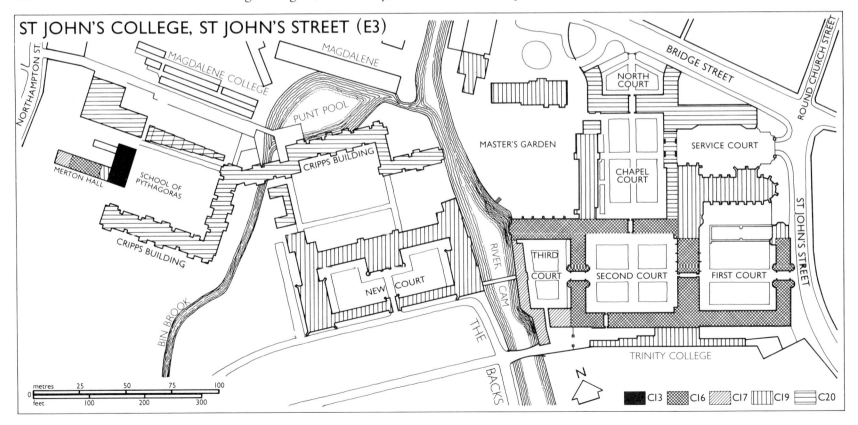

ST JOHN'S COLLEGE, ST JOHN'S STREET (E3)

of the polygonal apse (apparently inspired by the Sainte Chapelle in Paris) creates an extremely awkward gap in the court's north-east corner to the street. The statue above the archway in the west range is of the Foundress (for the gatehouse see front cover & figs. 457 & 466).

Second Court (figs. 333 & 337) was built mainly with donations from the Countess of Shrewsbury, whose statue is placed in a niche on the gate tower in the west range (Shrewsbury Tower, see fig. 467). The original drawings for this court, by Ralph Symons, still exist in the college library and are of special interest since they are the earliest surviving for any Oxbridge college (late sixteenth century).

Third Court (figs. 341 & 342) was begun with the building of a new Library (fig. 342), comprising its north range, with money donated by Bishop Williams of Lincoln. The initials I.L.C.S. on the top of the oriel gable of the river elevation stand for Iohannes Lincolniensis Custos Sigilli. The west and south ranges were added later, the south range being of particular importance as the first occurrence in Cambridge of chambers two rooms deep, this new plan being soon commonly adopted throughout the university. The west range cloister is interesting as the central archway has been designed larger than the others, and the whole of its upper storey facade accentuated in a Baroque manner, forming a sort of substitute gatehouse (fig. 341).

The rather drab collection of courts to the north of Second Court and the chapel are the result of 'semi-modern' work by Sir Edward Maufe. Scott's chapel and F.C. Penrose's west range of Chapel Court (fig. 338) were linked by Maufe's Chapel, North (fig. 339) and Service Courts, with what appears to be little regard for the urban domestic character of St John's and Bridge Streets.

On the west bank site, the next major building after Third Court was New Court (figs 346 & see 29). This early, neo-Gothic design, dubiously employing certain classical motifs, was built on an 'E' plan with the outer arms being connected by a vaulted cloister walk. It was intended here to continue the tradition of the college's brick buildings, but after a decision late in the day the south, east, and west elevations were faced in Ketton stone, the north elevation being of white gault brick with stone dressings. It is very decorative and has, for obvious reasons, been nicknamed the 'wedding-cake building', and creates a romantic composition when viewed from Trinity across the Backs (eg fig. 346).

One of the most successful examples of collegiate planning in recent years is to be found at St John's in the Cripps Building (figs 343, 344 & see 140, 176) by Powell & Moya. The most interesting aspect of this meandering structure is its relationship to the site (see fig. 331), the main line of building pulling together the two halves of the west bank by bridging the Bin Brook and creating two new three-sided courts. Subsidiary to the main building, is the single storey JCR projecting towards the west arm of New Court, and the conveniently placed punt-pool facing the rear of Magdalene's Lutyens range. Although the building is based upon the fragmentary idea of the broken line, a certain unity of form is established by the use of the traditional staircase motif, repeating

itself eight times, and providing a necessary, and welcome, point of reference. The four-storey structure is topped with a number of Fellows' penthouses, and constructed of reinforced concrete piers with in-situ concrete floor slabs. The building is faced with Portland stone. (A similar donation was later made by the Cripps Foundation to Queens' College, and Cripps Court, also by Powell & Moya, has recently been completed there, see fig. 313). The 'School of Pythagoras', the oldest surviving house in the county, and Merton Hall (fig. 345 & see 5) form the west side of Cripps' west court and were, until 1959, owned by Merton College, Oxford (since 1270).

See also figs: 5, 29, 35, 53, 67, 93, 106, 107, 108, 140, 176, 457, 466, 467, 479, 500, 501 & gatehouse on front cover

Chronological Summary of Buildings

Date	Building/Occurrence	Location/Details
1200?	'School of Pythagoras'	Cripps W Ct., W bank
1208?	Hospital of St John established	Area of the First Ct.
1511-20	First Court (S, E, W ranges)	E court of site
1516-19	Hospital chapel adapted	(dem.) S of chapel
1584-85	Hospital infirmary adapted	(dem.) S of chapel
C16	Merton Hall	NW extension of 'Pythag.'
1598-1602	Second Court	W of First Court
1623-28	New Library	Third Court, N range
1662-63	Statue of St John over entrance gate carved	Main gatehouse from street (see p. 168)
1669-72	Third Court completed	W of Second Court
1671	Statue of Countess of Shrewsbury on Second Court gateway	Second Court, W range (Shrewsbury Tower)
1674	Statue of Lady Margaret in First Court	Entrance from First to Second Court
1696-1712	Kitchen Bridge and gate piers	SW of Third Court
1772-76	First Court, S side, ashlared	(by James Essex)
1773	'Capability' Brown consulted over Backs landscaping	Area to SW of river
1826-31	New Court (Rickman & Hutchinson)	W of river and Third Ct.
1831	Bridge of Sighs (see p. 183)	Connects Third & New Cts.
1863-69	New Chapel (G.G. Scott)	First Court, N range
1863	New Master's Lodge	W of North Court
1869	Old chapel demolished	S of new chapel
1873	Cricket Pavilion	W of Queens' Road
1885	Chapel Court, W range	N of Second Court
1938-40	Chapel Court completed	N of Second Court
	Service Court & North Court	N & NW of chapel
1954	Garden Pavilion (D. Roberts)	W of New Court
1959	'School of Pythagoras' bought from Merton College, Oxford	Cripps W Ct., W bank (much restored int.)
1963-67	Cripps Building, Squash Courts, Workshops, Car Park, etc.	NW area of W bank site
1967	Groundsmans House	W of Queens' Road

332

333

334

335

336

337

338

339

331 St John's site plan. **332** The college front to St John's Street. **333** The north-east corner of Second court with the nineteenth century chapel beyond. **334** The west range of First Court containing the hall. **335** Sir G. G. Scott's Gothic-Revival Chapel (1863-69) in First court. **336** First Court from above showing the plan marks of the original medieval chapel of the Hospital of St John (see p. 58 and figs. 107 and 108). **337** The west range of Second Court containing the Shrewsbury Tower. **338** Chapel Court. **339** North Court.

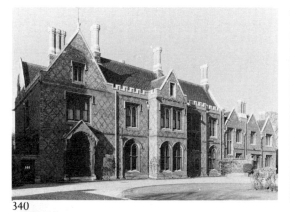

340

342

343

341

344

345

346

340 The new Master's Lodge of 1863 by Sir G. G. Scott. **341** The west range of Third Court of 1669-72. After passing through the first two older courts of St Johns, with their medieval ranges and traditional battlemented gatehouses, one is here confronted with a curious variation on that theme: a cloistered range of closely set round-headed arches is interrupted by a slightly projecting central bay taking the place of the gatehouse. The detailing of the bay is classically inspired though of a Baroque character crowned by an open segmental pediment. This classical detailing was derived from Wisbech Castle (demolished) and Thorney Abbey, designs of c. 1660 (Pevsner) **342** The College Library as the north range of Third Court – 1623-28, probably designed by the carpenter Henry Man. The lower storey was designed as chambers with the library above. The large two-centred, two-light Gothic windows are unusual for a building of this period. **343** A novel entrance staircase to the western ranges of the Cripps

Building, of 1963-67 by Powell & Moya **344** Cripps from the west *(see also figs. 35, 140 and 176)*. The JCR (Junior Combination Room) complex is in the foreground. **345** Merton Hall and the south-west end of the 'School of Pythagoras'. These buildings originally belonged to Walter de Merton, the founder of Merton College, Oxford, who owned property in both university towns. St John's bought the buildings from Merton College in 1959 and converted them to college use. Merton Hall is a sixteenth century, half-timbered house with a seventeenth century extension to the north-west and a nineteenth century rebuilt connection to 'Pythagoras'. As far as is known the 'School' was never actually such and was probably a private house, in fact the earliest in the county as it is of c. 1200 (the west end was rebuilt in 1373, and the hipped roof is of the nineteenth century). It is a valuable example of one of the earliest domestic buildings surviving in the whole county *(see also fig. 5)*. **346** New Court, of 1826-31 by

Rickman & Hutchinson. This Tudor-Gothic composition provides a pleasant backdrop to the northern end of the Backs. Built at a cost of £77,878 it was the first building by St John's on the west bank of the river and is connected to the older courts of the college by the Bridge of Sighs, also designed by Henry Hutchinson in 1831 *(see figs. 61 and 500)*. Although in essence a Gothic Revival building the planning of the composition is classically inspired with a slightly projecting centre flanked by far projecting wings. The wings are in turn connected by a cloistered walk which is interrupted by a central gateway which also has a classical feel about it with its traceried and pinnacled pediment. New Court's nickname of 'the wedding-cake building' is a result of the tall, elegant, circular staircase housed within the projecting middle section which is crowned with a glazed lantern supported by thin flying buttresses and pinnacles creating a central crescendo.

Emmanuel College

Like Jesus College and Sidney Sussex, Emmanuel is on a site previously occupied by a religious house, in this case that of the Dominicans, or Black Friars. The college was founded in 1584 by Sir Walter Mildmay, Chancellor of the Exchequer to Elizabeth I, and was thus the first completely post-Reformation college in Cambridge.

The site, though strictly confined, is fairly spacious, with a concentration of building in the western half towards St Andrew's Street. The eastern half contains one of the most pleasant gardens in Cambridge with a large pond (probably the fishpond of the priory) as its central feature. The early twentieth century North Court is situated away from the main site on the north-west side of Emmanuel Street.

The only surviving buildings of the priory are the Hall and Old Library which form the south and east ranges of New Court (fig. 351), the original court of the college. The south range was part of the Dominican church, the east range probably the refectory, and the architect responsible for the conversion from priory to college was Ralph Symons. The first major addition to the converted priory buildings was Brick Building (fig.352 & see 92), a range of seventeenth century chambers with an array of garrets and dormers in the roof.

By the middle of the seventeenth century, the old chapel had become far too small and was in need of repair. Christopher Wren was the architect of the new Chapel (1668-74, fig. 349 & see 95), the prototype for which may have been that at Peterhouse completed a few decades earlier (see p. 88). Though the two chapels differ in style, the Emmanuel Chapel is classical while that at Peterhouse is Jacobean Gothic, there are similarities between them in their location - forming the main court's east range - and planning (compare figs 349 & 189). Only a few years earlier Wren had completed his first Cambridge commission, Pembroke College Chapel, and if these two buildings are compared, particularly their facades, it will be seen that the earlier is in a purer classical style, while Emmanuel is heavier, more baroque, with a pedestal containing a clock breaking through the pediment to support a cupola. Over the next hundred years the rest of the Front Court was gradually changed to harmonise with it, firstly with the Westmoreland Building (fig. 350) as the south range, and then James Essex's rebuilding of the whole of the college's west front (fig. 348). At this time the main entrance was relocated to its present position in Emmanuel Street.

Much building has taken place in the twentieth century, Leonard Stokes built the Library (fig. 353) and North Court (see fig. 117), each similar in style, and based on Tudor-Gothic and Georgian models. Robert Hurd built the Second Hall (fig. 355) as the west range of New Court, leaving the Tudor wall facing into the court intact but employing an eclectic, Scottish vernacular style elsewhere in the building. In the sixties Tom Hancock added the new Master's Lodge (see fig. 141) and South Court (fig. 352), one of the most satisfying aspects of which is the handling of its relationship to Chapman's Garden. Instead of building a

range across the south side of the court, thus closing off the garden, Hancock projected the two wings of South Court away at unequal angles to it, thus retaining a feeling of space within the garden. The court blends well with the Brick Building to its north, the horizontal bands of concrete with brick infill harmonising with the similar pattern of its seventeenth century neighbour.

See also figs: 92, 95, 99, 117, 141, 168, 494

Chronological Summary of Buildings

Date	Building/Occurrence	Location/Details
C13	Dominican Priory established	Area of New Court
1538	Priory dissolved	(Diss. of Monasteries)
1584	Foundation charter granted	(by Queen Elizabeth)
1589	Conversion to college complete	(Ralph Symons)
1633-34	Brick Building (Westley & Man)	SE of Front Court
1668-74	Chapel and cloisters (Wren)	Front Court, E range
1719-22	Westmoreland Building	Front Court, S range
1769-75	James Essex rebuilds W front	Main entrance front
1824-25	N range of New Court (A. Brown)	N of Front Court
1883-84	Stained glass in chapel	(Heaton, Butler & Bayne)
1886-94	The Hostel (W.M. Fawcett)	Far E corner of site
1894	Emmanuel House (J.L. Pearson)	E end of pond
1909	Lecture Room bld. (L. Stokes)	S side of gardens
1910-14	North Court (L. Stokes)	NW side of Emmanuel St.
1929-30	Lecture Rooms conv. to Library	S side of gardens
1957-59	Second Hall & Kitchens (Hurd)	New Court, W range
1960	Barnwell Hostel (Bird & Tyler)	Newmarket Road (E.Camb)
1963-64	New Master's Lodge (T. Hancock)	E of New Court
1964	Pond altered to present shape	Centre of gardens
1965-66	South Court (T. Hancock)	S W corner of site
1972-73	New wing added to Library	(Cruickshank & Seward)

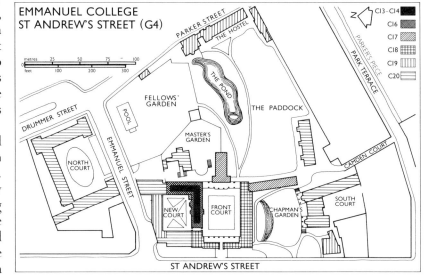

EMMANUEL COLLEGE
ST ANDREW'S STREET (G4)

348

349

350

351

352

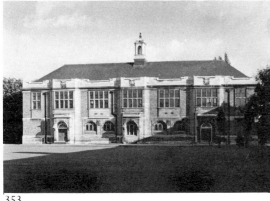

353

354

355

347 Emmanuel site plan. **348** The College front to St Andrew's Street – classicised in 1769-75 by James Essex. **349** The chapel, of 1668-74 by the young Christopher Wren. **350** The Westmoreland Building as the south range of Front Court – 1719-22. **351** New Court, the original court of the college. **352** Brick Building, of 1633-34 *(see also fig. 92)*, and part of the modern South Court of 1965-66 by Tom Hancock. **353** The early twentieth century library range by Leonard Stokes. **354** The Hostel (right) of 1886-94 by W. M. Fawcett, and Emmanuel House of 1894 by J. L. Pearson. **355** Second Hall and kitchens, of 1957-59 by Robert Hurd.

Sidney Sussex

Sidney Sussex was the second Elizabethan foundation at Cambridge, and like the first, Emmanuel, occupies the site of a suppressed religious order, the Franciscans', or Grey Friars' Priory. The college was posthumously founded by Lady Frances Sidney, Dowager Countess of Sussex, in 1594.

The main area of building is along the western boundary of the site to Sidney Street, with large gardens behind. Much twentieth century development has taken place along Sussex and King Streets in the southern part of the site.

Sidney has been referred to as the least attractive of the older colleges of the university; an observation which is undoubtedly due to the extensive work carried out in the early nineteenth century by Sir Jeffrey Wyatville (see pp. 58-9). If one looks at engravings of the college prior to this (fig. 357), there is nothing unattractive about the buildings and the appearance of the college is nearer that of a large Elizabethan country house. None of the original buildings of the priory remain and, once again, the architect responsible for the founding buildings was Ralph Symons. Some of Symons's buildings survive and, in fact, the majority of Hall Court (fig. 358) is sixteenth century, although much altered and hidden by Wyatville's nineteenth century neo-Gothic facades.

Sir Jeffrey Wyatville was one of the earliest exponents of the Elizabethan Revival, his most famous commission being the transformation of Windsor Castle for George IV in 1824-40. At the outset of his work at Sidney Sussex, Wyatville offered two alternatives to the college for their requested enlargement and alterations; Elizabethan Gothic, or the restoration of, and addition to, the genuine Elizabethan buildings; unfortunately the former was chosen. In 1821 he carried out repairs and alterations to the garden front of the Hall (see fig. 103), adding ten buttresses for necessary support, and rebuilding the upper part, adding another full storey below an embattled parapet. Ten years later he was again employed to carry out major alterations, in the same style, to the main courts, and in so doing completely changed the appearance of the college. This was done mainly by the addition of crow-stepped gables and battlements, chimneys with corbelled tops, and hood-moulds over all the doors and windows. The whole was then covered in Roman cement to provide a uniform surface to the new details and old walls. Wyatville also changed the layout of the college from two separate courts to a unified composition of one court on an 'E' plan. He accomplished this by moving the entrance to the west end of the south range of Hall Court (previously it had been in the centre of Hall Court's west wall in the form of a grand archway, itself relocated in the north-east corner of the gardens, fig. 359).

The twentieth century development of the southern part of the site began in 1923 with the neo-Georgian Garden Court (fig. 362) by T.H. Lyon. Next came E.R. Barrow's south range along Sussex Street, innovatory in the introduction of a dual purpose: accommodation for

students above commercial property. Completion of this area was finally achieved with the building of Blundell Court (fig. 363) in the late 1960s, by Howell, Killick, Partridge & Amis. An irregularly shaped block with rooms placed in echelon around the main staircases, this idea may have given rise to interesting external relief, but has contributed to the unfortunate destruction of King Street.

See also figs: 44, 103, 133, 151, 491

Chronological Summary of Buildings

Date	Building/Occurrence	Location/Details
1240	Franciscan Priory established	W area of site
1538	Priory dissolved	(Diss. of Monasteries)
1546	Priory conveyed to Henry VIII	(and Trinity College)
1589	Death of Lady Frances Sidney	(Executors proceed)
1594	Foundation charter granted	(by Queen Elizabeth)
1600	Founding buildings completed	Hall Court, W centre
	Chapel Court begun	S of Hall Court
1628	Sir Francis Clerke's Range	Chapel Court, S range
1749-52	Hall 'repaired and beautified'	
1762	New classical gate built	Hall Ct. (J. Burrough)
1776-82	New Chapel (James Essex)	Chapel Court, E range
1821	Garden front of Hall altered	(Sir Jeffrey Wyatville)
1831-32	Alterations to main courts	(Wyatville)
1831	Classical gate moved to garden	Jesus La. wall, N corner
1833	Chapel repaired	(Dr Chafy, Master)
1890-91	Cloister Ct., E range (Pearson)	N of Hall Court
1910-12	Chapel lengthened to E	(T.H. Lyon)
1923-25	Garden Court (T.H. Lyon)	E of Chapel Court
1937-39	Sussex Street range (Barrow)	S boundary of site
(1960	Oliver Cromwell's skull buried	Antechapel)
1967-69	Blundell Court (H,K,P & A)	SE corner of site
1981-83	Cromwell's Court (David Roberts)	King Street

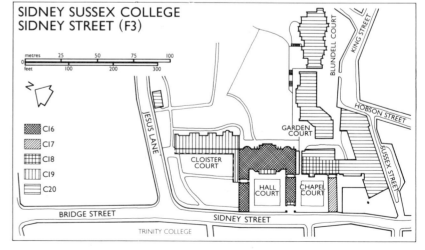

SIDNEY SUSSEX COLLEGE
SIDNEY STREET (F3)

C16
C17
C18
C19
C20

357

358

359

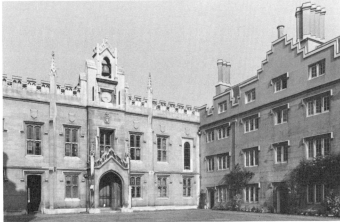

360

361

362

363

356 Sidney site plan. **357** The college pre-Wyatville's nineteenth century alterations – looking more like a large Elizabethan country house (from David Loggan's *Cantabrigia Illustrata* of 1688). **358** Hall Court from the west. **359** A classical arch designed by Sir James

Burrough in 1762 – formerly the main entrance gate to the college, but now located in the north-east corner of the gardens. **360** The east and south ranges of Chapel Court: the south, or Sir Francis Clerke's range, is of 1628; and the east range contains the chapel of 1776-82

by James Essex (much rebuilt in 1912 by T. H. Lyon). **361** Cloister Court. **362** The neo-Georgian Garden Court. **363** Blundell Court of the 1960s.

Downing College

Downing was founded posthumously at the beginning of the nineteenth century by Sir George Downing, 3rd Baronet of Gamlingay Park, whose grandfather was responsible for the building of Downing Street and Horse Guards Parade, London. The college was designed by William Wilkins and was one of the first major buildings of the Greek Revival, its novel plan being the earliest example in collegiate architecture of the spacious campus layout (see p. 79).

The present day site covers only just over half that of the original 17-acres, as the northern part, today known as the 'Downing Site', was sold to the university at the turn of the century. The east and west ranges are the original early nineteenth century buildings (though much added to, see p. 79), with the twentieth-century north range and additions to the northern area of the site, and recent expansion in the south-west corner. Unfortunately, much building has taken place to the immediate north and west of the college grounds, which has interrupted the skyline of both those ranges. The east range (see title page) was the only undisturbed side of the college from which one could fully appreciate the subtlety of Downing's unique character. However, even this side has now been interrupted by the lift service-core on top of the college's new commercial development beyond, thus breaking the classical lines when viewed from the west. The Catholic church, in the distance to the south-east, creates a pleasant though stylistically contrasting composition with the college paddock in the foreground (see fig. 59).

In the late nineteenth century E.M. Barry filled in the open spaces between the individual blocks of the east and west ranges and thus changed Wilkins's original layout from ordered groups into continuous ranges. The first half of the twentieth century saw further disregard for Wilkins's concept with the addition of the north range, or Graystone Buildings (fig. 371), including the new Palladian-style Chapel (fig. 370). Although the north range superficially merges with the rest of the college, mainly because of the use of the Ketton stone facing, it fails in its attempt to combine the classical grand manner with the low ceiling heights of modern requirement; the insertion of three storeys instead of two inevitably resulting in underscaled cramped proportions.

Although Downing's south range was never built (fig. 365), the buildings to east and west of it exist as the Master's Lodge (fig. 367 & see 100) and Hall (fig. 366 & see 27), the porticos surrounding both providing a strong termination to the east and west ranges and a visual connection across the open space between them. In the late 1960s this idea was extended westwards and a third component added to the line in the form of the Senior Combination Room (fig. 368 & see 37,145), architecturally the most satisfying addition to the college since Wilkins. The practice responsible for the SCR - Howell, Killick, Partridge & Amis - were faced with integrating a contemporary building into a formal, historic setting. The strong character of the adjacent Hall obviously could not be ignored, and in the design of the new building an equally forceful statement was necessary. The resulting single-storey pavilion is a very successful solution to this difficult problem, and well illustrates that modern reinterpretation, skilfully handled, can be preferable to the more generally accepted solution of a pastiche or reproduction.

See also figs: 27, 37, 59, 100, 145, 152, 171-173, 495 & title page.

Chronological Summary of Buildings

Date	Building/Occurrence	Location/Details
1749	Death of Sir George Downing	3rd Baronet
1771	James Essex consulted on design of college	
1784	Plans of James Wyatt	(1800: appointed arch.)
1796	Two sites agreed with town	Parker's Piece, Pound Hill
1798	Doll's Close site chosen	Now New Square
1800	Foundation charter granted	by George III
1801-04	Final site: Pembroke Leys	E of Pembroke College
1804	Further plans of Wyatt	(also Byfield's plans)
1806	Voluntary designs submitted: Wilkin's designs selected	(by Lewis Wyatt, and William Wilkins)
1807-13	Master's Lodge, Professor's house, lower block of chambers	S half of E range
1818-20	W range (including Hall)	(1821: students enter)
1834	Porters Lodge, gates to Regent St., wall to Tennis Court Road	(Tennis Court Road was set out in 1807)
1873-76	E and W ranges filled in	(E.M. Barry)
1896-1902	'Downing Site' sold to univ.	N of existing site
1929-32	Graystone Buildings (Sir H. Baker)	N range, E & W corners
1951-53	Chapel added to Graystone Bldgs.	N range, centre (A.T. Scott)
1959-62	Kenny Court (A.T. Scott)	NW corner of site
1966-70	SCR, Parlour, Kitchens, etc.	W of Hall (H,K,P & A)
1981-84	Commercial Development	Regent Street (Hughes & Bicknell)
1985-87	'Villa of Pleasure'	West Lodge Garden (Quinlan Terry)

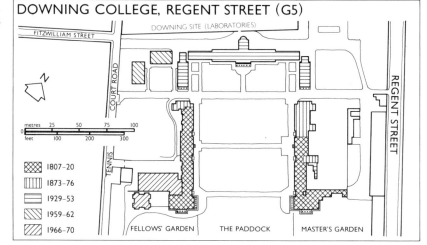

DOWNING COLLEGE, REGENT STREET (G5)

FITZWILLIAM STREET — DOWNING SITE (LABORATORIES) — COURT ROAD — REGENT STREET

metres 0 25 50 75 100
feet 100 200 300

1807-20
1873-76
1929-53
1959-62
1966-70

TENNIS — FELLOWS' GARDEN — THE PADDOCK — MASTER'S GARDEN

365

366

364 Downing site plan. **365** The intended south range which was never built, flanked by the terminations of the executed east and west ranges with their Ionic tetrastyle southern porticos – in the foreground the Hall and in the distance the Master's Lodge – the south range containing the library and chapel (print by J. Le Keux, 1841). **366** The Hall from the south-east with its hexastyle portico facing into the court. The chambers to its north were originally separate from it and the connection was built later in the nineteenth century *(see p. 79 and fig. 172)*.

141

367

368

369

370

371

367 The Master's Lodge – the first completed building of 1807-10. Its connection north to the neighbouring, though originally separate block of chambers, was made in 1873-76 by E. M. Barry *(see fig. 172)* 368 The Senior Combination Room, 1966-70, a pleasing modern addition to the neo-classical environment of Downing *(see also figs. 37 and 145)*. 369 Part of the original, elegant two-storeyed buildings of Wilkins, with the twentieth century three-storeyed north range of Sir Herbert Baker. 370 The chapel of 1951-53 by A. T. Scott. 371 Graystone Buildings of 1929-32 by Baker. 372 The east-west axis through the college from Kenny Court. 373 The rear of Downing's new commercial development to Regent Street, of 1981-84.

372

373

Newnham College

Two women's colleges were established at Cambridge in the early 1870s; Newnham in 1871, and Girton in 1873 (the latter was founded first, in fact, in 1869, but was initially located in Hertfordshire, and the buildings of Girton were begun earlier, in 1873.)

The North of England Council for Promoting the Higher Education of Women was the organisation responsible for the founding of Newnham (see p. 34). The college occupied two smaller sites before moving in 1875 to its present location in Newnham village - from which it takes its name. The buildings of the college are best viewed from the extensive gardens to the south, which are particularly beautiful in the autumn.

As with Waterhouse at Girton, red brick was again employed here and the new corridor plan was further exploited (see p. 80). However, in welcome contrast to Girton, the architect of Newnham, Basil Champneys, introduced a different style to distinguish this new kind of college. Instead of building in the traditional Gothic and Tudor manner characteristic of the men's colleges, he chose the domestic, neo-Dutch 'Queen Anne' style with its dainty decorative brick details and neat, white woodwork, which brought a distinct air of femininity to this area of west Cambridge. Before his death in 1935, Champneys completed the building of the four main component parts of the college: Old Hall (fig. 374), Sidgwick, Clough, and Piele Halls.

In 1938 Cambridge received its first building designed by a woman, the Fawcett Building (fig. 375), appropriately at Newnham, by Elizabeth Whitworth Scott. The local practice of Lyster & Grillet were responsible for two major additions to the college in the 1960s. The Library Extension (fig. 378) successfully conveys a femininity similar to that of Champney's original work, and the large 'Y' plan Strachey Building (fig. 375 & see 177) also maintains the domestic atmosphere, with its short faceted walls of red tile. Recently, a further extension has been added to the library along Sidgwick Avenue (figs 378, 379) by Joanna Van Heyningen of London.

Chronological Summary of Buildings

Date	Building/Occurrence	Location/Details
1875	Old Hall built	E side of gardens
1880	Sidgwick Hall	N E side of gardens
1882	W wing added to Old Hall	
1888	Clough Hall	N side, centre
1893	Gatehouse, or Pfeiffer Bldg.	N of Old Hall (fig. 473)
1897 & 1905	Library. Kennedy Buildings	N range, centre and W
1910	Peile Hall	W side of gardens
1938	Fawcett Building (E.W.Scott)	N range, E
1948-50	Porters Lodge (Buckland & Heywood)	NE corner of site
1956	New Principal's Lodge (L. Osman)	Newnham Walk, S side
1961-62	Library ext. (Lyster & Grillet)	N range, N side, mid.
1966-68	Strachey Bld. (Lyster & Grillet)	NE corner of site
1981-82	Library extension (J.v.Heyningen)	Sidgwick Avenue

374

375

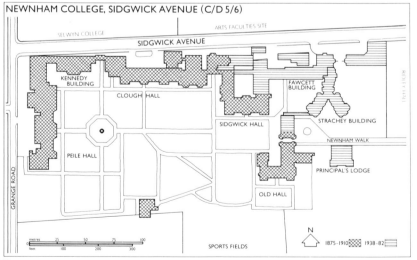

NEWNHAM COLLEGE, SIDGWICK AVENUE (C/D 5/6)

376

377

378

379

374 Old Hall, the first completed building of 1875.
375 A wing of the modern Strachey Building by Lyster
& Grillet *(see also fig. 177)*, with the Fawcett Building
beyond by Elizabeth Whitworth Scott of 1938. **376**
Newnham site plan. **377** Kennedy Buildings of 1905.
378 The Library extension of 1961-62 by Lyster &
Grillet. **379** A further extension to the Library, for
rare books, of 1981-82 by Joanna Van Heyningen.
380 The Dining Hall, within Clough Hall by Champneys
of 1888. *(See also figs. 31, 112, 177, 473).*

380

Girton College

Girton was originally established at Benslow House, Hitchin, Hertfordshire, in 1869, and moved to Cambridge in 1873. Emily Davies was the main figure responsible for the founding of the college, and she played a major part in the fight for women's education in the university. This was the second women's college (see p. 144) and for reasons of Victorian respectability was located two miles north of the town centre to discourage marauding male undergraduates. The site is very large, over 45 acres, and lies to the south of Girton village - from which the college takes its name - with the main buildings along the south-west boundary to Huntingdon Road.

The architect chosen was Alfred Waterhouse, who had already built a number of buildings in Cambridge in his characteristic red brick and terracotta. He applied the same style to Girton, but within its neo-Tudor Gothic facades Waterhouse introduced the innovatory corridor plan, later to be taken up in both Oxford and Cambridge (see p. 80).

Three generations of Waterhouses, Alfred, Paul and Michael, built at Girton; in 1962 David Roberts made a clear and expressive architectural statement at the college, perhaps rebelling against the dominating Waterhouse red brick. The Mistress's Flat (fig. 384) is a light design reminiscent of the work of Mies van der Rohe, its wooden frame and extensive use of glass in stark contrast to its Victorian surroundings. In the early 1970s, Roberts & Clarke further increased this break with the rather heavy, institutional character of Girton, with Wolfson Court (figs 387, 388). Situated about two miles from the main college, this new complex of five courts (phase 1) is inward looking, unlike the traditional Cambridge college which normally opens out onto its gardens. The reasons for this were twofold; firstly because the surrounding area was very vulnerable to development, and secondly for security reasons which, at the time, were a prominent requirement of the design brief. The informality of the plan was deliberate and this, along with the domestic scale, the choice of materials and detailing of the buildings, has created a relaxed and rather Scandinavian atmosphere.

Chronological Summary of Buildings

Date	Building/Occurrence	Location/Details
1869	College started at Benslow Hse	Hitchin, Hertfordshire
1873	Old Wing (A. Waterhouse)	Emily Davies Ct., N
	Mosaic clock face (Powell & Sons)	E. Davies Ct., N side
1876-79	Hospital Wing	E. Davies Ct., W range
1880	Gate Lodge at main entrance	Huntingdon Road entrance
1884	Orchard Wing	N of Hospital Wing
	Stanley Lib. Old Dining Hall	Cloisters Ct., SW corner
1887	Tower Wing (P. Waterhouse)	Main Gatehouse wing
1900-02	Cloisters Court completed	Main central court
1931	Woodlands Court (M. Waterhouse)	E of Cloister Court
1962	Mistress's Flat (D. Roberts)	Eliza Baker Ct. E
1969	Wolfson Ct. (Roberts & Clarke)	Clarkson Road (B/C3)

381

382

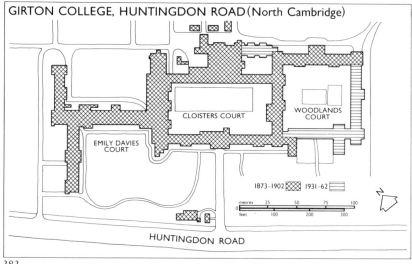

GIRTON COLLEGE, HUNTINGDON ROAD (North Cambridge)

EMILY DAVIES COURT

CLOISTERS COURT

WOODLANDS COURT

1873-1902   1931-62

metres 0 25 50 75 100
feet 100 200 300

HUNTINGDON ROAD

383

384

385

386

381 Old Wing in Emily Davies Court, the first completed building of 1873 by Alfred Waterhouse in his characteristic red brick neo-Tudor. 382 Tower Wing and the gatehouse, of 1887 by Paul Waterhouse, Alfred's son and later partner from 1891 (see also fig. 472). 383 Girton site plan. 384 The Mistress's Flat above the north-east range of Eliza Baker Court, of 1962 by David Roberts – a strong statement rebelling against the traditional Waterhouse styles. 385 The Hall as the north-west side of Eliza Baker Court. 386 The east range of Woodlands Court, of 1931 by Michael Waterhouse. 387 & 388 The domestic scale of Wolfson Court, Clarkson Road, of 1969 by Roberts & Clarke.

387

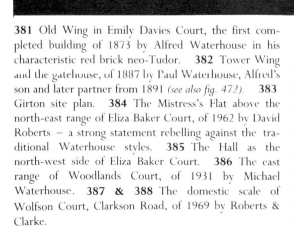

388

Selwyn College

Selwyn was founded in 1879 partly to maintain Anglican culture in response to the University's Test Act of 1871 (see p. 33); and also in memory of George Augustus Selwyn, an important ecclesiastical figure of the nineteenth century.

The founding buildings of the college were designed by Sir Arthur Blomfield between 1882-95, and included the West Range and Gatehouse (fig. 389 & see 471), the Master's Lodge, the north range (fig. 391) and the Chapel (fig. 395), all in red brick Tudor-Gothic. The 'Elizabethan' Hall (see fig. 116), of 1908-09, contains some interesting eighteenth century panelling, taken from the former English church of St Mary at Rotterdam in 1913.

Most of Selwyn's plans for contemporary development of any promise seem to have been rejected, either by the college or by the planning authorities, including interesting proposals by Stirling & Gowan and Robert Matthew, Johnson-Marshall & Partners in the late fifties and early sixties. The only notable addition to the college in recent years has been the latter's Senior and Junior Combination Rooms (fig. 393) as an infill block in the south-west corner of the main court.

Mr Cripps (Cripps Foundation), the benefactor of so much good modern architecture in Cambridge, donated Cripps Court (fig. 392), which uncharacteristically does not have the quality generally associated with other Cambridge buildings bearing his name (eg at St John's and Queens' Colleges). As usual, Mr Cripps specified his architects, this time Cartwright, Woollatt & Partners, from his home town of Nottingham. The building has been severely criticised and its main failing is, indeed, in the too-varied mix of materials, resulting in an unattractive, four-storeyed, three-sided court of brick, reconstructed stone, and knapped flint facing panels; summed up by Booth & Taylor as '...crematorium-modern monumentality...the kind of obvious collegiate images that one would expect in a "B" film set in modern Cambridge...' Recently the college kitchens have been extended by Purcell, Miller, Tritton & Partners, of Norwich (fig. 394).

Chronological Summary of Buildings

Date	Building/Occurrence	Location/Details
(1878	Death of Bishop Selwyn	Bishop of New Zealand)
1879	Constitution formed	(mod. on Keeble, Oxford)
1882	West Range and Gatehouse	Grange Road frontage
1883	Master's Lodge	Main court, SE corner
1884&89	N range: staircases C&D, E&F	Main court, N range
1893-95	Chapel (glass by Kempe 1900-03)	Main court, E side
1908-09	Hall (Grayson & Ould)	Main court, S side
1930	Library (T.H. Lyon)	NW of N range
1963-64	SCR and JCR (RMJM & Ptnrs)	Main court, SW corner
(1964	RMJM's proposal: rejected	Cranmer Road site)
1966-68	Cripps Ct. (Cartwright Woollatt)	Cran. Rd. W of main ct.
1980-81	Kitchen extension (PMT & Ptnrs)	SW to Sidgwick Avenue

389

390

SELWYN COLLEGE
GRANGE ROAD (B/C5)

CRIPPS COURT

PINEHURST

LECKHAMPTON

CRANMER ROAD

GRANGE ROAD

NEWNHAM COLLEGE

SIDGWICK AVENUE

OLD COURT

MASTER'S GARDEN

GARDENS

N

1882-95
1908-30
1963-81

metres 0 25 50 75 100
feet 100 200 300

391

392

393

394

389 The west range and gatehouse of 1882, and part of the north range of 1884-89 – red brick neo-Tudor by Sir Arthur Blomfield *(see also fig. 471).* **390** Selwyn site plan. **391** North range, south elevation from the Hall *(see fig. 116).* **392** Cripp's Court, Cranmer Road, of 1966-68 by Cartwright, Woollatt & Partners. An austere building ". . . which is a nasty throwback to the pre-1958 sort of trite hostel . . . 'Traditional forms used in an up-to-date manner' is the usual cant description" (Booth & Taylor, see bibliography). **393** Combination Rooms in the south-west corner of the main court, of 1963-64 by Stirrat Johnson-Marshall of Robert Matthew, Johnson-Marshall & Partners. **394** Kitchen extensions of 1980-81. **395** The Chapel, set directly on axis with the gatehouse to its west, of 1893-95 by Blomfield – the most attractive facade at Selwyn and reminiscent of King's College Chapel *(see fig. 299).*

395

Fitzwilliam College

Although today a completely modern complex of buildings forming a whole college, Fitzwilliam is not a twentieth century foundation but came into existence as part of the Cambridge non-collegiate community in 1869 as an establishment for students not attached to an endowed college (see p. 34).

The college first occupied rooms at 31 Trumpington Street in 1874 which, owing to its location opposite the Fitzwilliam Museum, soon came to be known as 'Fitzwilliam Hall'. In 1922 the name was changed to 'Fitzwilliam House', and then upon receipt of full collegiate status in 1966, to 'Fitzwilliam College', by which time it had moved to its present 7½ acre site on the northern edge of town.

Sir Denys Lasdun was the architect chosen for Fitzwilliam and his contribution is obvious in the idea and layout, but the buildings as executed are disappointingly boring. This is at least partly due to the fact that the college lacked any form of private endowment and Lasdun had therefore to work under the stringent economic restraint of the University Grants Committee.

Owing to the lack of finance, Lasdun's approach was to design a growing organism around a central nucleus, and for this he based his plan on the spiral, or snail-shell idea; a centrally-placed block of public rooms established the focal point around which a community could gradually evolve as the funds became available (see fig. 180). So far, the first two stages have been completed, but the buildings do not match the ingenuity of the idea - which was further hindered by increases in building costs, not met by the UGC budget. The uniformity of the elevations, with the floor-to-ceiling ranks of slit windows, contained within brown, engineering bricks and exposed concrete floor slabs, is an image typical of the early sixties (see fig. 135). In contrast, the extravagant Hall (fig. 397) counteracts the repetitiveness of the residential ranges, the canopy of parabolic hoods for clerestory lighting being a strange motif reminiscent of the East, as with New Hall's dome next door.

See also figs: 135, 180, 483

Chronological Summary of Buildings

Date	Building/Occurrence	Location/Details
1869	Camb. non-collegiate comm. founded	
1874	Rooms rented at 31 Trump. St.	
1892	House bought ('Fitz. Hall')	(house renovated)
1922	'Fitzwilliam House'	
1939-45	Disbandment of establishment	(temporary)
1946	Intake of over 400 men	(5th largest in univ.)
1961-67	New college bldgs (stages 1,2)	Huntingdon Road site
1966	Full collegiate status granted by university	

396

397

398

Location: Huntingdon Road (C1). **396** The Hall, with its eastern-like canopy of glazed parabolic hoods, and the north range *(see fig. 135)*. **397** The Fellows' Parlour with the Hall beyond. **398** The regimented, typically 'sixties' elevation of the south range to Storey's Way.

Hughes Hall

Hughes Hall was a late nineteenth century independent foundation, then known as the Cambridge Women's Training College, as the initials over its front porch testify. It was yet another response to the lack of opportunity available to women wishing to pursue further education (see pp. 34, 69) and it was initiated by discussions in the rooms of Miss Clough, the first Mistress of Newnham College, in 1885.

The college was originally located in a house at Newnham and its first principal was Miss E.P. Hughes, a graduate of Newnham, from whom Hughes Hall later took its name. A move to the east side of town was made in the late 1880s and the college occupied various houses before it finally settled on its present site, next to the Fenners cricket ground, which it obtained in 1893 from Gonville & Caius College. In 1949 it gained the status of a 'recognised institution', and then in 1968 was elevated by the university to collegiate status as an 'approved society'. From this time it has also admitted men and pursued a wider variety of subjects.

Like Newnham, Hughes Hall was built in the appropriately feminine neo-Dutch style. The architect was William Milner Fawcett, a local man who set up his practice in Cambridge after graduating from Jesus College and who built much else in and around the town. The building is best viewed from the lawns of Fenners to the west (fig. 399), from where the decorative details of the school of Flemish Renaissance, in deep red terracotta, form a contrasting backdrop to a game of cricket on a hazy summer afternoon. An extension to the south was added in 1937 by Verner Rees in a simple neo-Georgian manner (fig. 401). To the rear of the house are gardens and tennis courts.

399

400

401

Chronological Summary of Buildings

Date	Building/Occurrence	Location/Details
1885	Discussion about such a college	Newnham College
	College opens at Newnham	(CWTC)
1885-99	Principal: Miss E.P. Hughes	(Graduate of Newnham)
1888	Move to E side of town	Queen Anne Terrace,
		Warkworth St. & Terrace
1893	Site in Wollaston Rd bought	(from Caius College)
1894-95	Main building (W.M. Fawcett)	Wollaston Road
(1925	Death of E.P. Hughes)	
1937	Extension to SE (V. Rees)	SE of main house
1949	Status of 'recognised instit.'	(previously known as Camb.
	Name changed to Hughes Hall	Women's Train. Coll.)
1968	Full collegiate status gained from university	

Location: Wollaston Road, off Mill Road (south-east of H5). **399** The west elevation of the college from Fenners Cricket ground. **400** The original building of 1894-95 by W. M. Fawcett – red brick with decorative gables. **401** The neo-Georgian extension of 1937 by Verner Rees.

Homerton College

Homerton is the Teachers' Training College in Cambridge. It became an 'approved society' in 1976 when the university took it under its wing in response to the threat of possible extinction under the then Labour Government's education cuts. Its affiliation to the university was contentious; when the deciding vote was cast by the Senate (Dons voted 2 to 1 in favour), the academic standing of the college came under considerable attack.

The older, red brick neo-Tudor buildings were built by Giles & Gough in 1876-89 (fig. 402), and were originally the home of Cavendish College which was founded in 1873 to cater for poor, male undergraduates. Cavendish ran into financial difficulties and closed down in the early 1890s. Homerton moved in from London in 1894. The site today comprises a muddled collection of several groups of buildings as there have been many additions, two of particular interest: the rather Arts & Crafts Gymnasium (fig. 403) of 1913-14 by Herbert Ibberson, and the Nursery School (now Geography and Physical Sciences) of 1940-41 by Maxwell Fry, a pioneer of the Modern Movement in Britain at that time (see p. 49 & fig. 130).

In 1962 David Roberts was employed to draw up a plan for future expansion. Two years later, he handed over the job to his former assistant, Christopher Grillet, who embarked upon developing the very difficult site to the north of the main buildings, already dotted with other extensions. The result is a collection of pre-fabricated, black steel-frame buildings with white painted, pre-cast concrete infill panels (figs 405, 406), possibly inspired by Fry's Nursery School. More recently, Lyster, Grillet & Harding added the Biology Labs & Lecture Theatre (fig. 407) to the far west of the main college buildings. A low and simple complex, employing red brick and tile with some weather-boarding, this block achieves a satisfying synthesis of buildings and landscape, and is a refreshing addition after Grillet's harsh graphic treatment of the sixties.

Chronological Summary of Buildings

Date	Building/Occurrence	Location/Details
1695	Congreg. churches fund estab.	London (Founders)
1768	Society moves to Homerton	East London
(1873	Cavendish College founded	Hills Rd, Cambridge)
1876-89	Original bldgs (Giles & Gough)	Site centre, E-W axis
(1894	Cavendish College closes	Homerton moves in)
1913-14	Gymnasium Wing (H. Ibberson)	W. ext. of original blds
1940-41	Nursery School (E.M. Fry)	SW of car park (conv.)
1955-56	Gatehouse block (Seely & Paget)	SE ext of main buildings
1960-61	Science Range (Gardner & Ellis)	N of main buildings
1965-70	Major extensions (C. Grillet)	N area of main buildings
	Dining Hall, Common rms, Lib.,	Studios, Geog. etc.
(1976	Affiliation to university)	
1978	Biology labs & Lecture Theatre (P. Sparks of L,G & H)	NW corner of site

402

403

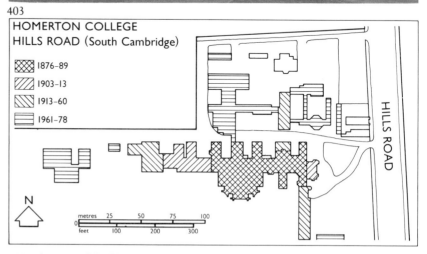

404

402 The original buildings of 1876-89. **403** Gymnasium Wing of 1913-14. **404** Homerton site plan. **405 & 406** Grillet's buildings of 1965-70. **407** Biology Labs and Lecture Theatre of 1978 by Lyster, Grillet & Harding.

St Edmund's House

St Edmund's House originated from the English College at Douai in Flanders, founded in 1568, via St Edmund's College in Ware, Hertfordshire. It was established in Cambridge in 1896 by Baron Anatole von Hugel, with the support of Cardinal Vaughan and the 15th Duke of Norfolk, and was originally a Roman Catholic lodging house. Official recognition as an 'approved society' was gained in 1965 and it then became an 'approved foundation' in 1975. It is now one of the five graduate colleges in the university.

Prior to its being occupied by St Edmund's, the house was known as Ayerst Hostel, after William Ayerst, a Gonville & Caius don who had housed students there from 1884-96. The buildings are of no particular architectural interest, and much has been added to the original Ayerst Building (fig. 408), The Chapel (fig. 409) was built at the west end of the range in 1915-16 by Benedict Williamson. The new dining hall, or New Wing, at the north-east end of the house, dates from 1940 and 1952. In 1973-74, the local practice of Lyster, Grillet & Harding, built the maisonettes for married students to the rear of the chapel (fig. 410).

408

409

410

405

406

407

St Edmund's House:
Mount Pleasant (C2)   **408** Ayerst Building.   **409** The Chapel of 1915-16 by Benedict Williamson.   **410** Graduate Flats of 1973-74 by Lyster, Grillet & Harding.

New Hall

The fifth women's college at Cambridge, New Hall, was founded in 1954 and for the first ten years of its life occupied a house in Silver Street, now part of Darwin College. The new Huntingdon Road site of 6.2 acres was given by the Darwin family and the college was relocated in the early sixties when the new buildings were constructed between 1962-66.

The architects for the college were Chamberlin, Powell & Bon, best known for their Barbican scheme in the City of London. The late Peter Chamberlin once said that '. . . The fundamental element that an architect deals with is space', and at New Hall this design philosophy is well demonstrated, giving rise to a fascinating scheme which so far is only about two thirds complete owing to lack of funds and a life tenancy on The Grove which occupies part of the site (for the buildings yet to come see fig. 413).

The college is planned around a central spine, running on a northwest to south-east axis, along which are a series of structures involving both gardens and water juxtaposed with the buildings. The design was developed around two main 'generators', and it is interesting to see how these criteria dictated the external appearance and internal layout of the finished buildings. Firstly, Chamberlin chose to concentrate on the smallest residential element of the college - the individual study bedroom - and to develop his ideas of space and plan from there (figs 411, 412). He was, as was Denys Lasdun next door at Fitzwilliam, working to the strict University Grants Committee budget (though also aided by the Wolfson and Nuffield Foundations) and thus decided to economise on space as much as possible by building-in the main units of the living area; the cupboards, wash-basins, and beds. A variety of types were developed, and the idea behind them, that of punched-out spaces, is expressed in the external modelling of the walls and window pattern, as well as in the varying internal corridor widths. Secondly, the concept behind the larger-scale public buildings was greatly influenced by constructional practicality; the size, and to a degree, the shape, were dictated by the pre-cast concrete units of, for instance, the Dining Hall dome (figs 414, 415 & see 179) and the barrel-vaulted roof of the Library, the sixteen units of the dome being finely calculated with regard to the lifting capacity of the site crane.

The structure throughout is of reinforced concrete framing or brick cross walls. The architects intended to use concrete only, but this proved too expensive and the Sevenoaks white faced bricks were later introduced. There are no applied finishes and the concrete and brick are left bare both inside and out. The concrete is composed of Ballidon limestone and white cement, and is treated in different ways depending on its location; bush-hammered for beams and ceilings, and polished for columns and rails in walkways and stairways. The sections of the hall dome are made of ferro cement, after Pier Luigi Nervi's structures in Italy (eg the buildings for the Rome Olympic Games of 1960) and were, apparently, the first use of this type of unit in England.

In its outward appearance New Hall projects an intriguing image, easy to pass off as mere 'historicism'. The question has been asked why the minarets and domes? One possible answer, put forward by Booth & Taylor, is that with a disintegration of religious belief within university circles, traditional values with a kind of 'post-Christian pomp' were at the time desired. Maybe, but there seems to be no really convincing answer. As with Basil Champneys new interpretation for one of the first ladies colleges at Cambridge in the late nineteenth century (see p. 144), so these white skinned and curvaceous buildings at New Hall similarly exude a feminine aura, but of a more blatant era.

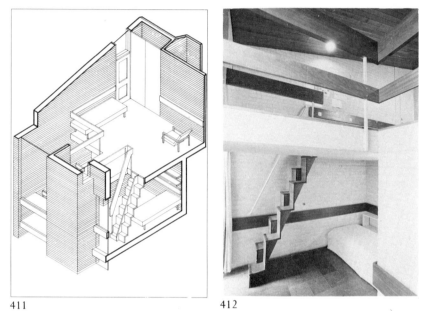

411   412

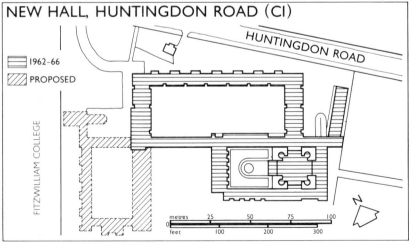

413

411 & 412 The individual study bedroom: isometric projection (drawing by Chamberlin, Powell & Bon) and internal photograph. **413** New Hall site plan.

414

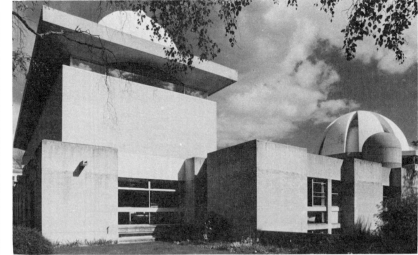

415

416

417

414 & 415 The pure white Byzantium forms of New Hall. **414** The domed Hall from the sunken court. **415** The barrel vaulted Library, the south range and the Hall dome. **416** The Library interior. **417** The north range showing the repeated relief pattern which represents the variety of room types within. **418** Hammond & Clover Houses to the south-west.

418

155

Churchill College

In 1955, at the age of 81, Sir Winston Churchill retired from British politics, and in 1958 Churchill College, Cambridge, was founded as a monument to this great Englishman.

The college was to place a strong bias on the sciences and the scale was to be extremely large for a modern foundation: 540 students and 60 Fellows. A limited two-stage competition was held for the design for the large 42 acre site in 1958-59, with 21 of the nation's top architectural practices invited to submit ideas. Four finalists were selected for the second stage: Chamberlin, Powell & Bon; Howell, Killick & Partridge; Richard Sheppard, Robson & Partners and Stirling & Gowan (see bibliography). Richard Sheppard's scheme was finally chosen and in its subsequent realisation has borne out the good judgement of the assessors who were Sir Basil Spence, Sir William Holford, Sir Leslie Martin, Noel Annan, and Sir John Cockcroft, the first Master of the college. The college was built in seven stages between 1959-68.

The main entrance is from Storeys Way, where one is confronted by the monumental brick columns of the gateway (see fig. 474). Behind this runs the 68-metre-long main circulation spine of the central buildings taking one into the heart of communal activity, and terminating in the buttery which is surrounded by a collection of students and dons' common rooms. Above this is the main Dining Hall (fig. 420), with its triple barrel-vaulted roof. To the south-west is the Bracken Library (fig. 420) behind its strong, vertically-ribbed concrete facade, and the much-envied and extremely well equipped Wolfson Hall; a lecture theatre with a seating capacity of 250 facing a proscenium stage and containing, among other things, an instant four-way language translator. The residential areas, in the form of ten courts (fig. 423 & see 178), surround these communal buildings, while the Chapel (fig. 421) is set apart and the Sheppard and Wolfson Flats (figs 425, 426) are located in the far western part of the college grounds. A service road runs along the northern edge of the site off which are located car parks and various service buildings, including the boiler house with its massive 'Corbusien' concrete exhaust ducts (see fig. 136). The Master's Lodge (fig. 424) is also located off this road, which continues further to provide access to the sports pavilion, chapel and flats.

The original winning scheme consisted of twenty peripheral courts forming one large central court, within which the central block of public buildings is situated. This was gradually whittled down to ten courts, but with a corresponding increase in size so that there are seven larger courts 22.8m square (from 19.8m), and three smaller ones 16.7m square (from 13.7m). The courts were designed on the cloister idea, with the larger courts being grassed and the smaller ones concrete paved. They are laid out on the traditional staircase plan with staircases located in the corner of each court and serving 12 study bedrooms. The rooms themselves appear more spacious than they are in reality owing to the clever treatment of the wide bay-windows which are punched-out of the

actual floor area, providing an attractive interior feature of a terrazzo-covered window seat which also contains the central heating unit.

The hall roof is the most interesting structural feature in the college (fig. 420), and is made-up of three cylindrical reinforced concrete shells spanning 18.5m unsupported.

Richard Sheppard's scheme has given birth to a modern college incorporating the best ideas of traditional Cambridge planning. The ingenious layout of a court-within-courts-within-a-campus, and the quality of the buildings, conveys a strong feeling of community spirit and academic prowess. Now, twenty years on, at the telling point at which so many modern buildings seem to have failed to wear well, Churchill is maturing gracefully in the manner of its finest historic Cambridge neighbours. The choice of materials, and in particular, the warm brown Stamfordshire brick, are complemented by the sensitive planting and landscaping by Sheila Haywood.

See also figs: 34, 136, 178, 474 & 496.

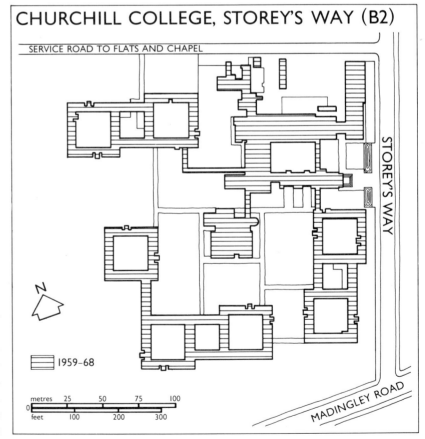

CHURCHILL COLLEGE, STOREY'S WAY (B2)

SERVICE ROAD TO FLATS AND CHAPEL

STOREY'S WAY

N

1959-68

metres 25 50 75 100
0
feet 100 200 300

MADINGLEY ROAD

420

421

422

423

424

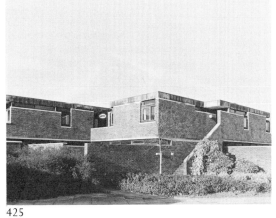

425

426

419 Churchill site plan. **420** The Bracken Library with the Hall in the distance. **421** The Chapel, in the far western area of the site – designed on the Byzantine plan of the inscribed cross, and 'a masterpiece of internal space' (Pevsner). **422** The north-west group of residential courts, with Barbara Hepworth's sculpture *Four Squares (walk through)* of 1963 in the foreground. **423** A typical court interior showing the study bedrooms with their spacious feature of cantilevered bay windows punched-out of the room space. **424** The Master's Lodge. **425** Research flats of 1959-60. **426** The Graduate, or Wolfson Flats by David Roberts & Partners.

Lucy Cavendish College

Lucy Cavendish was Britain's first college for mature women. It was born out of discussions in the early 1950s between three eminent university ladies: Dr Anna Bidder, Mrs Margaret Braithwaite, and Dr Kathleen Wood-Legh. The college is named after Lady Lucy Cavendish, wife of the murdered Lord Frederick Cavendish, the Chief Secretary for Ireland. During her long widowhood Lady Lucy devoted much time to the cause of women's education, and her efforts were greatly admired by many Cambridge women.

Discussions about such a college first began over weekly lunches in the Regent House Members Combination Room in 1951, and for the following fourteen years the 'society' continued to dine at a number of locations, gradually increasing its numbers and the strength of its cause. They first established themselves in a room in Silver Street in 1965, but soon moved on to larger premises in Northampton Street, rented from Magdalene College. Here a firm and positive base was established until the final move was made, just around the corner, in 1970, bringing them to their present site where they now occupy three large Victorian houses in this very pleasant north-west residential area of town.

The houses were built for married fellows after the repealing of the celibacy requirement in the late nineteenth century (see p. 33). They were owned by St John's College and originally occupied by senior members of the university and their families. They are, from east to west: College House (fig. 427, formerly Torrisdale), Barrmore (fig. 428) and Strathaird (fig. 429). The gardens of all three have been joined together to form one large open space so thickly wooded on its southern slope that one might well be in a secluded country house in Scotland, rather than next door to the flat Cambridge Backs. The houses are of no particular architectural merit but are good examples of the sort of building that went on at the time in west Cambridge. Minor additions include a porch to Barrmore and a dining conservatory to Strathaird, both by Berryl Green, a graduate architectural student of the college.

427

428

429

Chronological Summary of Buildings

Date	Building/Occurrence	Location/Details
1883	Torrisdale for A. MacAlister	(Prof. of Anatomy)
1895	Barrmore for D. MacAlister	(Sen. Tutor, St John's)
1890s?	Strathaird for J.D. Duff	(Tutor at Trinity)
1951	Dining Society formed	(by three ladies)
1951-65	Meetings at: Regent House	
	Copper Kettle, Harvey Court	(and Churchill Coll.)
1965	Granted status as 'Appr. Soc.'	Room in Silver Street
1966	Move to Northampton Street	(rented from Magdalene)
1970	Torrisdale leased	Lady Margaret Road
1976	Purchase of freeholds	(of the three houses)

The three houses which comprise Lucy Cavendish College: **Location:** Lady Margaret Road (C/D2) **427** 'Torrisdale' of 1883, now College House. **428** 'Barrmore' of 1895. **429** 'Strathaird' of the 1890s.

Darwin College

Darwin was set up in 1965 by Gonville & Caius, St Johns', and Trinity Colleges as the first all-graduate foundation at Cambridge.

Charles Darwin (1809-1882), author of the famous *Origin of Species,* was a student at Christ's College between 1828-31. His son, George (1845-1912), bought the family house and business premises of the Beales family in 1885: 'They were Cambridge corn and coal merchants . . . and their granaries, warehouses, cow-houses, stables and yards ran along the west bank of the Cam, up-stream from Silver Street Bridge. The house had no name, nor had the road; all that part of Cambridge was simply called Newnham; so my father named it Newnham Grange' wrote Gwen Raverat, Darwin's grand-daughter (see bibliography). The Darwin famiy lived in Newnham Grange, the original building of the college, until 1962 when Darwin's grandson, Sir Charles Galton Darwin (Master of Christ's 1936-62) died. The family then left Cambridge and gave the house and its gardens for the founding of the college.

Before recent addition, the college buildings consisted of three main parts: Newnham Grange, the Old Granary (fig. 433) which was largely reconstructed and now contains student accomodation, and the Hermitage, another early nineteenth century house, which was the first home of New Hall until 1965 when it was relocated in its new buildings on the northern edge of town. Darwin's trustees then bought the Hermitage with the idea of expanding the college by connecting these two main houses. Considerable benefactions from the Max Rayne Foundation enabled this expansion to take place in 1966 to the designs of Howell, Killick, Partridge & Amis.

The new residential block (figs 430, 431) forms the link between the two houses and is of three storeys, and though its neighbours are two storeyed retains a corresponding roofline. Below the mansard roof, the brick facade has paired buttress shafts and boxed-out windows, a characteristic device of this practice. The new octagonal Dining Hall (fig. 432), the first of that form in Cambridge, is located just around the corner in Newnham Road. Raised on four concrete pilotis, providing covered parking and a view through to the college gardens and river, it is constructed of brick on supporting concrete beams and has some interesting features such as a circular concrete staircase. At the same time, the Hermitage underwent major internal reconstruction with the inclusion of new kitchens at first floor level to connect with the adjoining dining hall, common rooms, and a reading room. Howell's scheme pulled together the isolated parts of the site to form not only a physically united community, but also a most successful piece of urban infill on this very prominent corner of West Cambridge. An extension was added to the east end of Newnham Grange in 1980 to designs by David Roberts in a manner reminiscent of Palladio and the Italian villa.

430

431

432

Location: Silver Street (E5). **430** The college front to Silver Street: In the foreground is the east-end of The Hermitage, an early nineteenth century villa; the modern infill block, of 1966-70 by Howell, Killick, Partridge & Amis, connects The Hermitage with Newnham Grange beyond, another early nineteenth century house of pre-1830; and in the distance is the new building of 1980 by David Roberts, with the Old Granary at the far end. **431** The picturesque south front of the college towards the gardens and river – Newnham Grange and the Roberts' building from The Island. **432** The octagonal dining hall.

159

433

434

433 The Old Granary at Darwin College from Laundress Green. The granary was originally part of a collection of outbuildings belonging to Newnham Grange *(see p. 159)* and when the Darwin family bought the property it was adapted to their needs by J. J. Stevenson in c. 1890. Upon becoming part of the new college in 1965 it was converted into student accommodation.

Clare Hall: Herschell Road, off Grange Road (B/C4). **434** The centre of the college looking north up Scholar's Walk towards the pedestrian entrance: to the left is the President's Lodge with its upper floor cantilevered over the point of entry, and to the right the kitchens and dining room. **435** The entrance hall to the communal rooms looking up towards the common room and dining area. **436** The West Strip consisting of houses and flats in an irregular block rising from two storeys to three and containing nine bed-sitters, three two-bedroom flats and a day nursery. *(see also figs. 181, 183).*

Clare Hall

Clare Hall was founded in 1965 by Clare College with help from two American benefactors: the Ford Foundation and the Old Dominican Trust. It is a graduate college particularly designed to take visiting scholars and their families.

The three-acre site was obtained from St John's College and is set amongst large Victorian houses, of which Elmside (see fig. 118) was the initial home of the college during the construction of the new buildings between 1966-69. The newly founded Robinson College is located opposite.

The architect chosen by Clare was Ralph Erskine, English-born and educated but who, at the age of 25, left England for Sweden in 1939. Erskine was attracted to the Swedish idea of the Welfare State and the prospect of a more egalitarian society, and his design philosophy reflects this social concern. His best-known building is probably the massive Byker housing scheme in Newcastle of the early seventies and which illustrates his very personal approach of participation with the prospective inhabitants of his buildings. There is, as one might expect, a strong Scandinavian atmosphere to this interwoven collection of buildings, courts and patios, with characteristic use of natural materials; the 'organic' philosophy is further expressed by the building being not only on, but sunken into, the ground. The site is not as complex as it may first appear (see fig. 183). The rectangular area is divided into three north-south strips: the West Strip (fig. 436) is an irregular block diminishing from three storeys to two (from north to south) containing flats, bed-sitters, a day nursery, and four terrace houses; the Central Strip (fig. 434) contains the two-storey President's Lodge to the street, with its cantilevered upper floor over the main entrance to the college, while behind this are three four-bedroomed courtyard houses; the East Strip is the facilities block, containing the common room and its patio, the reading room with its courtyard surrounded by studies and workrooms (see fig. 181), and the dining room and kitchens. Open-plan living areas are employed in the houses and flats. There are three main route ways: the Family Walk which separates the west and central strips; the Scholars Walk between the central and east strips; and an east-west cross walk through the central courtyard houses. All the buildings are constructed of brick and timber boarding supporting monopitch roofs of timber covered with aluminium. The whole site is slightly elevated along the northern side by a semi-basement car park, providing a north-south slope to take advantage of sunlight in the courtyards and patios.

435

436

Wolfson College

University College was founded in 1965 in Bredon House, Selwyn Gardens, and was the first college to be established by the university itself (see p. 69). This was another graduate foundation and was to be financed by an annual grant of £20,000 for ten years, after which time it was expected to be self-supporting. However, in 1972 a gift of £2 million was made by the Wolfson Foundation, and the name changed to Wolfson College in January 1973.

The four acre site is situated between Selwyn Gardens and Barton Road, and surrounded on three sides by residential properties. Apart from Bredon House, other houses were also purchased in the immediate area and the site was developed in response to these and their gardens. The College is designed on an 'E' plan, with the two outer arms returning at right-angles towards the centre and creating two semi-enclosed courts: East Court (fig. 438) and West Court (fig. 439). Main Court (fig. 437) is in the centre.

The architects chosen by the college were Ferry & Mennim of York. Mr A.M. Mennim had been engaged with the college on feasibility studies since the late 1960s, and the eventual design, which was executed in 1972-77 by Mr Mennim with later associates C.S.G. Liversedge and R.J. Carr Archer, gave the college the sort of character that it had requested - friendly and domestic, with a definite sense of order. The layout is on the traditional Cambridge plan; courts with rooms in the residential blocks accessible from staircases. The difficult job of incorporating Bredon House (fig. 438) with the new buildings has been sensibly handled, although the junction between new and old is harsh in places.

East and West courts flank the central block of public rooms located in the middle arm of the 'E'. The entrance hall, at the south end of the arm, is paved in granite from the old London Bridge, and behind this is the Club Room, the focal point of the college, with the Hall, Combination Room, and Council Room above on the first floor. West Court contains most of the residential accommodation in double-fronted, terrace houses of three storeys containing a mixture of flats and bed-sitters; the south block consists of the same kind of accommodation but with special attention paid to the needs of the disabled. In East Court the south block houses the seminar room below with the library above, while the east range has the same sort of accomodation as West Court, but here of only two storeys. As many of the trees were retained as possible and some of the chestnuts which had to be cut down were used for the panelling of the Council Room. An appropriate differentiation of function is made in the use of materials; the central block of public rooms is of stone, while the other, mainly residential, buildings are of a good quality facing brick in mixed shades of light browns and reds.

437

438

439

Location: Barton Road, south-west Cambridge (see D6). **437** The front of the college, or Main Court, The central block of communal rooms, built of stone, are beyond the main entrance gate, with a residential block to the right. **438** Part of East Court incorporating Bredon House. **439** West Court.

162

Robinson College

Robinson is the most recent college foundation at Cambridge and is unique in that its founder and benefactor, Mr David Robinson, is still alive. The college was founded in 1974 and the first stage of building was completed between 1977-80. It was the first Cambridge college to be conceived for both men and women and also to be designed as a college during the academic year and a conference centre during vacations.

The 12½ acre site was purchased from St John's College and included a number of large houses and their gardens containing much mature woodland. The choice of this site for university development met with severe opposition, as it was an area zoned for residential use only. However, the trustees of the college were determined to build there and a limited competition took place in 1974, with ten practices invited to take part. A short-list of four were chosen: Eric Lyons with Cadbury-Brown, Metcalfe & Cunningham; Fielden & Mawson; Gillespie, Kidd & Coia: and MacCormac & Jamieson (see bibliography). The successful proposal was that of Gillespie, Kidd & Coia, a Glaswegian firm who had in 1971-72 built highly praised additions at Wadham College, Oxford. The senior partners were Isi Metzstein and Andrew Macmillan.

The main buildings are designed as a double perimeter ring which wraps itself around the eastern edge of the site, a substantial garden strip separating it from the street (fig. 440 & see 183). The massive, inner ring contains the main residential staircases (figs 443, 444), while the lower, outer ring includes most of the public buildings, such as the Chapel and Library (fig. 442) and the administrative offices (fig. 445). An 'alley' (figs 443, 444 & see 184) separates the two rings and contains four courts: Front Court (fig. 442), Long Court (fig. 443), High Court (fig. 446), and Herschel Court (fig. 448). Extensive gardens and more buidings, yet to come, will fill the rest of the site to the west (fig. 440).

Several factors had to be taken into consideration in the design of this building, most obviously the site and its gardens, through which flows the Bin Brook. The fact that only part of the site was free for building, owing to long leases on many of the existing houses, also dictated the layout to a large degree. Within the proposed building itself its function as a co-residential community was all-important, as was its dual role as a conference centre during vacations - a necessary financial sideline of many colleges these days. In every way Gillespie, Kidd & Coia's proposal was convincing to the client: its utilisation of the site along traditional lines, where the main mass of college building faces the public street and behind which the gardens provide a serene private adjunct to college existence; its regard for the conflicting needs of its permanent and transient members; the co-residential aspect; vehicular problems (hide them underground); conference usage; building and fire regulations; consideration for disabled people; and, of course, cost. The site is so far only about two-thirds complete and the whole development cannot be fully realised until the end of the century.

One of the most dominant visual aspects of the buildings is the way in which the architects have exploited their materials, in particular the extensive and creative use of brickwork (for instance, the corbelled door-surrounds, fig. 450, and the 'V' shaped brick piers within which are copper down-pipes). The whole concrete structure is covered in this non-loadbearing 'skin' of 1¼ million hand-made Dorset bricks, with some accompanying tile-hanging (see fig. 149). However, it was obviously apparent to the designers that the vast expanse of bland brick walls were somewhat repetitive in places, and that something was needed to break the monotony. Thus the dominant decorative trellises were introduced during construction (absent in the original drawings) as a device to provide some play in the long facade to Grange Road (fig. 441). The grid design of the trellis arose from the window frames which project out from the walls and it is used in various permutations throughout the college. A high standard of craftsmanship was achieved throughout the building, and the main contractor was 'Joint Venture', a combination of the firms Johnson & Bailey Ltd., and William Sindall Ltd. The architects were initially assisted by the local practice of Whitworth & Hall. The year after building had commenced, the firm of Yorke Rosenberg Mardall were brought in as 'executive architects' to work with Gillespie Kid & Coia in order to rationalise the scheme.

Foliage should eventually play a very important role in these buildings as the long, austere balconies are desperately crying out for an organic foil - so noticeably absent on this vast, brick-clad concrete monolith - and the colour combinations produced by extensive planting with the red brick could be quite striking.

There are many individual parts to Robinson which deserve high praise; such as the library and chapel, definitely the showpieces of the college, and there are also some beautiful features, such as the massive stained-glass window of the chapel by John Piper (fig. 449).

See also figs: 38, 149, 182-186 & 475.

ROBINSON COLLEGE, GRANGE ROAD (B/C4)

441

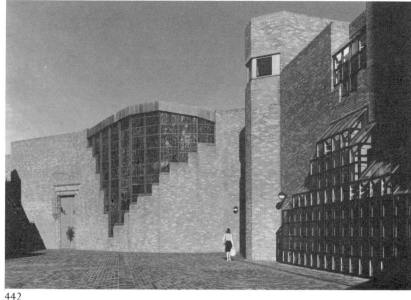

442

443

445

446

444

447

440 Robinson site plan. **441** The extensive fortress-like college front to Grange Road. **442** Front Court with the Library and Chapel at the south and east sides. **443** Long Court looking north, showing the tiered balconies of the main residential west range *(see also fig. 184).* **444** Long Court looking south.

445 The Bursary and Warden's office facing the west range of Long Court. **446** High Court. **447** The Hall and residential Terraces from the gardens in the west, showing the oversized bridge which provides access aross the Bin Brook pond to Thorneycreek House beyond. **448** Stacked study bedrooms in Herschel

Court facing Herschell Road. **449** The large stained-glass chapel window by John Piper. **450** The chapel door showing the architects' imaginative use of brickwork (1¼ million bricks cover the reinforced concrete frame structure).

448

449   450

Theological Colleges

As well as the 31 university colleges, there are also five independent theological colleges in Cambridge. These are all comparatively young institutions with the exception of Cheshunt College (originally founded in 1768 in a remote house in Wales), which today exists in name only, having ceased to have an independent identity in 1967, when it left its site in Bateman Street, its Master and Office now being housed within Westminster College. All five colleges were established in Cambridge in the late nineteenth and early twentieth centuries in response to the generally poor provision for theological teaching at Cambridge at that time, and in an attempt to re-assert and strengthen religious belief after the abolition of the university Test Act in 1871 (see p. 33).

Architecturally, the buildings are all fairly similar in style; ecclesiastic, red brick, neo-Tudor, exuding a pretty, friendly character, serene in their domestic scale. All of the architects involved in the initial buildings also built elsewhere in Cambridge and were of a similar mould.

Charles Luck built **Ridley Hall** (fig. 451) in 1879-81, the sister college of Wycliffe Hall, Oxford. Next came the north range of **Westcott House** (fig. 452) in 1899, Grayson & Ould's first building at Cambridge. Many additions were made to Westcott House early this century, and in 1960 C.J. Bourne added another storey to Horder's Cloister. The Ecoles des Beaux Arts-trained E.T. Hare built **Westminster College** (fig. 453 & see 115), also in 1899, the most grand of the five buildings. The roof turret with its squat lantern provides a charming motif, and, though the overall design is Tudor in origin, there is also much seventeenth century cartouche work.

The buildings of the now extinct **Cheshunt College** (fig. 454) in Bateman Street, designed by Morley Horder and built in 1913-15, are today occupied by the Freemasons, the Marlborough Secretarial College, and Hobson's Press. An architect of village halls, country houses, and many other important educational buildings (eg Nottingham University: 1922-28), this was Horder's first building in Cambridge and is an attractive composition. It is a pity that Cheshunt vacated this site, for the whole atmosphere of the buildings is particularly apt for its original purpose.

Finally, **Wesley House** (figs 455, 456) was founded in 1921 and originally occupied No. 2 Brookside, just around the corner from Cheshunt College with whom it worked in close co-operation until moving to its present site in Jesus Lane in 1925. The original buildings were designed by Maurice Webb and built between 1925 and 1930, and the new South Range (fig. 456) by Whitworth & Hall in 1972.

Chronological Summary

Date	Building/Occurrence
	Cheshunt College Bateman Street
1768	Expulsion from Oxford of six Anglican students.
	Lady Huntingdon founds *(Methodist)* Theological college at Travecca, Brecon, on 24 August.
1791	Death of Lady Huntingdon
1792	College moves to Cheshunt, Hertfordshire
(1871	Abolition of religious tests at Cambridge University)
(1879	Selwyn College founded *Church of England)*
(1896	St Edmund's House founded *Roman Catholic)*
1906	Cheshunt College moves to Cambridge
1913-15	New buildings in Bateman Street (Morley Horder)
1967	Cheshunt disbanded, office moves in with Westminster Coll.
	Westminster College, *Presbyterian,* Madingley Road (D2)
1844	Presbyterian church in England found a training college in London
1864	College occupies Queen Square House, London
1892	Offer of a Cambridge site made
1895	Offer accepted and site plus £6000 given by Mrs Margaret Gibson and Mrs Agnes Lewis (sisters)
1899	Westminster College, Cambridge (E.T. Hare)
1921	Chapel added (donated by Lord & Lady Kirkley)
	Ridley Hall, *Evangelical,* Ridley Hall Road (D5/6)
1876	Proposal to found theological colleges at both Cambridge and Oxford
1877	Ridley Hall, Cambridge (Wycliffe Hall, Oxford)
1879+	Buildings designed by C.F. Luck
1881	College opens under Revd. Handley Moule
1891-92	Chapel and New Block (W. Wallace)
1912	West Block
1949	Chapel reredos and neo-Georgian decoration (A.E. Richardson)
	Westcott House, *Church of England,* Jesus Lane (F/G3)
1881	College founded - occupies No 20 King's Parade
1884	Moves to larger rooms in St Mary's Passage
1889	Moves to 6 St Mary's Passage
	Moves to present building, N range (Grayson & Ould)
1901	Death of B.F. Westcott, Regius Professor of Divinity
1902	College named Westcott House
1912	W range (H. Simpson)
1914	E range, S half (T. Moore)
1923-29	Additions by Morley Horder
1960	New upper storey added to W wing (C.J.Bourne)
	Wesley House, *Methodist,* Jesus Lane (F3)
1921	Wesley House founded
1921-25	Occupies No 2 Brookside
1925	Site purchased in Jesus Lane, from Jesus College New Buildings (M.Webb)
1928	E wing
1929	Principal's House
1930	Chapel
1972	S range to Jesus Lane (Whitworth & Hall)

451 The east range of Ridley Hall, of 1879-81 by Charles Luck. 452 Westcott House of 1899 by Grayson & Ould. 453 Westminster College of 1899 by E. T. Hare *(see also fig. 115).* 454 The buildings of the disbanded Cheshunt Theological College by Morley Horder. 455 The north range of Wesley House including the chapel, of 1925-30 by Maurice Webb. 456 The modern south range of Wesley House to Jesus Lane, by the local practice of Whitworth & Hall.

457 St John's College Gatehouse, built with the rest of the First Court between 1511-16 of red brick with dressings of freestone and clunch *(see also front cover & figs 332 & 466)*. Along with its contemporaneous ranges the gatehouse is an important brick building of this period as it has, fortunately, escaped the fate of so many other buildings which were faced with stone during the seventeenth and eighteenth centuries. The ground floor is fan-vaulted. The Tudor linenfold oak door, within a four-centred arch, has two leaves, with a wicket in the north half, and is the work of the carpenter Thomas Loveday of Sudbury of *c.*1516. Above the entrance is a superb display of heraldic carving which should be compared to Christ's College gatehouse *(fig. 465)* as both colleges were founded by Lady Margaret Beaufort and thus bear her coat of arms and similar devices, such as the rose of Lancaster, portcullises and coronets. The two animals are yales - characterised by their antelope bodies, goats' heads and elephants' tails - supporting the foundress's coronetted coat-of-arms. The background of the composition is a field strewn with daisies, germander plants, rabbits, and a fox with a goose. All of this carving was re-painted and re-gilded in 1934-35 under the direction of Professor Tristram, and the whole gatehouse was restored in 1983. The niche above the heraldic panel contains a figure of St John the Evangelist carved by George Woodroff in 1662-63 for the sum of £11. The college treasury was located on the second-floor of the gatehouse. St John's is a perfect example of the typical Cambridge gatehouse with its lofty proportions, accentuated octagonal corner turrets (providing closets for the rooms within, though it can be seen here that the south-west turret is wider than the others as it contains a staircase), and battlemented upper storey. **458 & 459** The gatehouse of Great Quad, New College, Oxford, of 1380-86 by William of Wykeham. founder of the College and a former Clerk of Works to Edward III (see p. 74). This was the first occurrence of the gatehouse as a feature in collegiate architecture and set the pattern for many of the succeeding Oxford Colleges. Here there is little or no vertical accentuation of the gatehouse as an individual structure in the entrance range, on either the outer (fig. 458) or inner (fig.459) court side - very different from the form generally adopted at Cambridge.

457

4 College Gatehouses

This is an interesting little group of buildings which are unique to Cambridge. Although Oxford also possesses a number of gatehouses, they are of a different kind, being almost unaccentuated parts of the ranges in which they are located, whereas from early times the Cambridge gatehouse has been an individual structure in its own right.

Gatehouses became a fashionable architectural feature during the fifteenth and sixteenth centuries for large houses - for instance those at St James's Palace and Hampton Court - and are clearly derived from the medieval castle. In the earliest Cambridge colleges, such as Peterhouse, Clare Hall, Pembroke, Gonville Hall, and Corpus Christi, the entrances to the courts were very simple, usually a small archway in the range on to the street. The gatehouse as such first appeared at Oxford, in the east range of Queen's College's Old Quad (completed by 1355, but now demolished) though the forerunner of the Oxford 'type' was that built a few decades later by William of Wykeham at New College (figs. 458 & 459). The prototype at Cambridge was that at King's Hall, founded in 1337 (later to become part of Trinity College), and is now known as King Edward's Tower in the north range of Trinity's Great Court (fig. 460). With its fortified, sturdy, and solid appearance, the Cambridge 'type' is much more reminiscent of a castle than those at Oxford, and it is not surprising that in medieval times their upper floors were often used as the college treasury.

The form of the Oxford gatehouse, following Wykeham's gatehouse at New College, built at the same time as the rest of the quad in 1380-86, is simply a subtle accentuation of that part of the facade by which one enters the college; there is little vertical emphasis on the street side, apart from the setting back of the gatehouse so that its surface is not flush with the walls of the range (fig. 458). On the court side, its facade runs on exactly the same plane as the rest of the range (fig. 459). In their general form, every successive gatehouse at Oxford followed this example, with the exception of the seventeenth century Tom Tower at Christ Church, which is nearer the Cambridge type.

The pattern for the Cambridge gatehouses, set by King Edward's Tower in 1427, is much more bold, generally having four flanking turrets, one at each corner. Jesus College Gate (fig. 464) is the only exception to this and is, coincidentally, nearer to the Oxford type (particularly Wykeham's, and it has a similar alleyed approach). At Cambridge there is strong vertical emphasis, with the generally octagonal corner turrets often containing closets in their upper sections for the rooms in the neighbouring chambers, or staircases on the inner court side, as, for example, at St John's. All the gatehouses have sturdy wooden gates, of which the ones at Christ's are a fine intact medieval example (fig. 465).

There are 16 Cambridge gatehouses in this survey, with representative examples from many periods: among them the medieval structures of King Edward's Tower and Queens'; the very decorative Tudor facades of Jesus, Christ's and St John's; the nineteenth century neo-Gothic gates of King's and Corpus, both by William Wilkins, and neo-Tudor at Selwyn and Girton; the 'Queen Anne' Pfieffer Gatehouse at Newnham; and the modern gatehouses of Churchill and Robinson. The gatehouse of this last college is particularly appropriate to its overall castle-like composition, although its location within the college plan is very untraditional (see p.85).

Chronological summary:

Date	Gatehouse
1427	King Edwards Tower, Trinity College (moved & re-erected 1599-1600)
1441	Kings College Old Court (now part of the 'Old Schools')
1448	Queens' College
c.1490-1535	Trinity College, Great Gate
1500	Jesus College
1505	Christ's College
1511	St John's College
1596-97	Trinity College, Queens' Gate
1598-1602	St John's College, Shrewsbury Tower
1823-27	Corpus Christi
1824-28	King's College
1882	Selwyn College
1887	Girton College
1893	Newnham College, Pfieffer Gatehouse
1959-68	Churchill College
1977-80	Robinson College

458

459

460

460 King Edward's Tower, Trinity - the prototype Cambridge gatehouse of 1427-37 (see p. 92). **461** The gatehouse of the former King's College Old Court (see pp 116 & 190), begun 1441 but only half built, not completed until the nineteenth century by G.G. Scott (1864-67) and J.L. Pearson (1890).

462 Queens' College gatehouse of 1448. The gateway itself has an original lierne vault made from local clunch stone. **463** Great Gate at Trinity built between 1518-35 has, unlike other Cambridge gatehouses, a main entrance arch flanked by a smaller pedestrian entrance.

463

464

465

Five Tudor gatehouses: **464** Jesus College gatehouse of *c.*1500 (see p. 169). **465 & 466** Christ's and St John's gatehouses of 1505 and 1511. Both of these colleges were founded by Lady Margaret Beaufort, the very decorative gatehouses bearing her coat of arms (see also figs 277, 457). **467** The Shrewsbury Tower at St John's of 1598-1602, named after the Countess of Shrewsbury whose statue is in the niche above the arch. **468** The Queen's Gate in Trinity's Great Court of 1596-97, with a statue of Queen Elizabeth at its centre. **469 & 470** Two Gothic Revival gatehouses of the early nineteenth century, both by the prolific William Wilkins: **469** Corpus Christi's of 1823-27, and **470** King's (east side) of 1824-28 *(see also figs 28, 105, 287).*

466

467

468

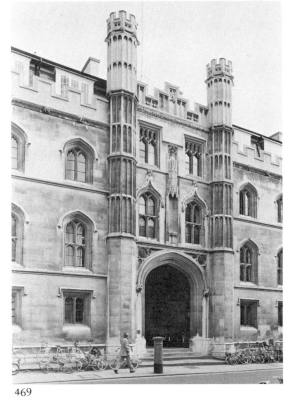

469

470

471

472   473

474

471 Selwyn College gatehouse to Grange Road, built as part of the founding buildings between 1882-95 by Sir Arthur Blomfield. A red brick neo-Tudor gatehouse with an asymmetrical facade, with only one octagonal corner turret and a pretty two-storey oriel window above the archway. **472** Girton College gatehouse to Huntingdon Road, of 1887 by Paul Waterhouse - continuing his father's red brick neo-Tudor tradition already established at the college (see p. 146). This very tall and slender gatehouse is, like Selwyn's, asymmetrically designed with only one octagonal corner turret. **473** The Pfeiffer gatehouse at Newnham College of 1893, by Basil Champneys. Here, at this ladies' college, a complete break with tradition has been made by employing the neo-Dutch or 'Queen Anne' style, as opposed to the Tudor Gothic of the older men's colleges (see p. 144) **474** The mini-monumental gateway of the modern Churchill College of 1959-68 by Richard Sheppard, Robson & Partners - a simplified version of the traditional gatehouse with a very strong two-dimensional feel created by its rather flat facade. **475** Robinson College gatehouse of 1977-80 by Gillespie, Kidd & Coia. This is possibly the most unfriendly and blatantly defensive college entrance in Cambridge: dauntingly dominating, fortress-like, approached by a brick ramp and surrounded by portcullis-like screens protecting windows and decorating blank walls - one almost feels there should be a bowman on top of the tower. Totally asymmetrical in its design and located in the corner of the front court this gatehouse is, like the rest of the college, rather unusual vis-a-vis traditional collegiate building and planning at Cambridge (see pp 84 & 163).

475

5 River Architecture: Boathouses and Bridges

This extremely attractive little group of buildings are all associated with the river. The nine bridges surveyed here are all located on the 'Backs', or middle section of the Cam, and the boathouses on the Lower River along the northern edge of Midsummer Common. On the whole, the boathouses are notable more for their playful and decorative elevations than for their architectural significance, as they are basically sheds fronted by often very elegant facades. However, several of the bridges are exceptional architecturally.

Boathouses

Rowing, probably the sport most commonly associated with 'Oxbridge', started at Cambridge in 1825, the first college boat club being established at St John's in the Michaelmas term of that year, and was soon followed by Trinity. The river must have been a peaceful place in those days compared to what it is today during the high points of the rowing calendar, at the end of the Lent and Summer terms. In 1826, there were only two racing boats on the Cam, but the new sport soon caught on, and by 1835 fifteen 'eights' competed in the summer races. Jesus College boat club was the next to be founded and was followed by Magdalene, Emmanuel, Christ's, Corpus Christi, and Peterhouse, between 1827-30; and in the early 1830s by Clare, King's, Pembroke, Trinity Hall, Downing, Sidney Sussex, and St Catherine's. However, this was not just a university sport and three town clubs were also founded: the Cambridge City Rowing Club in 1827, the Rob Roy Club in Victorian times, and the '99' Club in that year – 1899. The Cambridge University Boat Club's (CUBC) first official meeting took place in 1828 and led to the famous challenge being sent to Oxford on the 20th February 1829, for a race to take place on the Thames in or near London. Oxford accepted and the first Varsity Boat Race was rowed at Henley on the 10th June 1829, to become an annual event on the Putney to Mortlake course from 1856. The first women's club at Cambridge was founded by Newnham ladies in 1896.

Rowing in the early days was to many a way of life at Cambridge, and the social standing of a college to some extent depended on its position on the river after the annual May races. Today, it is still a very popular sport, although the heyday of Cambridge rowing, the 1880s and 1920s, has long gone, and with it the fervour and mythical stories associated with those times and famous names such as Steve Fairbairn and J.H.D. Goldie.

The original college boats were quite different to those of today, as they were comparatively heavy, clinker-built vessels without moving seats, and not just 'eights', but 'sixes' and even 'tens'. They were housed in commercial boatyards, which flourished on the northern edge of the river from Jesus Green to the far end of Midsummer Common. These yards built and stored the boats, and provided wharves on the banks

476 The combined boathouse of Magdalene and Queens' colleges. This large boathouse was built in 1934 by Banhams, one of the many commercial boatyards formerly located along the northern bank of the river. (Banhams at one time owned all of the riverside property from Victoria Bridge downstream to the Trinity boathouse). This particular building was originally used by several colleges, Magdalene being one of the first occupants. Queens' bought it from Banhams in the 1950s. It is one of the most attractive boathouses with its bright orange tiled roof, white-painted woodwork, and blue doors. **477** The typical riverside frontage on the 'lower river', with boathouses facing south across the river to Midsummer Common. Here, a college 'eight' returns home from an outing to Fen Ditton meadows, passing Clare and Pembroke boathouses en-route.

477

with hard slopes running down to the river's edge. By the end of the nineteenth century, most of the colleges had built, or started to build, their own boathouses, and today all of the commercial boatyards have disappeared.

The first college boathouse was Trinity's, built in 1872. This was re-built in 1896 and forms the basic fabric of the present structure, which was again re-built in 1935 (fig. 486). The CUBC boathouse (fig. 488), or 'Goldie' Boathouse (named after the famous oarsman who rowed for St John's and the university in the latter half of the nineteenth century), is the oldest surviving intact boathouse on the river, having been built in 1882. There are several other, very attractive, Victorian boathouses; such as those belonging to Jesus, Gonville & Caius, Emmanuel, Pembroke, Clare, Trinity Hall, and Christ's, which form the most notable collection of buildings on this stretch of the river. Both Jesus (fig. 489) and Caius (fig. 481) boathouses were architect designed, the former by Morley Horder, and the latter by W.M. Fawcett; both of whom carried out important buildings elsewhere in Cambridge. Other, pre-Second World War boathouses of note are Lady Margaret (St John's, fig. 479) Queens' and Magdalene (fig. 480), and St Catherine's (fig. 487). Only three boathouses have been built since 1945: the combined boat clubs of Corpus Christi and Sidney Sussex; the Cambridge City Rowing Club; and the also combined boat clubs of Selwyn, King's, Churchill, and the Leys School. Of these, the first, by David Roberts (fig. 491), is a most worthy 'modern' addition to these buildings of the lower river. In 1983 two boathouses burnt down — the Cambridge Rowing Association and the '99s. A new '99s clubhouse has been designed by the local architectural practice of Cound Page (fig. 485) and is, at the time of going to press, being constructed. A new CRA boathouse is apparently to follow.

The following photographs are organised in the sequence that occur along the river from Christ's in the north to Selwyn/King's/Churchill/Leys boathouse in the south.

479

480

478

481

482

483

484

485

487

486

478 Christ's College boathouse of 1887, next to the Victoria Avenue bridge of 1889. 479 Lady Margaret boathouse (St John's) of c.1905. 480 Magdalene and Queens' boathouse (see fig. 476). 481 Gonville & Caius boathouse of c.1880. 482 Peterhouse boathouse of 1928 which replaced a Victorian predecessor. 483 Fitzwilliam boathouse, built by Banhams and originally the home of Sidney Sussex boat club. 484 The wooden boathouse of the '99' Rowing Club destroyed by fire in 1983 and the Cambridge City Rowing Club. 485 The new '99's boathouse of 1984 by Cound Page Architects. 486 Trinity College boathouse of 1935. 487 St Catherine's boathouse, built in 1930.

488

491

489

490

488 The CUBC Goldie boathouse of 1882, the oldest intact clubhouse on the river, the first official meeting of the unversity club having taken place here in March 1883. **489** Jesus College boathouse of 1932 by Morley Horder, which replaced an apparently well designed and elegant Victorian structure destroyed by fire in September 1932. **490** Trinity Hall's Latham boathouse of 1905. **491** Corpus Christi/Sidney Sussex boathouse of 1958-59 by David Roberts. A steel-framed building divided horizontally into two distinct halves: the brick boatstore below and the glazed club/changing rooms above, flanked at either end by spiral staircases leading to the viewing balcony and upper rooms (see also fig. 133). **492** Clare boathouse of 1898-1900. **493** The decorative Pembroke boathouse of the 1890s (see also front cover) which originally had balconies running round the front and sides. **494** Emmanuel boathouse of c.1895, and a ladies coxless pair. **495** Downing boathouse of c.1895, formerly Waite's boatyard but with a new front added. **496** The asbestos clad 'warehouse' of the King's/Selwyn/Churchill/Leys School boatclubs.

493

494

495

496

Bridges

There are some fascinating bridges in Cambridge, appropriately in a town whose name means 'the crossing of the river'. The most interesting examples, nine in all, are to be found on the 'Backs', between, and including, the two road bridges of the Great, or Magdalene Bridge in the north, and Silver Street Bridge in the south.

Most of these nine bridges are successors to previous structures, all of which were, to begin with, made of wood and none of which have survived. At the outbreak of Civil War in 1643, Oliver Cromwell and his men destroyed all of the Cambridge bridges except the Great Bridge, in order to defend the town. The oldest today is Clare College Bridge (figs. 505 & 506), which was one of the earliest pieces of classical architecture to appear at Cambridge. Several eminent architects have been involved in the design of these nine bridges: Wren and Hawksmoor exerted a major influence on the form of the old bridge at St John's, built by the mason Robert Grumbold (whose father had built much of Clare College and its bridge some 70 years earlier); the local and very prolific architect James Essex designed the Trinity Bridge; the equally active William Wilkins the King's Bridge; Henry Hutchinson, the much admired 'Bridge of Sighs' at St John's, (built at the same time as Rickman & Hutchinson's New Court, the bridge providing the connection with the college's older courts across the river); and Sir Edwin Lutyens the Silver Street Bridge.

There is also a considerable diversity of style in these structures – ranging from the classical elegance of Clare Bridge; the almost oriental nature of Queens' Mathematical Bridge; the Gothic pinnacles and tracery of the Bridge of Sighs; the Victorian, cast-iron Great Bridge; and the most recent 80-foot, pre-cast concrete span of Garret Hostel bridge. By far the best way to see them all is to hire a punt at either the north or south end of the 'Backs', and to float up- or downstream underneath them. The following photographs are arranged in order from north to south.

497

498

499

500

501

497 College bridges on the Backs: King's is in the foreground with Clare and Trinity beyond *(see also figs: 63,64,67,69).*　**498** The bridge from which Cambridge takes its name - the cast-iron Great, or Magdalene Bridge of 1823, by Arthur Browne, replaced a stone bridge of 1754 which in turn superseded generations of wooden bridges. It is one of the earliest examples in Britain of the three-pin arch arrangement which allows for movement within the structure under load.　**499** Magdalene Bridge during repairs in 1982 showing the ribbed cast-iron structure joined together by yokes and ties.　**500** St John's College Bridge of Sighs of 1831 by Henry Hutchinson *(see also fig. 67 & p. 131).*　**501** St John's Old Bridge of 1709-12 by Robert Grumbold.

502

502 Trinity College Bridge of 1764-65 by James Essex. This replaced a previous stone bridge of 1651-52, materials from which were used in the new sub-structure with Portland and Ketton Stone ashlar above water level. **503 & 504** Garret Hostel Bridge (north and south views) of 1960 by T.G. Morgan, which replaced a cast-iron Tudor Gothic bridge of 1835-37 by Chadwell Milne. A unique modern structure for the very traditioal Backs and '. . . one of Cambridge's best post-war works of architecture' (Booth & Taylor). It is a concrete portal frame which has a clear span of 80 feet: the concrete contains an attractive aggregate of Cornish granite which has been exposed by pneumatic hammering, the upper deck is paved with York Stone, and the handrails are of satin-polished bronze. **505 & 506** Clare College Bridge of 1638-40 by Thomas Grumbold - built of Ketton stone ashlar at the same time as the college's east range (see p. 100). This very elegant bridge was one of the earliest classical structures at Cambridge and is the oldest surviving bridge over the Cam.

503

504

505

506

507

508

509

510

507 King's College bridge from the south-west with the Chapel beyond *(see also fig. 497)*. The location of the previous bridge at King's was about 45 yards north of the present bridge on axis with the centre of Gibbs Building to the east. The first bridge was constructed sometime before 1472 and was rebuilt several times, the last in 1627 by George Thompson. That bridge survived until 1818 when it was decided to build a new one to the south, which was designed by William Wilkins and built in 1819-20, a few years before his major works at the college (see p. 116). The bridge is built of Fifeshire stone

ashlar. **508 & 509** Queens' College Bridge or, as it is commonly known, the Mathematical Bridge (508 shows the bridge during a May Ball covered with a temporary white awning). This intriguing structure was designed in 1749 by an undergraduate, W. Etheridge, and constructed in 1749-50 by James Essex. It has since been rebuilt twice, in 1867 and 1902. It is interesting to note that Etheridge had visited China while an undergraduate, as the bridge has a strong Oriental flavour to it. It is also interesting that a certain James Essex was involved with one of the former Garret Hostel bridges in the seven-

teenth century (presumably the father or grandfather of the famous James Essex, born 1722) which was also nicknamed the 'Mathematical' Bridge because of its very similar structure, as shown in Leach's engraving of 1785 when that bridge was still in existence. **510** Silver Street Bridge of 1958-59 to a design of 1932 by Sir Edwin Lutyens. There was a bridge here as early as the fourteenth century and there have been many 'editions' since. The present structure, which replaced a cast-iron bridge of 1843, is of concrete faced with Portland stone and sits on a raft foundation.

6 University Buildings

Origin of the Universities

The word university comes from the Latin *universitas,* which, translated from Medieval Latin, means any collective body of men. The adoption of the word to refer specifically to an academic body came about in medieval times, and means a collection of scholars and students pursuing higher branches of learning. The degree awarded by a university to its graduates was regarded as a licence to teach - hence the term licenciate - and awarded with it was the privilege of *ubique docendi,* permission to teach at any university in Christendom. In medieval times the more common term for a group, or guild, of teachers, was *Studium Generale,* and Cambridge was officially proclaimed such in a Papal Bull issued by Pope John XXII in 1318, although the university itself was established well before that date.

The university movement started in the twelfth and thirteenth centuries, basically in response to the unprecedented growth of organised communities. Towns and cities had dramatically increased in size and population, with a consequent flourishing of commerce, and with this came the requirement for learned and professional men to co-ordinate the surge in activity and communication, and that the teaching of reading, writing and arithmetic should be more widely available. Until this time, education had taken place within the ecclesiastical system of cathedral and monastic schools, but these soon proved inadequate for the study of such secular and practical subjects as medicine and civil law. The universities gradually became the new centres of learning.

The earliest universities originated in Italy, at Salerno and Bologna, and were followed by Paris which soon became the intellectual centre of Europe. It was from Parisian origins that Oxford developed as the first British university, the earliest organised teaching taking place in about 1133 when Robert Pulleyn, the Parisian academic, is thought to have taught there. Later, in around 1167, a larger group of scholars from Paris went to Oxford and a *Studium Generale* began to take shape. By the beginning of the following century the university was well organised on the model of Paris, but was experiencing severe teething problems in its relationship with the townspeople. A riot between 'Town and Gown' in 1209 led to the university receiving its first royal charter of privilege. The Oxford riots of 1209 also resulted, indirectly, in the formation of a university at Cambridge.

Legend attributes the founding of Cambridge University to Cantaber, a mythical Spanish Prince, or to the Anglo Saxon Sigebert, King of the East Angles in the seventh century; but, in fact, the earliest authentic date at which Cambridge is described as a centre of learning is 1209 when, as a result of the riots in Oxford, a group of scholars fled from there and established themselves at Cambridge. In 1229 a further group of students left Paris, under similar circumstances, and also migrated to Cambridge. It was at this date that the university and its chancellor were legally recognised. As at Oxford and Paris the university at Cambridge had to struggle to establish its independence both from the indigenous community and the local governing diocese of Ely. No other English universities were established for over six hundred years after the founding of Oxford and Cambridge, until Durham and London in the first half of the nineteenth century, though in Scotland, St Andrew's, Glasgow and Aberdeen Universities were founded in the fifteenth century, Edinburgh in the late sixteenth century, and at the same time, Dublin University in Ireland. Today there are fifty universities in the British Isles. In 1919 the University Grants Committee was formed to administer the allocation of public money to the universities, and thereafter this organisation controlled the establishment of new foundations.

The growth of the university at Cambridge

Why, in the early thirteenth century, a university was formed in a little market town on the edge of the desolate East Anglian fens, and why scholars decided to settle in Cambridge, is difficult to ascertain, but perhaps it was its very isolation that was its main attraction as it appears initially to have been a harbour for academic refugees from Oxford and Paris. However, it soon started to develop into one of the most important European universities, the traditional competition between Oxford and Cambridge starting at a very early stage. Today, Cambridge without a university is impossible to imagine, as the city is, in effect, a campus, with both 'Town' and 'Gown' now living in harmony.

The dominating, physical presence of the *university,* as opposed to the colleges, came about in a relatively short period, roughly in the last 150 years, as before the nineteenth century there were few university buildings in Cambridge. This survey is of the buildings that comprise the university as an individual entity. The colleges and the university are, of course, inseperably linked, but the university buildings have developed in response to different functions and responsibilities.

511 The centre of university ceremonial - the east elevation of the Senate House to Trinity Street (E4) with the Old Schools' east range beyond *(see also front cover & figs 19, 513, 520, 521).* In 1722 the London-based architect James Gibbs proposed a scheme for a three-sided court to house university offices, a library and Senate house (see p. 190). Only the Senate House was built, between 1722-30, at a cost of £13,000. This is one of Gibbs's most important works designed in '. . . a most elegant blend of the English Wren tradition with the new Palladianism . . . and with what Gibbs in his youth had seen in the Rome of about 1700.' (Pevsner). The building is faced with Portland stone. Inside, the reredos and other woodwork is by the elder James Essex and the coffered ceiling by Atari and Bagutti. The iron railings around the building date from 1730 and are amongst the earliest in the country.

The function of the university

The university at Cambridge has three roles: it is the body that awards degrees; it shares the teaching role with the colleges; and it enforces its jurisdiction over its members. It was the increase in the teaching role of the university in the latter half of the nineteenth century which led to the majority of its buildings, now so prevalent in and around the city.

The medieval curriculum at Cambridge university consisted of the 'trivium' and 'quadrivium', undertaken by students of 14 or 15. The trivium was the first three years of study, equivalent to the present day Bachelor's degree, and consisted of a year of grammar, a year of rhetoric (Latin style), and a year of logic. The quadrivium was the succeeding four years and consisted of the study of arithmetic, geometry, music (the science of harmonies), and astronomy, at the end of which the Master's degree was awarded. If the student wished to remain at the university, he then studied theology, achieving his doctorate after about a further ten years. Thus, in medieval times a PhD could take from 17 years to achieve, whereas today a bright scholar at Cambridge can do so in a minimum of six years. For the teaching of these subjects, no special university buildings were required, as the teachers, or 'clerks' as they were often termed, simply had classrooms in their own houses or in rented accommodation.

The preparation for the examinations was undertaken by teachers in the individual colleges or by freelance tutors. During the sixteenth century the university began to establish professorships as endowed teaching posts, and in so doing started to take a more active role in the curriculum. From this point on, the number of subjects taught in the university slowly began to increase, reaching its zenith in the mid nineteenth century. By this time, the choice of subjects offered at Cambridge was so varied that an inter-collegiate supervisions system of teaching developed, as the teaching fellows at the individual colleges could not cope with the large number of subjects now demanded (see chapter 3). Thus, in order to avoid specialisation (ie colleges housing only lawyers, or entirely medics, or philosophers, engineers or mathematicians etc) the system of interchange evolved. In the same way, and particularly in the nineteenth century, with the massive growth of practical subjects such as the experimental natural sciences, the individual colleges could not afford to provide the laboratories and lecture theatres needed solely for their own students. This led to the university becoming actively involved as a teaching body, as its responsibility was now to provide all of the necessary facilities and to co-ordinate the teaching of these new subjects, the relationship between the university and the colleges becoming much closer in the process.

The colleges and the university have their own individual statutes, and although the colleges are not administered by the university they are subject to its jurisdiction. The colleges do, however, have two direct responsibilities to the university: they contribute to its income in proportion to their individual wealth, and they are obliged to reserve a number of fellowships for university professors. This is one of the most important links between the two bodies in that almost all university teachers, ie Professors, Lecturers, Readers, or Demonstrators, collectively termed Dons, hold college fellowships (the colleges also contain a number of non-teaching research fellows who may, however, tutor at the supervisions level). In their university role the Dons are linked to faculties or departments, each concerned with its own subject and each responsible for the organisation and setting of its individual curriculum and examinations. The head of the university is the Chancellor, who is often a member of the Royal family, an eminent Civil Servant or Politician (at present it is HRH Prince Philip, Duke of Edinburgh). However, the role of the Chancellor is mainly that of a figurehead, and during his customary absence the active head is the Vice-Chancellor, who is elected for a two year period from amongst the Masters of the colleges. He is the head of the Council of the Senate, the governing body of the university, of which the General Board of Studies is the most influential committee as it controls both teaching and research. The Regent House, composed of all MAs resident in Cambridge, can oppose decisions of the Senate Council, and if more than ten of its members are agreed in their opposition then a ballot is forced. This democratic constitution is very similar to that of Oxford. News of events and other university happenings are published weekly in the official journal the *Reporter*.

Other university posts are also filled by college fellows; such as that of the Registrar, who is responsible for supervising the clerical work of the university and who edits its official publications, or the university Librarian. Until fairly recently, probably the most widely recognisable of all university officers were the Proctors, who are responsible for enforcing university law. Helped by their Pro-Proctors and Deputies they would patrol the streets of Cambridge every night during term, with their belligerent bowler or top-hatted assistants, or 'bull-dogs' as they were

512

known, on the look-out for misbehaving undergraduates, or simply those out after dark without their gowns – which in the past constituted an offence.

The first university buildings and modern expansion

It was not until the latter half of the fourteenth century that the first purpose-built university building was begun, the Divinity School (fig. 512). This was completed by 1400 and was followed by the Schools of Law and Arts and the old University Library, all completed by 1475 and forming the quadrangle known today as the 'Old Schools' (fig. 513). By this time a number of colleges were well established, there were in fact thirteen by 1475 (see p. 87), and their presence was beginning to dominate the town. No other purpose-built university buildings were then erected until James Gibbs built the Senate House, next door to the Old Schools, in 1722-30, and Stephen Wright then replaced the Old Schools' east range with a new building in 1754-58. C.R. Cockerell added an extension to the Library, the north range of the Schools, in 1837-42. In the early nineteenth century, the Old Court of King's College, immediately next door to the Old Schools, was sold to the university, thus becoming part of the precinct. So, over a period of more than 400 years, the only area of university development was in this vicinity to the north of King's College.

As a result of the increased teaching activity of the university in the nineteenth century, its buildings have become almost as numerous as those of the colleges. Architecturally, the result of later nineteenth and early twentieth century expansion was vast in quantity but, on the whole, poor in quality. The main area of development at that time was to the north and south of Pembroke and Downing Streets; the New Museums site and the Downing site respectively. The majority of post-war development has taken place in the southern area of the town around Trumpington Street and Lensfield Road, and more recently to the west of the river on the Sidgwick Avenue site and to the south of Madingley Road. The modern pattern of university and college expansion in Cambridge has been to abandon the packed centre and to build in the more spacious areas on the west side of the city.

There is no single building, or single group of buildings, at Cambridge that can be referred to as 'the University'. The buildings that comprise the university; its faculties and laboratories, administrative and ceremonial buildings, and its library, are dispersed throughout the city and around its perimeter. Excluding the colleges, the buildings associated directly with the university can be divided into three areas:

1. University buildings in the city centre

2. University buildings in the southern area of the city

3. University buildings west of the river

512 The oldest university buildings at Cambridge - the north and west sides of Cobble Court, the Old Schools (E4). Built c.1350-1400, the first completed building for university teaching was, as one might expect, the Divinity School, on the ground floor of the north range of this small court, with the original Senate House (Regent House) and a chapel above (the upper floor is now the University Combination Room). The north range stood alone for several years but in c.1430-1454 was joined by the (former) School of Canon Law with a library above. Both buildings are of brick and rubble construction, ashlar-faced in places, with dressings of Barnack and Portland stone. The Divinity School has unusual perpendicular windows with very straight-sided arches. The west range was much altered by James Essex in 1732; notably the depressed round-headed arches of the windows (see also fig. 515). **513** The Old Schools precinct from above: the Senate House and its lawn are in the foreground; the classical eighteenth-century front of the Old Schools' medieval Cobble Court, with the nineteenth-century University Library to its north; and beyond is the former King's College Old Court which was sold to the University in the nineteenth century (see p. 116). King's College Chapel is to the south, the Old Court of Clare to the west, and, in the far distance, the tower of the modern University Library.

513

1. University Buildings in the City Centre

Old Schools precinct and the Senate House (E4)

This group of buildings is the heart of the university, forming its ceremonial and administrative centre. The original court of the Old Schools (figs 514 & 512) initially contained all that was necessary for the running of the university; a meeting place for the Senate, the Registry and its offices, a library, and lecture rooms for all of the professors of the different faculties. However, with the increased activity of the university in the nineteenth and twentieth centuries more buildings were required and today this precinct forms only a small, though very important, part of the whole.

During the eighteenth century various schemes were proposed by a number of architects to expand the original court, resulting in the building of the Senate House and the re-building of the Schools' east range. With the purchase of the Old Court of King's College by the university in 1829, the extra space gained temporarily halted the need for expansion, the new library range being added later. The older, western half of the site consists of two enclosed courts; the Old Schools Court (known as 'Cobble Court') and the Old Court of King's, both having on their northern side the old University Library. In the eastern half of the site is the Senate House and its 'Yard', that is the area of grass to its south enclosed by low walls and iron railings. The medieval Cobble and King's Old Courts have, unfortunately, undergone extensive alterations; namely the interior re-modelling of Cobble Court by Murray Easton in 1935; and the virtual rebuilding of King's Old Court by Sir George Gilbert Scott in 1862-67 and J.L. Pearson in 1890 although leaving the splendid gatehouse in the west range intact (see fig. 461).

In 1278, a strip of land was given to the university by a doctor, Nigel de Thornton, in the area of what is now Senate House Passage and Caius Court of Gonville & Caius College. In the 1350s the first building on the site was begun, the Divinity School, as the north range of Cobble Court (see fig. 512), with the original Senate, or Regent House, above it being completed by 1400. It was followed in 1430-57 by the west range (fig. 515), then containing the School of Canon Law with the Library above. The brick south range (fig. 515) was then built between 1457-70, housing the School of Civil Law with the Lesser Library above. The east range (now demolished) was the last to be built in 1470-73, and contained the Consistory and Doctors' Vestry, above which was another part of the library. It was during the building of the west range that Henry VI started work on the first court of King's College in 1441. A few years later Henry obtained the enlarged site he wanted and began to develop his foundation to the south, away from the original court that was to be sold off to the university nearly 400 years later (figs 516–518), and now containing entirely administrative offices.

The eighteenth century was a very active period with regard to ideas for the development of this central city site. Firstly, Nicholas Hawksmoor put forward fascinating plans for this whole area, based on a classical forum, as part of his larger scheme for the whole city centre, but nothing came of it (see p. 30). Then, in 1722, James Gibbs submitted a scheme for a three-sided court immediately to the east of the Schools. This court was to be open towards the east so that it did not obstruct the view of King's College Chapel from the street, and was to contain a Royal Library as its east range (modelled on Wren's Trinity College Library, with an open undercroft below the library itself, to be entered by large staircases at the north and south ends); a Senate House as its north range; and an identical south range housing the Registry and Consistory below with the University Printing House above. Only the Senate House (fig. 520 & see 511) was built, between 1722-30. The plan is a parallelogram, 100 x 50 feet, and the building is designed in a Classical Baroque style, a mixture of Wren, Palladio and Rome, where Gibbs had spent several years training under Carlo Fontana. From the external modelling of the building one anticipates a complex interior, suggested by the projection of the three central bays on the south side, and by the two-storeyed arrangement of the windows, but, in fact, the interior is one large unbroken space, entered at the east end via an ante-room, and surrounded on three sides at first floor level by a continuous gallery.

In 1754-58 Stephen Wright rebuilt the east range of the Schools (fig. 521). Once again this was only one side of a proposed three-sided plan, similar to Gibbs's idea, and forms what Gibbs had intended to be the Royal Library and, indeed, has the open undercroft proposed in his scheme. It is an attractive, Palladian style building, and is an appropriate neighbour to the Senate House. A decade or so after this, the old town buildings to the south of the Senate House were demolished to create a clear north-south vista along King's Parade terminating at the north end in the Senate House (see fig. 42).

The next requirement was for improved and enlarged library facilities. Plans were submitted by Robert Adam in 1784 but nothing materialised. In the late 1820s the university held a competition between four architectural practices to decide who should design the library: Rickman & Hutchinson, William Wilkins, a Mr Burton and Charles Robert Cockerell, with Cockerell winning the job. His scheme, however, covered virtually the whole area of the two medieval courts, and it was not until he had amended and re-submitted his plans that the existing building evolved as, once again, only one side of a more ambitious proposal. The (old) University Library (fig. 519 & see 101) was built between 1837-42.

Perhaps it is the mixture of medieval and classical architecture, combined with an area of grass and the large horse-chestnut tree fronting the Senate House, that makes this the most attractive of all the university precincts in Cambridge. The area around the Senate House is one of the most pleasant to pass through, and in which to linger, in the whole city, this being at least partly due to its attractive approaches: from King's Parade in the south, Trinity Street in the north, the market place in the east, or from the Backs in the west.

514

515

516

517

518

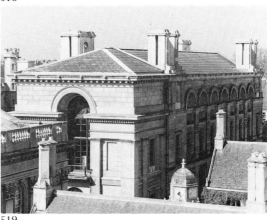

519

520

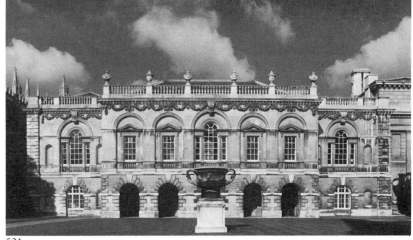

521

514 The north and east sides of Cobble Court: the late fourteenth century Divinity School and the mid-eighteenth century east range. 515 The west elevation of Cobble Court, with the old University Library to its north. 516 The north-west corner of the former King's Old Court, rebuilt in the nineteenth century. 517 King's Old Court from the south-west. 518 The south front of King's Old Court and Cobble Court with Great St Mary's church beyond. 519 The former University Library (now the Squire Law Library), of 1837-42, by C.R. Cockerell *(see also fig. 101)*. 520 The Senate House, south elevation *(see fig. 511)*. 521 The east range of Cobble Court, of 1754-58, by Stephen Wright.

The Union Society and the Selwyn Divinity School (F3)

It is appropriate to look at these two buildings together as they have much in common. They are not dissimilar in their outward appearance, particularly in the use of materials — red brick with stone dressings — and were built within a few years of each other, the Union Society in 1866, the Divinity School in 1877-79, by two interesting Victorian architects who also built extensively elsewhere in Cambridge; Alfred Waterhouse and Basil Champneys.

The Union Society (fig. 522) was the first Cambridge building by the young Waterhouse whose prolific output, here and elsewhere, is recognisable by his use of richly coloured terracotta and red brick, employed in a mixture of styles from Romanesque and Gothic to French Renaissance.

The Selwyn Divinity School (fig. 523) by Champneys is particularly interesting when compared with his masterpiece, Newnham College, begun a few years earlier, and which had brought a breath of fresh air to Cambridge architecture. At Newnham, Champneys succeeded in introducing a style appropriate to these new female colleges, as opposed to simply re-using the traditional styles associated with the men's foundations. In contrast the Divinity School is, in Champneys own words, in an 'English Gothic [style] of the early part of the sixteenth century...', very different to his 'modern' treatment of Newnham, for which he employed the fashionable 'Queen Anne' style. He no doubt considered the ecclesiastical Gothic more appropriate for a School of Divinity. Champneys estimated that the building would cost £11,523, in fact it cost £15,074.12s.7d.

522   523

2. University Buildings in the southern area of the City

New Museums Site and the Downing Site (F4/5 & F/G5)

With the increase in the teaching of the sciences at Cambridge during the nineteenth century, and particularly the Natural Sciences, the university had to acquire extra space to cater for the needs of these laboratory-requiring subjects. This resulted in these two large sites, just south of the city centre and divided only by Pembroke and Downing Street, being developed in the nineteenth and early twentieth centuries.

The Natural Sciences course became part of the university curriculum in 1848, and a few years later development began on the north side of Pembroke Street to house the new faculties. At that time only about a half of the present area of the site was university property, consisting of the original Botanic Garden, established there on five acres of land in 1760. The site was gradually enlarged, building later spread southward and the Botanic Garden relocated to its present site around 1852. In 1896 the university purchased two acres of land from Downing College, to the south of Downing Street. In the following year more land was acquired from Downing, and a further 6½ acres in 1902, this comprising the whole of the so-called 'Downing Site'.

The lack of organisation on both these sites has resulted in a number of oversized structures sited too close together, forming a depressing and harsh environment. Bricks and mortar, concrete and tarmac, here predominate and overwhelm. The northern site, in particular, is disorganised, and the southern site, although on a predetermined plan clearly trying to imitate the college-type atmosphere, is not much better.

The majority of the New Museums Site buildings were constructed between 1863-1914, and the Downing Site buildings between 1904-39. Clearly, a great opportunity has been missed here to create something worthy of the pioneering work that has been carried out in these buildings, where X-rays and electrons were given birth, and where such men as Rayleigh, Thomson, Rutherford, and Cockcroft were rewarded with numerous Nobel prizes for their discoveries in the famous Cavendish Laboratories. As Booth & Taylor lamented in the 1960s 'Those of us who still adhere to that passionate discovery of English architectural philosophers a century ago, that the quality of buildings is closely related to the quality of thought and organisation, even of morality, of the society which produces them, are floored completely by the dark and sordid muddle which is the physical expression of Thomson, Rutherford and Cockcroft. Why did Cambridge science, or even Cambridge physics by itself, not reflect in its labs and lecture theatres some of the lucid passion of experiment that possessed those for whom they were built?...'[16]

522 The Union Society, off Bridge Street, of 1866 by Alfred Waterhouse.
523 Selwyn Divinity School, St John's Street, of 1878-79 by Basil Champneys.

524

525

526

528

529

524-527 Four New Museums Site Buildings. **524** The neo-Tudor Gothic front of the old Cavendish Laboratory, Free School Lane, of 1874 by W.M. Fawcett. **525** The former Engineering Department, of 1893-94, by W.C. Marshall. **526** The Zoology Laboratory, 1900-04, by E.S. Prior. **527** The new Department of Zoology, built in the late sixties by Sir Philip Dowson of Arup Associates. **528** The Sidgwick Museum of Geology, of 1904-11, by Sir T.G. Jackson. **529** The School of Agriculture, of 1909-10, by Arnold Mitchell. **530** The Department of Pathology, of 1927, by Edward Warren. **531** The Department of Biochemistry extension of 1962-63, by Hammett & Norton: '. . . probably the best building on the whole site' (Pevsner).

530

531

Trumpington Street and Hills Road Area

The Pitt Building, Trumpington Street (E5)

Cambridge University Press moved out of this area to their extensive new site on the southern edge of the city in the 1960s but retained the Pitt Building (fig. 532) as central showrooms and office space. Designed by Edward Blore and built in 1831-33, it is in the Tudor Gothic style and consists of a central church-like tower flanked by two three-storey ranges to north and south (stone-faced to the street front and sides, but brick on the rear). In 1934-37 Murray Easton 'modernised' the exterior by altering the fenestration and removing the hood-moulds above the windows in the wings, changing the character of the building apart from the central tower. Changes to the interior were made in 1964-65, when Lyster & Grillet adapted it to its present form. The building is named after William Pitt the Younger (1759-1806), the British Prime Minister who was educated at Pembroke College, Cambridge, opposite, the money for its construction having been donated by the committee of the London Pitt Club in 1824.

The University Centre, Granta Place (E5)

Designed by Howell, Killick, Partridge & Amis and built between 1964-67 (fig. 533), this was the first major building at Cambridge by this practice and some of their characteristic motifs, such as canted forms and chamfered surfaces, are evident here, as in some of their later buildings (eg at Darwin and Sidney Sussex Colleges). The central feature of this four-storey, concrete-framed building is a double-storey cafeteria accessible from the second floor, with an exciting open pyramidal timber roof. Around the cafeteria are a number of common-rooms, an admirable feature of which is the way they can be sub-divided by sliding screens to provide a variety of smaller spaces.

Old Addenbrookes Hospital, Trumpington Street (F5/6)

John Addenbrooke died in 1719 leaving £4500 for the founding of a hospital. The land was purchased in 1728 and the original building constructed in 1740, part of which survives but is embedded within later accretions. From 1825 through to the 1860s there were numerous additions, the most extensive taking place under the direction of Matthew Digby Wyatt. Pevsner comments of Wyatt's work 'a depressing example of its date, with many rather dry, thin motifs, Italian as well as Tudor, assembled without any tension or accentuation...' There were further additions made during the 1920s.

School of Architecture Extension and Geodesic Dome (F6)

The Faculty of Architecture and History of Art is housed within the northern half of Scroope Terrace (built 1839) at the southern end of Trumpington Street. The School Extension (figs 535 & 536) was built in 1958-59 for the new Professor, Sir Leslie Martin, and was designed by his partner Colin St John Wilson (the present Professor) in association with Alex Hardy, both of whom were lecturers in the Department at the time. In this respect it was a real 'in house' job as the students at the School carried out the surveys and working drawings.

This small building is an excellent example of the modular architecture of this era, employing mathematical relationships developed for mass-produced schools and housing. It could be classified as 'architects' architecture' as its aesthetic values were, at that time, probably very unappealing to the man in the street. Booth & Taylor sum this up perfectly 'To the architect this building exudes geometric refinement. He will study the golden section, the modular relationships of shelf to blackboard to window. He will rejoice over the purity of the structure. The layman sees almost exactly the opposite: the deliberate (and very attractive) crudity of the massive brickwork, the rough-shuttered concrete and the self-consciously massive pulpit, which juts out into the lecture room and turns out to be merely a table for the slide projector.'[17]

Located to the south of the extension is a Buckminster Fuller-type geodesic dome (fig. 535).[18] This was built in 1958-62 and designed by David Croghan, another lecturer at the School. It is used for teaching purposes and research into the levels of daylight in buildings with the use of models. Based on Archimedes' truncated icosahedron, it is constructed of two surfaces: an outer skin of anodized aluminium, and an inner skin of translucent plastic. Between these two skins are 184 fluorescent lamps which provide the light source which is diffused through the inner plastic layer, creating an artificial 'sky' for use in experiments. The dome was also built by students at the School.

Towering above Scroope Terrace is the **Engineering Department** (fig. 537), and further to the south east, in Lensfield Road, the **Department of Chemistry** (fig. 538), both designed by Easton & Robertson, Cusdin, Preston & Smith. Also in Lensfield Road is the **Scott Polar Research Institute** (fig. 539), built in 1933-34 and designed by Sir Herbert Baker, its inspiration being largely geographical as, in the architects own words, 'The front is composed of two large arches suggesting the two poles. Small halls lie behind the arches vaulted with domes of the same arc as the polar regions of the globe'.

The **Local Examinations Syndicate** (fig. 540) in Hills Road, of 1960-64, was designed by Robert Matthew, Johnson-Marshall & Partners, and planned on a modular building system to allow for the flexible partitioning of the internal space. Finally, the **University Health Centre, Fenners** (fig. 541), of 1950-51 in Gresham Road, was designed by J.M. Macgregor and David Roberts. The building is notable for two reasons: it was one of the earliest non-traditional buildings in Cambridge after the war, and it was the first Cambridge building by the prolific David Roberts.

532 The Pitt Building, 1931-33, by Edward Blore. **533** The University Centre, 1964-67, by Howell, Killick, Partridge & Amis. **534** The recently vacated Old Addenbrooke's Hospital. **535** The School of Architecture extension and geodesic dome. **536** The Lecture Hall, School of Architecture. **537** The Department of Engineering (F6), 1949-52, by Murray Easton. **538** The Department of Chemistry (G6), 1953-60, also by Easton. **539** The Scott Polar Research Institute (G6), 1933-34, by Sir Herbert Baker. **540** Local Examination Syndicate, Hills Road. **541** The University Health Centre, Fenners, 1951, by Macgregor & Roberts.

534

538

535

532

536

539

540

533

537

541

The Fitzwilliam Museum, Trumpington Street (F5/6)

In his will, dated 18 August 1815, Richard, 7th Viscount Fitzwilliam of Merrion, bequeathed to Cambridge University his collection of paintings and etchings, together with his library, which contained 10,000 books and a collection of medieval illuminated manuscripts, and £100,000 worth of New South Sea Annuities. The income from the investment was to provide a building in which to house his collection, to support its upkeep and to purchase further works of art. He died in 1816 and the collection travelled to Cambridge, though the building to house it was not to be ready for over thirty years, and not fully completed until 1875.

A syndicate was formed by the university Senate to administer the bequest, as was the normal procedure, and to execute the building. The delay in this was caused by difficulties in choosing an appropriate site and, in fact, ten were chosen between 1816-21. A site was finally acquired from Peterhouse in 1823, but because of existing leases did not become wholly free for building until 1840. In 1834 the syndicate advertised the project in the national newspapers as an open competition, and invited architects to put forward plans and estimates. 36 schemes were submitted by 27 architects, including Basevi, Rickman, Salvin and Wilkins. The designs were exhibited, the members of the Senate voted, and Basevi's scheme won by an overwhelming majority.

George Basevi was one of the most renowned pupils of Sir John Soane. After leaving Soane's office in 1813, he entered the Academy School, and then in 1816 set out to study in Italy and Greece, where he spent the next three years. His design for the Fitzwilliam is thought to have been inspired partly by the remains of a Roman building discovered at Brescia in 1820. Basevi was trained and well versed in the classical tradition, and his most successful buildings are in a Graeco-Roman style. Tragically, at the age of 51, Basevi fell to his death while inspecting the west tower of Ely Cathedral.

Building started on the Museum in 1837 and by 1841 most of the major work was completed. In 1844 Basevi was authorised to proceed with the interior, but met his death at Ely before he could do so. C.R. Cockerell, who had recently completed the new University Library, was appointed to continue the work, and in 1846 submitted designs for the completion of the entrance hall and staircases which Basevi had never finished. Cockerell introduced a central lantern to light the hall in place of the three domes Basevi had intended, and also changed the staircase arrangement. The work was carried out in 1846-47. Work was then suspended due to lack of funds. However, the library and galleries were far enough advanced to receive the collection, which finally moved in in 1848. In 1870, when sufficient funds had been accumulated, E.M. Barry was appointed architect and completed the building between 1871-75.

Much has since been added to the south of Basevi's original building: in 1924 the Marlay Galleries were built on two floors as a south wing; the Courtauld Galleries followed in 1931, and the Henderson Galleries and the Charrington Print Room in 1936. All these extensions were built by Dunbar Smith and C.C. Brewer. In 1959 the Graham Robertson Room was opened and two more extensions added, in 1966 and 1975, the latter (fig. 543) containing the museum shop below with the Adeane Gallery for special exhibitions above. These most recent additions were designed by David Roberts.

543

542 The main entrance front of the Fitzwilliam Museum of 1837-41 by George Basevi. **543** The museum shop and Adeane Gallery of 1975 by Roberts & Clarke.

542

The Botanic Garden, Trumpington Road

The University Botanic Garden, off Trumpington Road, has two functions: primarily it is part of the Botany School, located about a mile away on the Downing site, for which it provides practical facilities for teaching and research; but it also serves as an unusual public park as it contains a fascinating collection of trees, shrubs, and other flora from all over the world.

The garden was first established between 1760-63 on a five-acre site north of Pembroke Street and in the area now known as the New Museums Site, today covered in concrete. It was founded there by Dr Richard Walker, the Vice-Master of Trinity, and was initially known as the 'Walkerian Botanic Garden'. In 1825 J.S. Henslow, the Professor of Botany (Charles Darwin's teacher), realized the need for expansion, and in 1831 the present forty-acre site was purchased and the garden moved there between 1846-52.

There are four buildings of interest here. Two are picturesque nineteenth century lodges: the small neo-Gothic Brooklands Lodge next to Hobson's Brook in the south-west corner of the site built some time before 1830, and the former Curator's House (now the garden offices) in the north-west corner towards Bateman Street, designed by W.M. Fawcett and built soon after 1830. There is also the row of teak-framed glasshouses along the northern edge of the garden (fig. 544 & see 60), first built in 1888-91 but rebuilt in 1932-33. The most important

building architecturally, however, is Cory Lodge (fig. 545) of 1924. It was designed by M.H. Baillie-Scott, one of the most competent English domestic architects in practice around the turn of the century, who also built several other beautiful houses in Cambridge (see fig. 119). Pevsner described Cory Lodge as 'a rare example of what perfection the neo-Georgian or neo-Colonial style could attain in the hands of an exceptionally sensitive architect...'

Cambridge University Press, Shaftesbury Road

CUP moved out to their extensive site in Shaftesbury Road in the early 1960s. The Press had previously been located in the city centre on a confined site in the Mill Lane/Silver Street area, and when they moved they kept the Pitt Building as a central showroom and office (see fig. 532). The new buildings were constructed between 1961-63 and the architects were Beard, Bennett, Wilkins & Partners.

The buildings are planned around a central spine, at the south end of which is the Printing House (fig. 546). This is an enormous single-storey structure which has the very characteristic feature of a steel-ribbed roof, curved in two directions. A massive internal span of 150 ft (46 m) provided by longitudinal ridge girders, allows large open spaces or smaller working areas, both necessary in a printing workshop. The most recent addition to the site is the large Edinburgh Building (fig. 547) designed by S.J. Currin of International Design and Construction, and built in 1979-80.

544

545

547

546

The Botanic Gardens: **544** teak-framed Palm House and Aquarium of 1932-33 *(see also fig. 60)*. **545** The neo-Georgian Cory Lodge, the Director's House, of 1924, by MacKay Hugh Baillie Scott whose earlier work belongs to the Arts & Crafts movement *(see fig. 119)*. Cambridge University Press. **546** The Printing House of 1961-63; **547** the Edinburgh Building of 1979-80.

3. University Buildings West of the River

The Arts Faculties Site, Sidgwick Avenue/West Road (C/D5)
This was the first site to be developed by the university after 1945, and like the University Library, built just before the Second World War, it is located away from the city centre to the west of the river. Building started in the mid fifties and today the site is about three-quarters complete (there remain a few buildings to come as funds are made available). So far three of this country's most eminent architects have contributed to the buildings here: Sir Hugh Casson and his partners between 1956-68 and again in the early eighties; James Stirling in 1964-68; and Sir Leslie Martin and his associates in 1975-80. The result is an improvement on other modern university development at Cambridge, and the buildings are extremely diverse in character: Casson's traditionally 'heavy' raised court and other box-like structures in the southern area of the site, Stirling's mechanistic and excitingly 'aggressive' History Faculty in the centre, and Martin's neatly packaged and 'friendly' Music School in the north-west corner.

Casson, Conder & Partners (1956-82)
The first building to be erected was the caretaker's house in the south-west corner in 1956. Then, in 1958-59, the Lecture Hall Block (fig. 548) was built in reinforced concrete and loadbearing brick, establishing the shape of things to come in the next decade. The raised three-sided Faculties Building (fig. 549) followed between 1959-61, housing English, Moral Sciences, Modern and Mediaeval Languages. It is raised above the ground on concrete columns, creating an open cloister all round. Closing the west side of this court, though separate from it, is the Economics and Politics Building, built at the same time.

In 1963-64 the Little Hall and Lady Mitchell Hall were built - both polygonal in shape, of load-bearing brick, and with unusual roofs as prominent features of their design. The Little Hall (fig. 548) seats 150, the Lady Mitchell Hall (fig. 550) 450 in its irregular octagonal space which is dominated, both inside and out, by the two massive pre-cast, box beams. The final building by this practice was the 'L' shaped block built in 1966-68 in the south-east corner of the site and intended to house the Faculty of Archaeology. Recently, the same architects completed the museum of Archaeology & Ethnology (fig. 548).

Casson, Conder & Partners remain the overall consultants for the development of this site and although they have produced some admirable structures here the overall effect lacks the picturesque quality intended in their original scheme from which much was pruned, including a 1000 seat Lecture Hall and an ornamental water court. The major decision to raise the main faculty court above ground level on this open site is rather questionable. If the intention was to create intimate cloisters in which students would linger, then the designers must have overlooked the strong winds that haunt Cambridge and gather even greater force in such confined undercrofts open on both sides, and most of the time these are draughty and empty places.

548

549

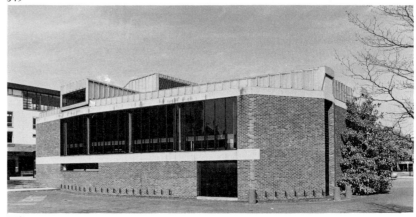
550

548-550 The founding buildings of the Arts Faculties Site by Casson, Conder & Partners. **548** The south-east corner of the raised court, the lecture hall block, and the little hall - all of 1958-64 - with the new Museum of Archaeology & Ethnology, 1981-83, in the foreground. **549** The main court of the site housing the faculties of English, Moral Sciences, Modern and Medieval Languages, 1959-61. **550** Lady Mitchell Hall of 1963-64.

Faculty of History: James Stirling (1964-68) (D5)

This must be the most controversial modern building in Cambridge (figs. 551 & 552 & see 36, 143), and reaction to it has been very mixed ranging from: 'So here is the answer of a younger man [Stirling was in his late thirties]. We must do away with beauty altogether. Don't be polite, be honest, even if it makes you brutal...People in 2068 will shake their heads at such self-confidence...anti-architecture...actively ugly...' (Pevsner); and 'something rather strange and original.' (Sir John Summerson); to 'visually striking...a great work of architecture...' (Booth & Taylor). It is enlightening to quote Stirling himself talking generally about architecture, and also specifically about this building:

'...All built form has weight and properties of stability or instability dependent on shape, and it is necessary to make a grouping of masses which is inherently stable...The History Faculty for Cambridge University is also intended to be read as a grouping of identifiable elements, i.e. lift and staircase shafts, and most obviously the large tent shaped roof indicating the library reading room below, the largest internal space.

A vast amount of modern architecture is banal, partly through the easy acceptance of compressing room accommodations into simple overall building forms. We usually try to retain the ideal shape of a room and avoid distorting it to fit a structural module or a pre-conceived building shape. In the History Faculty the room shapes are stacked to become the total building form and it is possible to see that the smaller rooms are on the top floors, increasing to larger and largest rooms at the lower levels.

The open steel truss roof, which leans across the reading room, allows daylight to filter into the library and, at the upper levels, it also allows daylight through into the circulation corridors. This roof is also a technical element, a controlled climate cushion containing heaters, ventilation louvres, fan extracts, lights, etc. automatically adjusting to the outside climate to maintain a constant atmosphere within. The thrust from this 'lean-to-roof' is stabilised by the buttressing effect of the 'L' shaped block, and the total building mass is a resolvement of various structural forces.

...The corridors are thought of as galleries running around the upper spaces of the reading room, they are glazed for sound and are the primary circulation system. The students moving about the building are visually in contact with the library, the most important working element of the Faculty. This inter-relationship was developed from an implication in the faculty's brief for the new building.'[19]

With the History Faculty, Stirling has not exercised any restraint - he does not believe in being 'polite' at the expense of his design philosophy. As Pevsner further lamented: '...the architecture hits you and that is what the facade - and the whole building - are meant to do'. This building makes one think about what is going on within it and offers simple and satisfying explanations. At last Cambridge achieved a building by this architect who had been unsuccessful in his two previous attempts (in the design for Churchill College in 1958, and for new buildings at Selwyn College in 1959). However, since its completion it has been plagued with a number of problems, such as a leaking library roof and the peeling-off of large areas of the red tile cladding. Furthermore, it has proved to be unpopular with those who use it, and the standard complaint is 'too hot in summer, too cold in winter'. Hopefully, these teething problems will soon be solved and the building restored to its intended state - without the scaffolding, which, in the past few years, almost seems to have become an integral part of it.

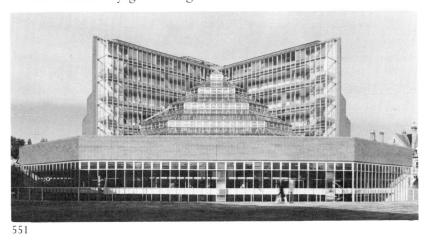

551

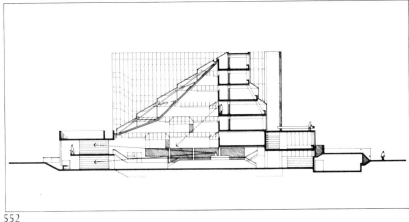

552

551 The History Faculty from the south-east showing the tent-like 'lean-to' glass roof of the library nestling between the seven storey L-shaped block which contains the faculty offices, seminar rooms, studies, and common rooms. The quadrant roof is constructed of tubular steel with industrialised glazing, the L-shaped block is concrete-framed clad in red engineering bricks with matching tiles and glazed corridors. **552** North-south section of the History Faculty (drawing by Stirling).

Faculty of Music: Sir Leslie Martin with Colen Lumley & Ivor Richards

The auditorium (fig. 553 & see 148) was built between 1975-77 and forms the centre of the complex. It seats 500 and also has practice rooms and a musical instrument store. This is surrounded by a single storey building with, on the east side, the main entrance foyer, common rooms, a bar, and a student area; extensive teaching and more practice rooms on the south and west sides; and a large rehearsal room and workshop on the north side, the rehearsal room doubling up as the backstage area. To the south-east of the main block, and connected to it by the student area, is a secondary block containing the library and administrative offices.

This is an attractive building with a telling structure. Like the neighbouring History Faculty Library, one immediately assumes that here is another building with a precise internal function, though in this instance the form is very solid (for acoustic reasons) as opposed to translucent. The interior of the auditorium has been designed for as much flexibility as possible in order to fulfil the differing requirements of teaching, as well as the needs of solo concert performances, and those of a full orchestra. Undoubtedly Sir Leslie is highly qualified for such a project as the Royal Festival Hall, London, was one of his earliest concert hall commissions.

553

553 The main entrance (east side) of the Faculty of Music, West Road. This building is similar in character to Sir Leslie Martin's (and Colin St John Wilson's) Harvey Court only a short distance away down West Road *(see figs 175 & 248)*. The roof is covered with zinc and the walls clad in a buff-coloured brick *(see also fig. 148)*.

The University Library (C4)

The Library at Cambridge University came into existence over 600 years ago, beginning as a small collection of books kept in chests in the university treasury. A building in which to house the library was not begun until the first half of the fifteenth century when the university began to develop its first site, now known as the Old Schools quadrangle (see p. 190). The collection slowly increased over the years until, in 1709, the library was made a copyright deposit under the first copyright act, which meant that it was entitled by law to receive, free of charge, every publication produced in the country, which subsequently led to expansion on an unprecedented scale; and in 1715 it was given the entire library of John Moore, Bishop of Ely, who had died in 1714 and whose collection of books was authorised to be donated to the neighbouring university by King George I. Moore's library contained approximately 30,000 volumes and more than trebled the size of the existing university library. The premises were extended in 1837-42, when a large new building was erected parallel to the north side of the Schools north range. This was designed by C.R. Cockerell (see figs. 101 & 521). From this point on the modern library began to take shape under the guidance of three industrious librarians in particular, who were largely responsible for transforming the collection into its present state: John Eyton Bickersteth Mayor (1864-67); Henry Bradshaw (1867-86); and Alwyn Faber Scholfield (1923-49). It was under the guidance of Scholfield that the important move was made to the present site in the early 1930s.

The library was designed by Sir Giles Gilbert Scott and built between 1931-34. It is a large symmetrical composition (fig. 554) comprising two inner courtyards, and is of russet coloured brick with red pantiles on the roofs. The high central tower (156 feet, 47.5 metres) is flanked by lower wings to the north and south behind which are the two courtyards separated by the catalogue room leading to the enormous main reading room, which closes the composition on the west side. There is a curious mixture of design elements in the main façade; the tall upright windows of the wings, spanning several storeys, provide a lightness of effect in contrast to the solid massing of the central tower capped with its pyramidal roof. Classical features and detailing, for example the central pedimented entrance with its giant arched doorway with rusticated surround, the treatment of the cornice, and the windows in the outer wings with their classical balustrades, overwhelm any attempt at something wholly contemporary here. As Pevsner comments, there is a certain unsureness in this facade between function and mere display.

Inside the building, Scott provided a large amount of 'open-stack' shelving, attractive for readers but not so practical for the modern needs of the library staff. To provide better working facilities for the library a large extension (fig. 555) was added to the west of the main building by Gollins, Melvin Ward & Partners, and completed in 1972. The brief required 60,000 feet of compact shelving in closed-stacks, more reading rooms, and more space for specialised work by the staff. Booth & Taylor refer to it as 'tactful...basically a warehouse added to a monument'.

The Observatory, Madingley Road

In 1704, Dr Thomas Plume, of Christ's College, left some £1800 in his will for the building of an observatory and the maintenance of a Professor of Astronomy and Experimental Philosophy. These funds were insufficient for his purpose and were temporarily invested until such a scheme was possible. However, the first Professor was appointed in 1706, Roger Cotes of Trinity College, and Plume's idea did lead to the building of a temporary observatory on the top of Trinity's Great Gate.[20] It was not until the early 1820s that sufficient money was forthcoming and the building of a proper observatory could go ahead.

In 1821 a site of 6½ acres was purchased from St John's College: '..which unites the advantages of a view all round the horizon, not now obstructed, nor likely to be obstructed hereafter in any direction, particularly in the essential one of the meridian; of sufficient elevation; of a clear air, never subject to be disturbed by the smoke of the town; of a dry soil; and of such a distance from the university as, all circumstances considered, they judge the most desirable'. The exact positioning of the building on this site was determined as follows '...the spot which has the tower of Grantchester Church in the meridian to the south, has been ascertained with sufficient accuracy; and this spot will determine the Western end of the Observatory.'[21]

Late in 1821 the design of the building was put out to open competition with a first prize of £100, and a second of £50. Thirteen architects submitted ideas; John Clement Mead won first prize, and William Wilkins came second. Mead's building (figs 556 & 557) was completed in 1822-23. It is a symmetrical composition in the Greek Doric Style, with a principal south front of about 160 feet (49 metres) and is entered through a tetrastyle (four-columned) pedimented Doric portico in the centre, behind which rises the copper covered dome (the portico was copied from the Temple of Minerva at Athens). The building is of two storeys throughout, with east and west wings projecting from the central domed section.

The wings eventually turn north providing accommodation in the east for the Professor, and in the west for his assistant, with the principal fronts of these apartments facing in those directions. The building sits on a base of Devonshire granite, the walls are of brick with Bath Stone ashlar facing, and roofs of lead with Westmoreland slate.

Another dome was built in 1838, the Northumberland Dome, just north of the main building, to house a telescope donated by the 3rd Duke of Northumberland. The dome has since been reconstructed. Also nearby is the Solar Physics Observatory built in 1911 and designed by T.D. Atkinson.

554

556

555

554 East elevation of the University Library from Clare College's Memorial Court. Both buildings were designed by Giles Gilbert Scott and completed in the same year on a very dominant east-west axis which connects eastwards across the Backs with the Old Court of Clare. The vista at this west end of the axis is about to be interrupted by a new octagonal library for the college, designed by Arup Associates, which will be placed in the centre of Memorial Court **555** Library extension of 1972. **556** The Observatory of 1822-23. **557** The Doric entrance portico of the Observatory.

557

The Science Faculties Site, Madingley Road (A3)

As with the decision in the 1950s to locate the Arts Faculties on a comprehensively developed site away from the crowded city centre, a similar idea was suggested in the mid sixties, when a committee, headed by Professor Deer, was established to investigate the future needs of the science faculties. The Deer Report, published in 1966, strongly recommended that the sciences should also vacate the city centre which could not accommodate further expansion, and should move to the western area of the city's perimeter. A site of some 300 acres was designated to the south of Madingley Road in the area of the Coton footpath, and Robert Matthew, Johnson-Marshall & Partners were commissioned to prepare a development plan. At the time, this idea was hailed by the local press as a 'Science City' and the development was also to include other faculties and residential accommodation, with a well-equipped communal centre. The site would be connected to the city via the Coton foothpath as a pedestrian and cyclist route, and by Madingley Road for vehicles. After this overall plan, the architects proceeded to prepare a more detailed layout for the Cavendish Laboratory (fig. 558)

which, along with the Department of Biochemistry, was most in need of expansion.

The scheme was criticised at the time by the Professor of Architecture, Sir Leslie Martin, who suggested that the whole project was moving too fast and had not been properly investigated. His main argument was that the land use was wasteful and that the real effects of the proposal on the neighbouring area of west Cambridge – around the Backs, Queens' Road, and Grange Road - had not been carefully enough considered. Sir Leslie's view was that the Science Faculties should be kept near the city centre, and he suggested that the Newtown area off Hills Road would be a possible site for expansion.

Prior to the Deer Report, the School of Veterinary Medicine had already been established on this site in a large red-brick neo-Georgian building (fig. 559) by Ian Forbes of 1954-55. Also, two other buildings were erected between 1965-68 before the overall development plan had been fully rationalised. These were both designed and built by Mowlem Ltd for the Institute of Theoretical Astronomy and the Department of Geology & Geophysics. The site remains to be fully developed.

558

559

The Science Faculties site off Madingley Road: **558** The Cavendish Laboratories north of the Coton footpath. **559** The School of Veterinary Medicine, south of Madingley Road.

Kettle's Yard, Northampton Street (D/E2)

Kettle's Yard is a unique phenomenon not to be missed when visiting Cambridge. It is a house containing the art collection of one man, Jim Ede, in a charming environment of converted cottages and an attractive modern extension. A gallery housing temporary exhibitions is located on the same site.

The best way to explain how this permanent exhibition, begun in 1957, evolved is to quote its creator:

'...I suppose it began by my meeting with Ben and Winifred Nicholson in 1924 or thereabouts, while I was an Assistant at the

Tate Gallery. It started of course before that; I was 15 at the Leys School in Cambridge and fell in love with early Italian painting and broke bounds to search the Free Library and Fitzwilliam Museum...

...it wasn't until I was nearly thirty that the Nicholson's opened a door into the world of contemporary art and I rushed headlong into the arms of Picasso, Brancusi, and Braque; not losing, however, my rapture over Giotto, Angelico, Monaco and Piero della Francesca.

Ben Nicholson shared this rapture and I saw in his work a simple continuity from them into the everyday world of the twenties and thirties...It was while we were still abroad in 1954 that I found myself first dreaming of the idea of somehow creating a *living place* where works of art could be enjoyed, inherent to the domestic setting, where young people could be at home unhampered by the greater austerity of the museum or public art gallery, and where an informality might infuse an underlying formality. I wanted, in a modest way, to use the inspiration I had had from beautiful interiors, houses of leisured elegance, and to combine it with the joy I had felt in individual works seen in museums and with the all embracing delight I had experienced in nature, in stones, in flowers, in people...

...Kettle's Yard is in no way meant to be an art gallery or museum, nor is it simply a collection of works of art reflecting my taste or the taste of a given period. It is, rather, a continuing way of life from these last fifty years, in which stray objects, stones, glass, pictures, sculpture, in light and in space, have been used to make manifest the underlying stability which more and more we need to recognise if we are not to be swamped by all that is so rapidly opening up before us.

On my side, I have felt strongly my need to give to others these things which have so much been given to me; and to give in such a way that by their placing and by a pervading atmosphere one thing will enhance another, making perhaps a coherent whole, in which a continuity of enjoyment, in the constantly changing public of a university, can thrive."[22]

The conversion of the cottages was carried out by Rowland Aldridge and Mr Ede in 1957, and they form part of this pleasant area of Honey Hill that has a quasi-village atmosphere about it created by the green, the old peoples home, the cottages, and the tower of St Peter's Church.

In 1969-70 the new buildings were added by Sir Leslie Martin and David Owers in two stages. The first stage was the extension to the cottages themselves (fig. 560), and the second the single-storey building that was to be the separate gallery for visiting exhibitions (fig. 562). As with the cottage buildings, the materials and finishes were kept very simple with the extensive use of white-painted rough plaster, brick and timber boarding (dark stained externally). The new building of the first stage followed the line of the existing buildings down the slope to Northampton Street, with access to the new extension via the old cottages. One enters the complex through a gap between the older cottages, ascending the spiral staircase to the first floor, then unlike the often tiresome passage through many museums and art galleries, the domestic scale entices the visitor to proceed and the changing spaces are continually refreshing. The visitor then enters the two-storey high space of the new extension which, in its purity of form and light, is a perfect foil, the white-painted plaster accentuating the exhibits therein.

The exhibition gallery to the east, like the house, has a domestic intimacy created by the use of materials — brick, brick paviours, white-painted rough plaster — and the division of the area into three spaces set in echelon and on slightly differing levels.

560

561

562

560 Kettles Yard - the house and its modern extension from the west on Honey Hill.
561 Interior of the extension at first floor level from the older cottage **562** Interior of the exhibition gallery next door to the house.

203

563 The church of All Saints in the Jewry, also called All Saints by the Hospital because of its location in medieval times opposite the ancient hospital of St John. The engraving, by John Le Keux *c.*1840, shows the church's western tower, St John's Street, with St John's gatehouse beyond and Trinity College chapel opposite. The church dated back to the eleventh century and was first mentioned when bestowed upon the monks of St Albans Abbey during the time of the Abbot Paul (1077-93). In 1180 the advowson (the right of presentation to a benefice or living) was given to the Benedictine nunnery of St Radegund and at the dissolution of that religious household in 1496 by Bishop Alcock, it passed on to Jesus College. The church dated mainly from the fifteenth and sixteenth centuries, with a chancel of 1726; it was demolished in 1865 in order to widen St John's Street. Only its churchyard remains and has recently been used as a craft market during the summer. The successor to the church, the new All Saints in Jesus Lane, was designed by G.F. Bodley and built between 1863-71 and although now redundant is one of the finest nineteenth-century buildings in the city (see p. 216). Some of the old church's fixtures and fittings were transferred to the new building, such as bells, books, brasses, some monuments and floor slabs, and marble and slate tablets, but most notably the Perpendicular octagonal font bowl decorated with pointed quatrefoils and shields.

563

7 Churches

Like most English cities, Cambridge possesses a considerable number of churches, including one or two exceptional examples. The city and its outlying parishes contain far too many churches to include them all here and the following is a selection of those of particular interest, all located in Cambridge itself or around its immediate perimeter.

About a third of all the churches in Cambridge were established by the early fourteenth century. A period of inactivity spanning several hundred years then followed as the existing churches met the needs of the town's inhabitants. Then, with the rapid increase in population in the nineteenth century, came a vigorous revival of ecclesiastical building, and the industrious Victorians more than doubled the number of churches in Cambridge, the final third of the total existing today being built in the twentieth century.

The medieval town of Cambridge evolved as two settlements, on the east and west banks of the river (see chapter 1), that to the east becoming the present city centre, and it was here that the Saxons built St Bene't's, today the oldest surviving church in the county. Another Saxon church, All Saints by the Castle, possibly even earlier in origin, existed in the western settlement around Castle Hill, the remains of gravestones dated between 975 and 1050 having been discovered there in the early nineteenth century.

A number of Norman churches were built in the years following the Conquest, of which two particularly fine examples remain: the Church of the Holy Sepulchre in the city centre, and St Mary Magdalene on the eastern outskirts. Of these the Holy Sepulchre is particularly important as it is one of only five round churches that survive fairly intact in the whole of England. St Mary Magdalene, which was originally part of a leper hospital (hence its location away from the town), is an almost completely unspoilt example of small scale Norman architecture.

By the middle of the thirteenth century there were 16 churches serving the town and of these 13 remain, though many have been extensively rebuilt, and three have been completely demolished: All Saints by the Castle, All Saints in the Jewry or by the hospital (this would have been the ancient hospital of St John, later St John's College), and St John Zachary in Milne Street (now Trinity Lane), which was demolished circa 1446 to make way for Henry VI's King's College Chapel. Of these All Saints in the Jewry provided a most interesting feature in St John's Street where, as Le Keux's engraving shows (fig. 563), there was an arch through the base of its tower under which ran the pedestrian footpath. The church was demolished in 1865 when St John's Street was widened.

Several of the colleges established in the late thirteenth century and mid fourteenth century, did not at first possess chapels, as they all do today. As a result some of the earliest foundations, such as Peterhouse, Michaelhouse, Gonville Hall, Corpus Christi, Clare Hall, and Trinity Hall, were granted permission to use their respective parish churches. Indeed, both Peterhouse and Michaelhouse took their names from their parish church: Peterhouse from St Peter-without-Trumpington-Gate (now St Mary the Less), and Michaelhouse (later part of Trinity) from St Michael's in Trinity Street. In order to accommodate their collegiate guests, the often too-small churches had to be adapted or enlarged, sometimes adding extra chapels, as was the case, for instance, at St Edward's, the chapel for Clare and Trinity Halls for many years. Also, if the church was situated close enough to the college a physical link was built to connect the two, as at both Peterhouse and Corpus Christi (Corpus with St Bene't's) which are joined to their parish churches by two-storey buildings.

The late Middle Ages saw much rebuilding in Cambridge but virtually no new churches. The most important event of the period was the almost complete rebuilding of Great St Mary's, the University Church, in the late fifteenth century and throughout the sixteenth century, on the same site as its twelfth century predecessor. The west tower of St Botolph's was built circa 1400; additional chancel aisles were added to St Edward's in 1446 to cater for the enlarged congregation mentioned above; transepts were added to the Church of the Holy Trinity in the late fifteenth century, at which time Little St Mary's was also extended westwards. After this, little of architectural importance appears to have taken place until the nineteenth century.

In 1801 the population of the parish of St Andrew the Less was 252, yet by 1841 it had risen to almost 10,000, and two new churches were built, both by Ambrose Poynter (figs. 583-585).

One of the most notable buildings of this period in Cambridge is G.F. Bodley's All Saints Church in Jesus Lane, containing much interior work by the firm of Morris, Marshall, Faulkner & Co. This building, which has been described as 'one of the most important works in the history of British Architecture - marking the very moment when the Gothic Revival, having exhausted the inspiration of Continental models, returned to its English roots'[23], was declared redundant in 1973, as has been the fate of many Victorian churches.

Twentieth century church building has, so far, produced nothing exceptional in Cambridge. St George's in Chesterfield Road of 1934, by T H Lyon, is an unusual and noteworthy example of the period; and equally representative of its era is the Arbury Road Baptist Church of the mid sixties by R.J. Wyatt. Of recent years two attractive ecclesiastical buildings have emerged from not so attractive and highly controversial redevelopment schemes in and near the city centre: Fisher House by Gerard Goalen & Partners in the Lion Yard and Petty Cury scheme of the early seventies; and, very recently, the newly completed Eden chapel in Fitzroy Robinson's 'Kite' development scheme.

St Bene't, St Bene't Street (F4) *(fig. 564 & see 2, 71, 72, 260, 262).*
St Benedict of Nursia, the patron saint of this church, was the patriarch of Western Monasticism and the founder of the Benedictine Order in about 529 AD. St Bene't dates from the early eleventh century and only about fifty years after its foundation one Edward of Cambridge and his mother gave the advowson of the church to St Alban's Abbey, although two centuries later in 1279 it belonged to a Sir Giles d'Argenteyn from whom it was purchased in 1350 by the town guilds of Corpus Christi and St Mary. These two guilds united in 1352 to establish the College of Corpus Christi and the Blessed Virgin Mary, and the following year conveyed the church to the College, from which time it served both the College and its parish until 1579 when Corpus built its own chapel (prior to this the chancel in St Bene't's was the area reserved for College use). For many years Corpus was known as 'Bene't College' because of its association with the church. The College remains its patron and appoints the rector.

St Bene't's is the oldest surviving building in Cambridge. The tower and parts of the nave and chancel are thought to have been built sometime in the first half of the eleventh century, probably around 1040, but alterations and additions were made in the thirteenth, sixteenth and nineteenth centuries. The original church consisted simply of tower, nave and chancel. Possibly owing to a fire in the thirteenth century the nave and chancel arch were rebuilt with the addition of narrow side aisles. In c.1500 the Master of Corpus, Dr Cosyn, joined the church to the college by building a two-storey chapel on the south side of the chancel. In 1853 the north aisle was rebuilt and enlarged by R. Brandon, as was the south aisle, and the north and east walls of the chancel, and the chancel arch, by A.W. Blomfield in 1872. Blomfield also replaced the clerestory windows and reconstructed the roofs of the nave and chancel.

The most notable feature of this church is the Saxon Tower (see fig. 71) and its internal arch (see fig. 72). The tower is built in three stages, each slightly smaller than the one below, with the belfry as the top section. The round-headed, twin openings in the bell tower were added later in 1586. The original entrance to the church would probably have been through the west side of the tower. The arch from the nave into the tower is an excellent example of Saxon construction and Pevsner throws interesting light on this 'valuable relic...It shows two things, both historically significant: that the masons had a notion of the construction and detailing of arches in Germany or France, and that their notion was vague and superficial. The cornice or entablure especially is obviously a rendering of something more correct by men to whom the logic of such a member meant nothing. The same is true of the weird idea of making the jambs of long-and-short-work but placing a demi-shaft and a demi-pillar to the left and right of the arch. The arch mouldings moreover do not continue what goes on below, but rest on two barbaric beasts or monsters...'

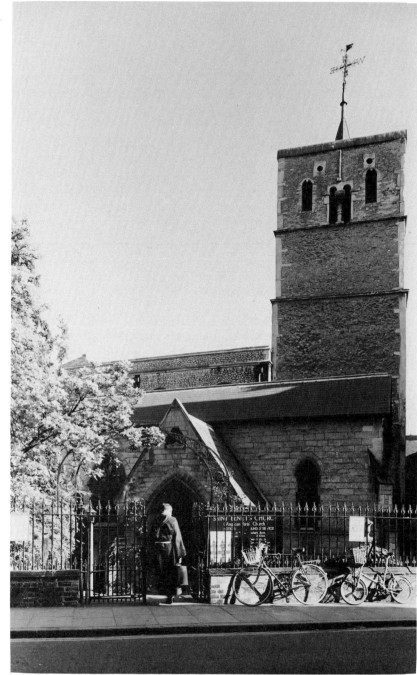

564 The north elevation of St Bene't's - the oldest church in the county - from the Eagle Inn on the opposite side of Bene't Street. This view shows the pre-Conquest tower at the west end of the fourteenth-century nave, with the rebuilt north aisle and new north porch, both dating from the mid-nineteenth century. The tower is constructed of rubble with characteristic Saxon 'long and short' quoins at the angles *(see fig. 71).*

565 The west elevation of St Mary The Less. The west end of the church dates back to the fifteenth century, with walls constructed of rubble (with brick repairs) and dressings of Barnack stone and clunch. The low Perpendicular window is presumably of the same period although its restored tracery is more characteristic of the fourteenth century (RCHM). The single storey extension was the start of a new west tower begun in 1892, now the choir vestry.

St Mary The Less, Trumpington Street (F5) *(fig. 565 & see 78)*

St Mary The Less is also known as Little St Mary's, but was originally called St Peter-without-Trumpington-Gate, for in medieval times it would have been located just outside the town's main southern approach. The former St Peter's served the earliest college, Peterhouse, which took its name from the church and which is sited to its immediate south. The beginnings of the church may well go back to pre-Conquest times, but by the early fourteenth century the original structure was in such a bad state that it was completely rebuilt between 1340-52. Upon its re-consecration in 1352 the new church was re-dedicated to the Virgin Mary and continued to serve Peterhouse, as well as its parish, until the college completed its own chapel in 1632.

There is no internal structural division in the body of the church between nave and chancel, and it has no aisles. It has been suggested by several authorities (including Pevsner and the R.C.H.M.) that the existing plan is the incomplete result of the fourteenth century rebuilding scheme, and that a larger church of the transverse antechapel type of arrangement was intended; the present building being simply its chancel. This theory is well supported by the form of the buttresses between the fifth and sixth bays (working from the east) which indicate that such an arrangement was contemplated. The five east bays belong to the rebuilding scheme of 1340-52, whilst the sixth bay was added later, in the fifteenth century, continuing the extension of the nave instead of expanding to north and south, as would have been the case in the intended building.

In the fourteenth century scheme, entry to the church had been via a porch and anteroom in the south-east corner, to the east of which a vestry was later added. In the fifteenth century an upper storey was built over both antechamber and vestry, with a gallery over the porch providing a link to Peterhouse. Originally an arch under the gallery led into the churchyard (then on the south side) from Trumpington Street. This arrangement, connecting church and college, is virtually the same as that at St Bene't's and Corpus, providing direct access for the scholars into the chancel which, likewise, was reserved for collegiate use. The next addition was not until 1892 when the choir vestry and the lower part of a new west tower were built as an extension to the nave (there had been a west tower here in the original church and this was still intact as late as the mid seventeenth century, but it either fell down or was demolished at an unknown later date). Finally, in 1931, T.H. Lyon added the south chapel.

There are excellent examples at St Mary's of Gothic window tracery from the Decorated period, including many characteristic forms of that elaborate style, such as ogee and dagger shapes (see fig. 79). Some interesting Saxon interlace work, and some Norman zigzag decoration, can be seen in the walls of the west end of the church, remnants of the original building. The Jacobean roof in the chancel was replaced by the present one during restoration by George Gilbert Scott in 1856-57.

Holy Sepulchre, Bridge Street (F3) *(fig. 566, front cover, 4, 74 & 75)*
The church of the Holy Sepulchre at Cambridge, or the 'Round Church' as it is commonly called, is one of only five such buildings in the whole country to survive fairly intact. The other four are the Temple Church in London; the Chapel at Ludlow Castle; and churches at Northampton, and Little Maplestead in Essex. These circular churches were normally associated with the Knights Templar and the Knights of St John of Jerusalem - the Orders founded to guard the Holy Land and the Holy Sepulchre - although that in Cambridge apparently has no direct connection with either, but was built by the local 'fraternity of the Holy Sepulchre' of which little is known.

The site was given to the fraternity sometime between 1114-1130 by Reinald, Abbot of Ramsey, and the church was built during the second quarter of that century. In the fifteenth century major work was undertaken and the building much altered when a polygonal battlemented bell tower was added above the clerestory of the nave, and most of the windows of the round aisle were altered and enlarged. Since then, however, mid nineteenth century restoration has done away with these additions and changes, the style of which can be seen in Ackermann's print of 1814 (fig. 567). In 1841 part of the vault of the east aisle collapsed, and a rather over-enthusiastic restoration scheme of the whole building was undertaken by the Cambridge Camden Society under the direction of Anthony Salvin, with the result that the present-day church has much Victorian addition.

This restoration scheme, which took place between 1841-43, has been much criticised for its too 'severe' (Pevsner) or 'drastic' (R.C.H.M) alteration of the fabric and many of the details. Salvin tried to restore the church to its original form, as he saw it, but in so doing he completely destroyed most of the fifteenth century work and replaced it with supposedly 'correct' twelfth-century features. The fifteenth century belfry was demolished and replaced with the stone vault above the clerestory; the contemporary Gothic windows of the clerestory and aisles were replaced with new 'Norman' windows, the design of which was apparently based on an example surviving from the original building; the vault of the aisle was dismantled and completely rebuilt and the chancel arch re-erected narrower than its predecessor. As the south wall of the aisle buckled under the thrust from the vault it was taken down to within six feet of the ground and also rebuilt. The west doorway was dismantled, the stonework thoroughly cleaned and repaired, and the whole re-erected (see fig. 74). Finally, much restoration and addition took place in the chancel to the east of the nave; the east and north walls were rebuilt, as was the north chapel, which was also extended east by half a bay; a bell-turret was added to the north-west angle of this chapel; the south aisle was built and a new arch inserted to connect it to the aisle of the nave. In 1892 the vestry on the north side of the north chapel was added.

Whether Salvin's work was based upon correct historical supposition is debatable, and many would argue that the church would have been better left alone. Nevertheless, in this church Cambridge possesses a valuable example of a rare form of Norman building.

566

567

566 Holy Sepulchre from the north-west showing the twelfth-century circular nave, the nineteenth-century bell-turret and the fifteenth- century north chapel.
567 The style of the church after fifteenth century alterations, current until the restoration of 1841.

St Mary Magdalene, Newmarket Road *(figs 568-570 & see 73)*
This little medieval church, also known as Stourbridge Chapel, is one of the finest examples of Norman architecture in the county. It was built sometime in the first half of the twelfth century, and was later associated with the lepper hospital that was established here soon afterwards. Although the chapel ceased to function as a regular place of worship in the sixteenth century, it survived fairly intact owing to its use by the famous Stourbridge Fair, initially as a lumber store but also at various times as a victualling house, a drinking booth, a stable and a barn.

In 1816 the church was bought by the Rev. Thomas Kerrich and then given to the university. In 1843-45 it was restored and once again resumed its intended role when it became a place of worship for the labourers employed to build the Eastern Counties Railway. In 1949 the university again restored the church, and in 1951 handed it over to the Cambridge Preservation Society, at which time the six acre field in which it stands (known as Chapel Close) was purchased.

This is a very simple church consisting solely of nave and chancel. Some changes were made in circa 1400 when the roof was repaired and the quadripartite vault of the chancel altered, though two of the vaulting shafts remain in the north-east and south-east corners and the line of the old vault can still be seen on the north, south and east walls. There were two nineteenth century restorations; in 1843 the east wall was partially rebuilt, and in 1867 Sir G.G. Scott rejuvenated the west wall.

There are some notable examples of Norman design and decoration at St Mary's, both inside and out. The chancel arch (fig. 569) is decorated with the chevron or zigzag pattern beloved of Norman masons, and can also be seen on the south doorway (fig. 73). Except for the east window of the chancel and the larger upper window in the west gable, both of which are nineteenth century additions, the windows are all twelfth century, with semi-circular heads and flanking shafts with capitals and bases (eg fig. 570).

The rural setting of this building has been somewhat spoilt by the development of the busy dual-carriageway to its south and the railway line to its west. In contrast, Chapel Close to the north and north-east provides a more apt setting, and it is thus best viewed from the south-west (eg fig. 568). There is something about this modest little building that is very alluring, and the medieval ambience of the interior gains from its lack of stature. The key is obtainable from the Old Station House down the side lane, and it is well worth the one and a half mile trek out from the city centre.

568

569

570

568 St Mary Magdalene from the south showing the simple form of its nave and chancel. The walls of the nave are constructed of flint pebbles (with later brick repairs) and dressings of Barnack or Weldon stone. The windows and nave door all date from the twelfth century *(see also fig. 73)* and the blocked-up chancel door is of uncertain but post-medieval date (RCHM). Characteristic chevron decoration ornaments all these Norman features. **569** The west face of the twelfth-century semi-circular chancel arch with beaded chevron patterning. **570** The south window of the chancel with chevron patterning on the arch head and on the western shaft.

St Botolph, Trumpington Street/Botolph Lane (F5)

St Botolph (fig. 571) may well date back to the late tenth or early eleventh centuries, as the cult of Saint Botolph was being widely promoted in the eastern counties at that time, and it is known that there was a church here prior to the existing one. However, nothing remains of the original foundation and the surviving church is mainly fourteenth century.

The nave and aisles were rebuilt first, sometime between 1300-50, consisting of four bays with arcades of two-centred arches. The sturdy west tower, with its four diagonally projecting buttresses, was added *c*.1400. Later in that century the south porch (originally of two storeys) and the south chapel were built, at which time also the aisle walls were heightened. The chancel was rebuilt in brick during the eighteenth century, but then rebuilt again in 1872 by G.F. Bodley. Also at that time, the new vestry and organ chamber were added to the north of the chancel. There were several restoration schemes in the nineteenth and early twentieth centuries. In 1924 the outer vestry was built on the north side of the organ chamber.

There are many notable features in this essentially Perpendicular Gothic church: the roofs of the nave, chancel, and south chapel, are all original fourteenth century work. The windows of the aisles were all renewed in the mid fifteenth century and are interesting examples of a fairly rare Perpendicular type, being topped with extremely depressed pointed arches. The font, with its seventeenth century casing, is particularly notable. There are interesting commemorations to two of the most prolific architects in Cambridge; a tablet to Robert Grumbold, against the outer south wall of the chancel (died 1720) and one to James Essex in the north aisle. Out in the churchyard there is a curious octagonal stone structure, designed in the Perpendicular style, which Pevsner thought might be a disused well covering.

St Edward King & Martyr, St Edward's Passage (F4)

Anglo-Saxon origins have been suggested for this church (fig 572), though no pre-Conquest architecture remains. This hypothesis is supported by the facts that the building is located in the neigbourhood of the original Anglo-Saxon Cambridge settlement south of the Cam (see chapter 1), very near the Saxon church of St Bene't; it is dedicated to Edward the Confessor, the last Saxon King of England (1043-66); and a Saxon coffin-stone was excavated on the site early this century. The advowson was initially held by Barnwell Priory until it was purchased by Henry VI in 1446, along with that of St John Zachary in Milne Street (Trinity Lane), which was demolished in that year as it was on the intended site for the chapel of his college. Prior to this the colleges of Trinity Hall and Clare Hall had worshipped at St John's, and to compensate them Henry gave the advowson of St Edward's to Trinity Hall, so that both colleges could continue to worship there.

The earliest part of the present building is the lower section of the west tower, which goes back to circa 1200. The original church would have consisted simply of the west tower with a nave and chancel, but much was added in the fifteenth and nineteenth centuries. In the early fifteenth century, the nave and chancel were rebuilt and the aisles added. In order to accommodate Clare and Trinity Halls the north and south chapels were added sometime around 1446. The north chapel and chancel were used by Trinity Hall, and the south chapel by Clare Hall. This involved the demolition of the easternmost bays of the aisles, and it is possible that the mason responsible for the building work was the prolific Reginald Ely who was a parishioner at St Edward's. The vestry and organ chamber were added to the north side of the north chapel in 1846. Since then there has been much restoration: in 1858-60 Sir George Gilbert Scott designed a new east window, and R. Brandon a west door and window, while in 1869 several other windows were renewed including those of the main facades of the north and south chapels. The twentieth century has also seen much restoration work: the chancel was restored in 1932, the nave in 1939, and more windows renewed, this time in the main elevations of the aisles by Professor Richardson in 1946 and 1949 respectively.

St Clement, Bridge Street (E3)

St Clement is of early thirteenth century construction but with a dominant nineteenth century tower attached to the main street elevation (fig. 573). The first mention of this church is in 1218, at around which time it was given to the nuns of St Radegund, the advowson later passing to Jesus College when Bishop Alcock took over the Benedictine Nunnery in the late fifteenth century.

The main body of the church was built, or perhaps rebuilt, in the first half of the thirteenth century; the first four bays of the nave are earlier than the fifth, which is thought to have been added later in the fifteenth century, and the slightly wider composition of which may indicate some form of earlier transept or transeptal chapels across the east end. In the early sixteenth century the north and south aisles were rebuilt and widened, at which time also the clerestory was added (a date of 1538 is carved in the roof). In 1726 the chancel was rebuilt and the present capitals of the responds of the chancel arch were constructed. The 'somewhat silly west tower' (Pevsner) was added in 1821 having been designed by Charles Humphrey and was initially topped by a spire (removed in 1928). A general restoration of the church took place in 1863 and the vestry, to the east of the north aisle, was added in 1866 on the site of the fifteenth century north chapel, the old doorway of which can be seen in the aisle's east wall.

St Peter, Castle Street (D2) *(figs 574-575)*

This little church, measuring only 15 x 35 feet (4.5 x 10.7 metres) is a Norman foundation dating from the twelfth century. The building that survives is only part of a larger composition which consisted of nave, chancel, aisles and a west tower with a spire. By the middle of the eighteenth century the old church had ceased to function and by 1772 it was apparently roofless and windowless. In 1781 it was largely rebuilt on a reduced scale, using the materials of the old church.

The western half of the nave, the tower and spire are fourteenth century, while the eastern half was rebuilt in the eighteenth century with an early nineteenth century window being inserted later. There are some interesting Norman details from the original church: in the north wall the doorway dates from the twelfth century (now blocked-up, the window to its east is fifteenth century), and the main door in the south wall is early thirteenth century. Inside the church, the bowl of the twelfth century font (fig. 575) is particularly notable; and is carved with Tritons pulling up their double tails behind them to form a loop-pattern which supports the lip of the bowl.

571

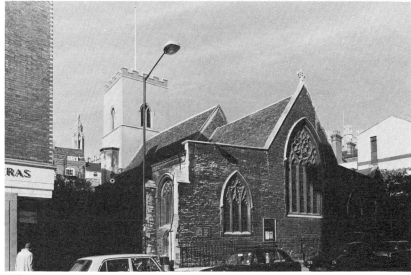
572

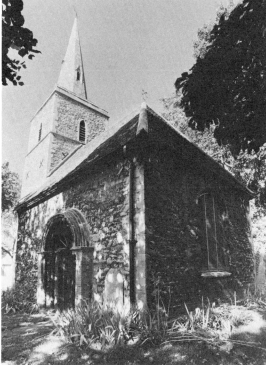
574

575

573

571 St Botolph from the south-west with New Court of Corpus Christi beyond. **572** St Edward from the south-east, showing the south chapel and the chancel with the thirteenth-century tower beyond. **573** St Clement from above showing the nineteenth-century tower with the medieval and sixteenth-century nave and aisles and the eighteenth-century chancel. **574** St Peter from the south-east. **575** The Norman font in St Peter's.

St Andrew The Less & Barnwell Priory, Newmarket Road
(figs 576 & 577)

The Augustinian Order came to Cambridge in about 1092, and eventually settled in the Barnwell district on the east side of the town where they established a priory circa 1112 (see chapter 1). Very little of their buildings has survived except for the ruins (fig. 576) on the corner of Beche and Priory Roads. After 1538 and the Dissolution of the Monasteries, the site served as a quarry, its stones being used for other buildings such as the new chapel that was being built at Corpus Christi in the last quarter of the sixteenth century. St Andrew The Less was probably built by the priory as the parish church, and it was served by the Augustinian Canons until the Dissolution.

The Priory buildings were probably all located to the north of the church, and it is thought that the surviving fragments formed the old kitchen which would have been in the north-west corner of the cloister. It is a vaulted room constructed of clunch rubble with dressings of Barnack stone and, in places, later brick patching.

The church was built in the early thirteenth century and consists simply of a nave and chancel, with no internal structural division. It too is built of clunch rubble with Barnack and other freestone dressings, although the walls have been extensively refaced with rough freestone ashlar. One of its most notable features are the three tall thirteenth-century lancet windows at the east end (see fig. 76), with a further restored lancet in the south side of the chancel, and a fourteenth-century window to its immediate west (see fig. 77). There are also two restored medieval lancets in the west wall. All the other windows appear to have been renewed during a nineteenth century restoration (1854-56) when the whole north wall was largely rebuilt under the direction of the Cambridge Architectural Society. The Vestry, on the north side of the nave, was added later in the nineteenth century, and the south porch in 1929 on the site of an earlier one. Because of the massive increase in the population of this parish in the nineteenth century, two new churches were built to accommodate the enlarged congregation, Christ Church and St Paul's, the former taking over as parish church in 1846.

St Mary the Great, King's Parade (E/F4) *(figs 578-580 & see 12, 26, 81)*

Also known as Great St Mary's, this large church is commonly referred to as the University Church because of its long association with both 'Town' and 'Gown'. The building was, in fact, the original centre of university ceremony and administration; congregations were held in it until the Schools were built nearby in the early fifteenth century, degrees were conferred there until the completion of the Senate House in 1730, and it was used as a general store for university documents throughout that whole period. Many official meetings between the university and the town were held at Great St Mary's in medieval times and, apparently, even the town's fire-fighting equipment was kept there — but it was its stronger connection with the university that provoked its ransacking by the rioting townsmen in 1381 (see p. 22).

There has been a church on this site since at least 1205, if not earlier, and the oldest parts of the present building date from the thirteenth century (lower sections of the chancel walls) with the main bulk of the fabric being the result of a rebuilding scheme which took place between 1478-1608. The original church was surrounded by timber-framed, thatch-roofed buildings and stalls of the market square, and a serious fire is recorded here in 1290, possibly ultimately resulting in the rebuilding of the church.

The foundation stone of the present building was laid in 1478, though little work was done until 1488 when the main body of the church was begun. The nave, aisles, chapels, chancel (extensively remodelled), south

576   577

porch (since renewed), and vestry (demolished), were all completed by about 1514. The west tower was begun in 1491, but by 1550 it had only reached half its full height, and it was not until 1593 that the bell-chamber was embarked upon (the first ringing of the bells took place in 1596). The tower was not fully completed, however, until 1608 when the four corner turrets were finished by the mason Robert Grumbold (an 80-foot spire was also intended but never built). The interior is largely faced with clunch (see p. 11), the exellent carving qualities of which have been used to full advantage. The timber for the roof was donated by Henry VII from the royal manor at Chesterford.

In 1735-36 galleries were added, providing over 400 more seats (making a total capacity of 1700), under the supervision of James Gibbs (two other galleries were added in 1754 and 1819 by James Essex and William Wilkins but were dismantled in 1863). In 1851 Sir George Gilbert Scott designed a new west portal for the tower in the Gothic style, replacing a classical one of 1576. The old vestry was demolished in 1857 and the chancel restored and ashlar-faced with Ketton stone by Anthony Salvin, who also inserted a new east window. In 1888 a new south porch was built — apparently a copy of the original one — and the tower restored in 1892. A general restoration took place in 1955 and the stonework of the facade was cleaned between 1982-84.

St Mary The Great is a notable example of late Perpendicular Gothic, built at a time when the classical style was slowly infiltrating Cambridge.

It is similar to other churches built in the eastern counties at that time, such as those at Safron Walden and Lavenham in Suffolk. Simon Clark and John Wastell were the freemasons contracted for the former in 1485, and both were employed as master masons at King's College Chapel (the final stages), opposite Great St Mary's. Thus, it is not improbable that Clark and Wastell were also employed on the University Church.

The embattled exterior is impressive (eg fig. 578 & see 12, 26), but, like King's College Chapel, it is the interior that is so compelling — a result of the proportioning of the tall and elegant forms of the Perpendicular style (fig. 579). There is some beautiful stone carving in the clunch spandrel panels of the arches of the nave, and on the chancel arch (fig. 580), all of which would originally have been brightly painted. The panelled ceiling of the tower room is also of clunch. The wooden roof of the nave and chancel are notable examples of Tudor construction, with large carved bosses at the main points of intersection. There are also some good examples of carved corbels in the aisles. Among other interesting features are the font of 1632, the early Georgian screens separating the north and south chapels from the chancel (apparently made up from a former large pulpit of c.1735), and the gilded wooden figure of Christ in Majesty, of 1960, by Alan Durst. All the original stained glass was unfortunately removed following the Reformation, the present glass being of the later nineteenth and early twentieth centuries.

578

579

580

576 The remains of the Augustinian Barnwell Priory - the 'CELLARERS CHEQUER' on the corner of Priory and Beche Roads. **577** St Andrew The Less from the south-west. **578** The University Church - St Mary The Great from the lawns of King's College. **579** Interior of St Mary's looking east with the slender shafts of the two-centred arches which seperate the aisles from the nave. **580** Details of the fine clunch-stone carvings in the spandrel panels of the chancel arch and the frieze above.

Holy Trinity, Market Street/Sidney Street (F4)

The original twelfth century church of the Holy Trinity, thought to have been a simple timber-framed and thatched building, was destroyed by the great Cambridge fire of 1174. Soon afterwards another church was begun and was completed by the time of the Magna Carta in 1215, though little now survives of that structure (only the lower parts of the west wall of the tower behind the north and south buttresses). Much rebuilding took place between the fourteenth and nineteenth centuries, resulting in the present church (fig. 581), which is unusual among medieval Cambridge churches in that it is cruciform in plan (ie it has transepts).

During the fourteenth century aisles were added to the existing stone-vaulted nave and chancel. Also at this time the tower was built from within the western bay of the nave, the massive buttresses being added for necessary support in the fifteenth century. In that century also, the transepts were rebuilt and the clerestory of the nave added, while later in the fifteenth century the north porch was built. During the sixteenth century the south aisle was widened and slightly lengthened westwards. The gallery in the south transept was built in 1806, and then in 1834 the old stone chancel was demolished and rebuilt in brick. In 1851 the transeptal arches were rebuilt, and in 1885 the chancel was redecorated by Bodley, and also refaced in stone. The organ chamber was added to the north side of the chancel at that date. The vestry is a modern addition.

An extremely thorough and recent cleaning of the facade of Holy Trinity has created a rather 'plastic' appearance, although it is only a matter of time before city centre grime gives it back its 'authentic' and more dignified character. The interior is refreshingly light owing to the many windows of the transepts. The fifteenth century roofs of the nave and transepts are notable examples of the period, employing very flat-centred, transverse arches. The church is famous for its connection with the Evangelical Movement, due to the 54-year ministry of Charles Simeon in the late eighteenth and early nineteenth centuries.

St Michael, Trinity Street (E/F4) *(fig. 582 & see 51, 80, 242)*

The original church of St Michael is first referred to in the early thirteenth century, but of this building nothing has survived. The existing church is almost entirely of the early fourteenth century having been very little interfered with since, and is possibly the most intact and original building of its date in Cambridge. Hervey de Stanton, Chancellor to Edward II, acquired the church in 1323 to serve the college which he founded the following year and named after the church; Michaelhouse. The college was located on the opposite side of Trinity Street, bordering St Michael's Lane and Milne Street (now Trinity Lane), and was later amalgamated into Henry VIII's Trinity College in 1546. Until then the church served both the neighbouring colleges of Michaelhouse and Gonville Hall (now Gonville & Caius College) and it in fact projects into Caius's St Michael's Court.

Hervey de Stanton proceeded to rebuild the church to serve both parish and college, and although he died in 1327 he charged his executors with the task of completing it, which was achieved sometime before 1350 (he was buried in the unfinished building). It is unusual in plan as the chancel is considerably larger than the nave (to cater for the collegiate congregation), and the tower is set off-centre, occupying the west bay of the south aisle. Nothing was altered in this building until the nineteenth century, when in 1818 the original lead-covered, wooden spire of the tower was dismantled; and then, due to a fire in 1849, the church was restored between 1849-50 by Sir George Gilbert Scott who rebuilt the north porch and the south doorway.

This beautiful little church is a noteworthy example of a medieval Decorated Gothic building. There are some excellent examples of flowing tracery in the windows, characteristic of that style (see fig. 80), which vary in construction from two-centred to four-centred arches. Of the interior details, particularly interesting are the fourteenth century Sedilia and Piscina in the south wall of the chancel; and the contemporary stone screen doorway between the chancel and south chapel. The superb oak choir stalls around the chancel are late fifteenth century.

Since 1908 the parish of St Michael has been linked with that of Great St Mary, and St Michael, although occasionally operating as a place of worship, has tended to become an active social centre housing a variety of events. The interior of the nave was adapted for this purpose by George Pace.

Christ Church, Newmarket Road
St Paul, Hills Road
St Andrew the Great, St Andrew's Street

The first three Victorian churches in Cambridge were all designed by the same architect — Ambrose Poynter — Christ Church in 1837-39 (fig. 583), St Paul in 1841 (fig. 584) and St Andrew The Great in 1842 (fig. 585). The two former were built in response to the huge increase in population in the parish of St Andrew The Less at that time, and St Andrew the Great was built on the site of the ancient church of St Andrew-without-Barnwell-Gate (demolished in 1842), the origins of which may well go back to the early twelfth century.

There are noticeable similarities between all three churches: the simple plan of nave and sanctuary under a single roof (before the later additions at St Paul's); the choice of the Tudor style, incorporating very similar interiors and details in all three, such as octagonal piers supporting the tall four-centred arches of the nave, with galleries behind in the aisles; and a mixture of straight-headed and four-centred Perpendicular windows. The similarity between the first two is particularly noticeable in the style and the use of materials, with emphasis on red brick with darker diaper work. In Christ Church (fig. 583) the architect was clearly influenced by King's College Chapel, as the basic form of the upright, rectangular box with polygonal corner turrets is reminiscent of that superb structure. The font is also similar to that at King's.

At St Andrew's there are some ancient remains in the wall at the west end of the south aisle; parts of the double capitals of two pairs of shafts thought to be twelfth century, and the lower section of a single-light thirteenth century window.

Additions were at Christ Church only minor, with the north porch being built later in the nineteenth century, and a minor restoration of the interior in 1946. However, at St Paul's much has been added; the aisled chancel of 1864 is by H.G. Elborne, and the shallow transepts of 1893 by Temple Moore. At St Andrew's the south porch was added in 1850, and the vestry in 1897.

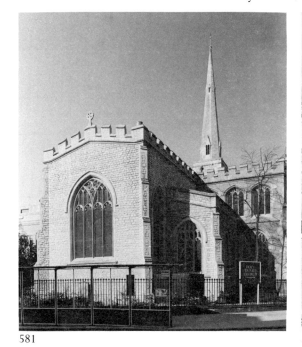

581

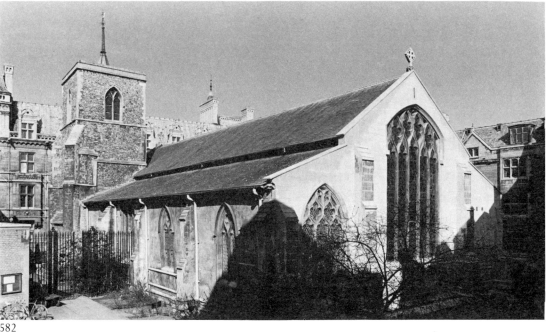

582

583

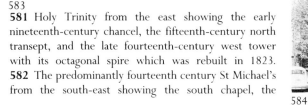

584

585

581 Holy Trinity from the east showing the early nineteenth-century chancel, the fifteenth-century north transept, and the late fourteenth-century west tower with its octagonal spire which was rebuilt in 1823. **582** The predominantly fourteenth century St Michael's from the south-east showing the south chapel, the chancel, and the asymmetrically placed western tower. **583-585** Three Victorian churches by Ambrose Poynter: **583** Christ Church from the south-east; **584** St Paul from the north-west and **585** St Andrew The Great from the south-east.

All Saints Church, Jesus Lane (G3) (fig. 586 & see 109)

The original church of All Saints in the Jewry was located in St John's Street, opposite St John's College, and dated back to the eleventh century (see fig. 563). It was demolished in 1865 when the street was widened, by which time it had also become too small for the increased population of the parish. All that remains is its churchyard in St John's Street, and its font in the new church.

G.F. Bodley was the architect chosen to design the successor to All Saints in the Jewry. He was predominantly a church architect who designed in the Gothic manner, having received a thorough training in that style as the first pupil (from 1845-50) of the eminent Sir G.G. Scott.

Bodley put forward his first design for the church in 1861, but when the tenders were received in early 1862, the scheme proved too expensive for the limited funds available. A revised plan still did not reduce the costs sufficiently and Bodley decided to start again, with the second scheme being accepted and built almost exactly as designed. This initial rejection may possibly have been fortunate, as the first design was an eclectic composition drawing heavily on French sources, whereas the subsequent scheme was derived from English models, in particular fourteenth century Gothic parish churches, resulting in such praise at the time as 'We note, with some satisfaction, that Mr Bodley has restrained himself to pure English forms. The time for a reaction from exclusively French or Italian types has at length arrived.'[24] The building has received more recent recognition from Stephen Wildman: 'All Saints stands out in the history of English Architecture, marking the point at which the Gothic Revival demonstrated the ability to learn from past styles and to build from their principles, rather than to plunder them for individual features and precedents.'[25]

Because only limited funds were available the church was built in two stages; the main body was completed between May 1863 and June 1864, at which time the tower was capped with a temporary pyramidal roof until funds were obtained to build the spire (not built until 1869-71). Bodley in fact preferred a simple tower, but the spire was insisted upon by the commissioners. The spire as built varied slightly from the intended design because of further financial restraint. The limited finances were a problem, but they were also a contributory factor in the design of the finished church and, to a degree, dictated the type of building to Bodley as '...the principle of getting effect by good proportion and a fair elevation, rather than by any rich or costly detail...' had to be adhered to. Bodley went on to say that 'The effect of height is not so manifest in drawings as it would be in reality...' and one can appreciate what he meant when standing next to, or inside, this incredibly tall structure (see fig. 109).

There is much decorative work of note in All Saints by Morris & Co and C.E. Kempe. The interior is extensively stencilled, on the ceiling as well as walls, with organic and geometrical patterns by both Bodley and Morris. The stained glass is a mixture of Morris & Co — in particular the east window of 1865-66 which includes work by Burne-Jones, Morris, and Ford Maddox Brown — and of Kempe, in the third and fourth windows from the west in the north wall, of 1891. To quote Stephen Wildman again 'If there is anything we can still learn from William Morris, it must be to recognise excellence, praise it when it is found, and do our best to preserve its finest fruits. All Saints is just such a lodestone. Its present state and uncertain future offer a sad reflection not on its creators but on ourselves.'

586 The Gothic Revival All Saints from the south-east; designed by G. F. Bodley and inspired by traditional fourteenth-century English parish churches.

587

588

589

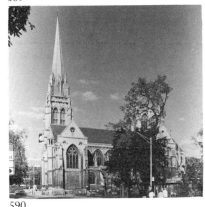

590

591

592

593

594

596

597

598

599

587 St Matthew, Geldart Street, of 1866, by R.R. Rowe. **588** St Giles, Castle street (E2), 1875, by T.H. & F. Healey of Bradford. **589** Emmanuel Congregational Church, Trumpington Street (F5), 1874, by Cubitt. **590** Our Lady and The English Martyrs, Hills Road/Lensfield Road (H6), 1885-90, by Dunn & Hansom. **591** St Columba Presbyterian Church, Downing Street (F/G4), 1891, by J. MacVicar Anderson. **592** St John the Evangelist, Hills Road, 1896, by Gordon Lowther & Gunton. **593** St Andrew's Baptist Church, St Andrew's Street (G5), 1903, by G. & R.P. Baines. **594** Methodist Wesley Church, King Street/Emmanuel Road (G3), 1913, by W.H. Gunton. **595** St George's, Chesterfield Road, 1938, by T.H. Lyon. **596** St Nicholas Ferrar, Arbury Estate (north Cambridge), 1957-58, by S.E. Dykes Bower. **597** St Martin's, Suez Road, 1960-62, by Paterson & Macaulay. **598** Arbury Road Baptist Church, 1965-66, by R.J. Wyatt. **599** The Eden Chapel, Fitzroy Street (H3), 1981-83, by Fitzroy Robinson.

600

601

602

603

600 The picturesque east side of King's Parade (E4) facing King's College, a mixture of sixteenth, seventeenth and eighteenth century houses all of which have had their ground floors adapted as shops, mostly with nineteenth century fronts. Particularly interesting are numbers 16 to 18 **601** The Grafton Shopping Centre (H3), of 1981-83, by Fitzroy Robinson Architects. **602** One of the most attractive houses in Cambridge - the late Arts & Crafts 'Upton House', 11 Grange Road (C6), of 1912, by A.J. Winter Rose. **603** The Italianate Railway Station of 1845 by Sancton Wood. Originally the arcaded loggia was open and matched on the opposite side by another - vehicles drew up on one side and trains on the other.

8 The Town

Cambridge 'Town' as opposed to 'Gown', never really had the resources to build sumptuous edifices. Cambridge has never been a major industrial centre, initially it was a commercial market town situated in a rich agricultural area, and as such carried on a busy river trade (see chapter 1). However, the coming of the university, and much later the railway, put paid to the river industry and from the latter part of the nineteenth century the university and the colleges became the main source of local employment. In recent years, however, the town of Cambridge has started to reap the benefits of being host to one of the world's most famous universities. Tourism provides a major income and the modern university has also been very influential in attracting light industry to the area in the form of high-technology companies and research institutes. Until recently the companies were located randomly around the town, but in the early seventies the Cambridge Science Park was set up and developed by Trinity College on its still-expanding site off the major roads bypassing the northern side of the city. With this continuing influx the town is quickly becoming a leading centre for high-technology industries.

Cambridge possesses only a few pre-twentieth century public buildings and, in the main, almost all commercial and industrial buildings are the result of modern development. These buildings range from domestic-scale Victorian shops to vast complexes such as the New Addenbrookes Hospital or the extensive Science Park buildings.

Cambridge housing falls into three distinct areas: that contained within the city centre, the historic old town; the extensive suburban 'sprawl' to north, east and south; and the more controlled, private development to the west, which could be described as the town's 'garden suburb'. Three quite different sorts of housing have evolved in the three areas: in the historic centre a varied collection of mainly terraced houses ranging from medieval cottages to modern blocks, including a few detached houses; in the more extensive suburban district a mixture of council housing with several large 'estates', mainly in the north and east, but also numerous streets with attractive terraced houses and larger detached houses, in addition to several well designed Housing Society schemes; and to the west an area full of large, private houses with equally large gardens. Architecturally, the three areas differ in many respects; the variety of buildings in the centre reflect its gradual evolution as the nucleus of the present area of Greater Cambridge; beyond it the outer district contains much property repetitive in style as dictated by the demands for mass housing since the nineteenth century, amongst which are some interesting council and private schemes alongside attractive Victorian and Edwardian terraces; and the smaller, and rather more 'select' area to the west, made up of a collection of houses representing the continuous change in architectural style since the early 1800s. The newer, peripheral growth now encompassing the old town, the mass of which has only come about during the last hundred years or so, covers an area many times the size of the historic centre, which has taken more than 800 years to evolve (see chapter 1).

There was little housing built outside the city before 1800, and in the historic centre itself examples are scattered at random. The oldest surviving private house in the town, in fact in the county, is the Norman stone building today known as the 'School of Pythagoras' (see figs. 5 & 345), which is now part of St John's College and is thought to have been built no later than c.1200. In the same vicinity, there are some late medieval cottages that have survived in Magdalene and Northampton Streets (see figs. 55 & 269) which, with their half-timbering and overhanging upper storeys, give a good impression of what the medieval town must have looked like.

The great East, or Barnwell, Field was Enclosed in 1802 (see p. 33), after which the main mass of suburban development soon started to spread east and north. Later, when the railway station was built to the south in 1845, development followed in that direction too. The great West, or Cambridge, Field was Enclosed in 1807, but it was not until the latter half of the nineteenth century that development in that area really got underway. At the time of Enclosure most of this land, from Barton Road in the south to the Huntingdon Road in the north, was acquired by the colleges, and their control on the building leases, by means of restrictive covenants, guaranteed a high level of design and materials for properties in this area, where the wealthier dons and professionals began to settle. For instance, in the late nineteenth century after St John's College had laid-down Adams and Sylvester Roads at the north end of Grange Road, they offered the building plots along them on 99 year leases, but with many restrictive clauses to ensure that high standards were maintained: plots had to be fenced on all unenclosed sides, either by a five foot high wall or by split-oak close-pale fences; there was to be only one private house per site, built at a cost of not less than £1,500; the houses had to adhere to a building-line at least 20 feet from the road; materials were to be red-brick or stone walls, with red-tiles for the roofs; and the architects' plans and sections were to be submitted to the college surveyors for prior approval.

The houses built in west Cambridge from the early nineteenth century through to the present day, record many of the changes that have taken place in English architecture, from the early Victorian villa to the modern house. 'Old English' and 'Queen Anne', Arts & Crafts, neo-Georgian, and the Modern Movement of the inter-war years, are all extremely well represented in the work of many eminent architects such as J.J. Stevenson, Basil Champneys, E.S. Prior, Ernest Newton, M.H. Baillie Scott, George Checkley, Marshall Sisson, and Raymnd McGrath, as well as many other equally competent local designers.

The following photographs (figs 600-627) are a very brief selection of a variety of town buildings (see also chapter 1).

604

606

607

608

605

609

604 The former Corn Exchange (F4), of 1874, built by R.R. Rowe in a byzantine style employing yellow, red and blue bricks.   **605** The Guildhall, Market Hill (F4), of 1936-37, by C. Cowles-Voysey.   **606** The old Police Station in Regent Street (G5), of 1901.   **607** The new Divisional Police Headquarters, Parkside (H4), of 1967-68, by P.R. Arthur and M.R. Francis of the County Architects Department.   **608** The University Arms Hotel (G5) from Parker's Piece, of 1903 & 1926-27, by G.J. Skipper.   **609** The late nineteenth-century Leys School, Trumpington Road (F6), by Robert Curwen. **610** The Perse School for Boys, Hills Road, of 1958-60, by Robert Matthew, Johnson-Marshall & Partners.

610

611

614

615

612

616

613

617

611-13 Three types of Cambridge housing which would have been erected after Enclosure in the early nineteenth century (see p. 32): **611** typical smaller terrace houses of which a huge amount were built mainly in the northern, eastern and south-eastern suburbs from the second quarter of the nineteenth century onwards. **612** The more elaborate larger houses of the Grange Road area of west Cambridge (C5/6) developed from the late 1800s under the control of the College landlords. **613** A rather select and very elegant row of late Georgian houses near the town centre - the Dolls Close section of Maid's Causeway (H3), with Willow Walk behind it, developed between 1815-26 by the local architect and speculative builder Charles Humphrey: '... of much interest as an example of a social and economic urban development of the early nineteenth century.' (RCHM). The plan of no. 8 is the most original with little modern addition. **614 & 615** Two neo-Georgian/'Queen Anne' houses of 1907 by Amian Champneys; Silbury and Whewell House, 60 and 62 Grange Road (C3). **616** The Modern Movement Thurso House, Conduit Head Road, of 1932, by George Checkley (*see also figs 121, 124*). **617** Laslett House, 3 Clarkson Road (B3), of 1957-59, by Trevor Dannatt. **618** Little Trinity, 16 Jesus Lane (F3), of *c.* 1725, notable for its elegant staircase and '... perhaps the most handsome private house in Cambridge ...' (Pevsner)

619

620

621

622

623

624

625

626

627

Select bibliography

Babington, Charles Cardale, *Ancient Cambridgeshire*, 1883

Booth, Philip, & Taylor, Nicholas, *Cambridge New Architecture*, 1970

Churchill College competition, *The Builder*: 14.08.1959

Gray, Arthur, *The Town of Cambridge*, 1925

Griffiths, Richard, *The Houses of West Cambridge* (M.A. dissertation), 1981

Pevsner, Nikolaus, *Cambridgeshire*, 1970

Raverat, Gwen, *Period Piece*, 1952

Roberts, David, & Cullen, Gordon, *The Town of Cambridge As it Ought to be Reformed*, 1955

Robinson College competition, *Architects Journal*: 20.11.1974; 27.11.1974; 05.08.1981

Robinson, Duncan, & Wildman, Stephen, *Morris & Company in Cambridge* (Fitzwilliam Museum catalogue) 1980

Royal Commission on Historical Monuments: *City of Cambridge*, 1959 (2 volumes and plans)

Steegmann, John, *Cambridge*, 1945

Victoria History of the Counties of England: *Cambridgeshire & The Isle of Ely*

Willis, Robert, & Clark, John Willis, *Architectural History of the University of Cambridge*, 1886 (3 volumes and plans)

619 The seventeenth and eighteenth century shops in Trinity Street (E3/4), known as the High Street until 1546 and the founding of Trinity College. **620** 14 Trinity Street of *c*.1600 - an attractive timber-framed building with much restored pargetting on its overhanging upper storeys and canted oriel windows. This building was a bank in the nineteenth century and prior to that the Turk's Head Inn. **621** 30 Trinity Street of the mid-eighteenth century. The timber shopfront, with its Gothic patterned glazing bars, dates from the late 1700s. **622** The interior of Heffers Bookshop, 20 Trinity Street a most successful scheme of 1970 by Peter J. Lord of Austin-Smith Lord, on four levels (mainly below ground) with a central exhibition well. **623** 21 Market Street (F4) - a recently uncovered original Art Nouveau shop front, probably dating from the turn of the century. **624** A modern office block in Downing Street (F4). **625-627** Three recent buildings in the Cambridge Science Park on the northern outskirts of the city, off Milton Road, by the Charter Building Design Group of Bedford *(see also figs 40 & 154)*.

Notes

1 Gray, Arthur, *The Town of Cambridge*, p.6

2 For a more detailed account of pre-history in the area see Pevsner's *Cambridgeshire*, p.259

3 Gray, Arthur, *The Town of Cambridge*

4 Ibid. p.1

5 Ibid. p.31

6 A brief chronological summary of the arrival of the early religious foundations at Cambridge: 1112 and 1135 Augustinian; 1133 Benedictine; c1224 Franciscan; c1238 Dominican; 1249 Carmelite; 1257 Friars of the Order of Bethlehem; 1258 Friars of the Penitence; 1290 Austen Friars.

7 Gray, Arthur, *The Town of Cambridge*, p.153

8 Steegmann, John, *Cambridge*, p.38

9 Cambridge preceded Oxford in womens education. The first ladies colleges there were: 1878 Lady Margaret Hall; 1879 Somerville College; 1886 St Hugh's Hall; 1893 St Hilda's College.

10 It is possible to see many of these former areas of Cambridge in old photographs kept in the Folk Museum, Castle Street.

11 Willis & Clark, *Architectural History of the University of Cambridge*, Vol. I, p.xxii

12 Ibid. Vol. I, p.xxxiii

13 Ibid. Vol. III, p.266

14 Ibid. Vol. III, p.574

15 Ibid. Vol. III, p.275

16 Booth & Taylor, *Cambridge New Architecture*, p.51

17 Ibid. p.59

18 Fuller, Richard Buckminster (1895-1983). Developed the geodesic dome, built on the space-frame principle.

19 Extract taken from a slide talk given by James Stirling to Bologna University in 1966. Reproduced in *James Stirling*, RIBA Drawings Collection, second edition.

20 See Willis & Clark, Vol. III, pp.190-191

21 Ibid. Vol. III, pp.193-194

22 Extract taken from the Kettle's Yard Handlist, 1970

23 Robinson & Wildman, *Morris & Company in Cambridge*, p.2

24 Ibid. p.30

25 Ibid.

Index